MR. DEATH

Manufactured in the United States of America.

FIRST EDITION

Playboy Press/A Division of PEI Books, Inc.

Library of Congress Cataloging in Publication Data

Rothman, David B.
    Mr. Death: the life of a CIA assassination expert—by his son.

    1. Rothman, Barry. 2. United States. Central Intelligence Agency—Officials and employees—Biography. I. Title.

JK468.I6R68   327.1′2′0924   [B]   81–50316
ISBN 0–87223–715–X   AACR2

Design by Tere LoPrete

*To all who contributed
but especially to those
who tried to stop me*

It was true that I had traveled great distances for one so young, but my spirit had remained landlocked, unacquainted with love and all but a stranger to death.

WILLIAM STYRON

MR. DEATH

1

Dad

Ten years ago. I am fourteen and contemplating his stature. I figure he stands five feet nine inches and weighs less than me, maybe 155. My mother says no, he's at least five eleven, maybe even six feet, and he must weigh more than that, probably closer to 165. I am convinced my mother is lying.

His skin has what might be called an olive tint. Sometimes it seems so dark I wonder if he is part American Indian. I've always wanted to be part American Indian, to be able to say that to a girl, so I ask him about his racial heritage. I am not shocked or even surprised when he says he believes he has some Mongolian blood in him. I know nothing about Mongolian blood, but it sounds right, because I know for a fact that Mongolia is in or near Asia, and those people are usually darker than the average white American. I know this little tidbit about Mongolia because I read an article about Mongol tribes in *National Geographic*. There was an article in one issue that told about Mongolian refugees and prisoners of war during World War II. It said that Mongolians had a better survival rate than other POWs because they seemed to have iron stomachs. It was not uncommon to see a Mongol POW scooping out a handful of rotten horse guts from a dead horse and eating them raw. The Nazis thought of them as dogs, possibly even as low and filthy as the Jews, but they survived while Jews died.

This fits my image of my father.

When I think of his body I always think of one part: his knees. I see him standing in his living room talking on the phone, or yakking with a neighbor, or rummaging through a book, and those knees catch my glance and hold it. I never think enough of them to ask him how they got that way, but they seem to bend in a direction that would be downright excruciating for most humans: They bend backward.

I see him walking up to the huge bookcase that covers the entire west wall of the living room, pondering for a second, and in that second locking his knees in place. This means he's going to be there for a while, pondering and rummaging. When he wants to move out of this position, first he unlocks, then he walks away. I've heard that Olympic swimmers feel blessed if they are born with hyperextended knees, but I have no reason to believe he feels blessed by them or any other part of his body.

I am calling him late one bitter-cold midwinter night from a phone booth on the streets of High Cliffs, New Jersey. I can't call from home because it's not private enough. Even if I could call from home, I would have to call collect because mom says it's the least he can do. Who needs that? Especially when I'm near tears because I'm thirteen and still a virgin.

"If you have a sixth sense about them and yourself and the world," he says, "you'll have no trouble finding girls and women who appreciate you."

I'm stunned. No one has ever talked to me this way. No one has ever said anything to me about females that makes this much sense—or sounds like it makes this much sense.

"After all," he says, "I'm no beauty, but I've been doing it since I was ten. I was trained to do it. Be direct. Take the cow by the horns. That's what I've always done, and, sure, I've gotten a lot of rejections, but I've also gotten a lot more. A lot more than if I just stood around waiting for things to happen. At least you know where you stand, but fast."

This is incredible, absolutely incredible. You mean that's actually how things work? You actually walk up to the chick and say: Hi. My name's Dave. Wanna fuck?

"Sometimes. I've done that. Gotten some pretty interesting

responses. Everything from let's do it right here right now to threats from police, older brothers, male cousins, Italian brotherhood who just happen to be standing across the street. But if it's any consolation to you, I've never been shot or stabbed or even punched in the line of duty."

I can't believe this. Are women the same as men? Do they get the hots the same way?

"Let me put it this way. If you're feeling good about a girl or woman, and you want her to know it, and you think that maybe she feels the same way toward you, proceed as if you know she feels the same way toward you. It's like I just said: You'll know where you stand, but fast."

But why is it so hard to tell?

"That's only because they've learned how to hide their feelings and disguise them and make them come out in all sorts of strange ways—ways that look strange to you. The trick is learning how to read the signals. I'll bet a lot more girls and even women have come on to you than you realize. I'll bet it happens to all men. I'm no different. But a long time ago I told myself I was determined to learn how to read the signals. Obviously I've been doing something right. I'm sure I've missed a few, and I'm sure you'll miss a few in your career. But you'll do fine once you put your mind into it. That's the key. Use your mind."

He always talks to me more like an older brother or a friend than a father, but this is the first time I really hear him.

I am six again, exploring in the bottom of his closet. I'm so absorbed in my discoveries that I don't hear the water running or the bathroom door open. Suddenly a huge shadow crosses my line of vision and I look up. I see his root, nestled in all that black silk. I'm afraid, not knowing what it is, because no man or woman has ever told me about the adult male or female body. I sense that he is shocked to find me so close, almost at his feet. He is afraid.

He has deep brown eyes and wears thick, black-framed glasses. I realize that his vision is an issue when I ask him why he always carries a gun when he leaves the house, even if he's only going to the post office or the grocery store.

"I've always known if I get in a fight and lose my glasses, I'm done for. And they're the first things you lose in a fight. I'm not too swift with karate or jujitsu, so I figure I should have some way of protecting myself."

I can understand. I know what it's like to get pushed around and feel defenseless. Happens all the time to me in school, supposedly because I'm "different," whatever that means. His explanation sounds quite reasonable, even though he seems to be one of the least fight-prone humans I've ever known.

I am very young and he is still young. I ask him why he's already lost so much hair. He tells me it's because he had to receive radium treatments when he was a boy. He had a tumor above his left eye and one at the base of his skull when he was eight or nine. They used the radium—an almost unknown miracle cure—to kill the tumors. He doesn't laugh when he says he wonders how they didn't manage to kill him, too.

Christmas vacation during my first year at Monarch College, which is located in St. Cloud, Minnesota. I have never spent more than a week with him twice a year since I was three or four, so these occasions are more than just visits. They're holy days. The Fourth of July and Christmas are my only true rituals, and neither has anything to do with the way everyone else celebrates these holidays. These are *his* holidays, *he* makes them special. Hill House on the Fourth of July and Christmas is the only place I ever feel truly at home, where I can park my bones and nourish body and soul. There is a feeling of gathering our loved ones in a circle and celebrating life's simple pleasures, even though our circle is somewhat motley by average American standards. No wonder I've been known to sleep twelve hours for the first couple days. The air itself makes me sleep better than I've ever slept. It's this magic, this mystery, that I love to come back to season after season.   I don't know if all boys need their fathers as much as I need mine, but every time I visit I take as much as I can get. I drink deep, recharge my batteries, feed my hunger, store up fat for the lean months ahead.

We've just had a wonderful week together. I've shot off plenty of fireworks in the driveway, "plinked" for hours up on the shooting range he built in the woods behind the house, watched TV late at night with Dawn and the kids, gone to see the latest James Bond "flicker," as he calls it.

I'm getting ready to catch a train down to New York to see my mother. I'm standing in the doorway to the kitchen, and he's sitting at the table. I need money, as usual, only now it's for college texts instead of butterfly nets or aquariums or maps of North America so I can hitchhike to God knows where. I've never asked him for money, even when I've really needed it. I'm always afraid to, I'm too proud. It's usually not that bad, because most of the time he drops a few twenties in my suitcase on the way out. But this time that's not enough.

"How much do you need?" My antennae pick up something unpleasant, something I've never heard aimed at me. There's something harsh under the surface tone. I try to convince myself I'm wrong. Can't back out now even if I wanted to. That would be a hell of a lot worse.

"Thirty for books, and then I think I need at least twenty for the train, and then about seventy-five for the plane back to Minnesota."

I haven't bothered to add it up, but I sense I should have before asking. My father isn't poor—at least he never seems to be —but still, I've never asked him for this much money. I may not have received this much from him in the past five years, but this has not occurred to me until now. I've never wanted money from him. I've always wanted more important things. Like time. Time to walk down Wood Mill Road. Just the two of us.

He pulls out three tens, a twenty, and quickly counts what he has left. There is enough to cover the rest of my request, but not by much. I feel like a thief when he hands me all those bills and only has a few left for himself. I try to find a way out, try to give some of it back, but he puts his wallet away and ends the conversation with a gesture that dismisses the entire concept of money. Deep in my heart, or, more precisely, the pit of my stomach, I know something is very wrong, but there it is, that paradox. We can talk about anything, anything at all. But then there are things we don't dare touch.

There I am, walking out into the frozen backyard behind the house he rented called Cricket Dell. This is before Hill House, before his marriage to Dawn. This is still the rolling green countryside of western Massachusetts, the land he says he loves.

I find molten white plastic blobs frozen into the trodden earth. I ask him what they are, and he tells me they are the remnants of some experimental white phosphorous grenades. He tells me about the horrible burns that phosphorous inflicts on the skin, how deeply and intensely the fragments burn, how nothing can put out those fires. He tells me that plastic might be the future for phosphorous grenades because that near-liquid metal flame disperses better from a plastic casing than a metal casing. I visualize one hell of an exploding ball of flame, hungry to oxidize with skin and eyes and hair. I wonder how I might make one, but I'm too scared to try.

Later I'll find loads of odd-caliber bullets lying around the house in shoe boxes and brown paper bags, on bookshelves and the kitchen table. With these, I fantasize about stealing the materials I might need to make a zip gun. But again, I'm too afraid to go all the way. I feel honored that he trusts me so much, that he only asks me not to put one through a neighbor, the dog, any of us, or the car.

When we're shooting a fireworks show over at the plant on the Fourth of July, I never think it strange that we have to drive through barbed-wire security gates and grin at man-eating Dobermans before we can get down to business. It's just part of his territory, and I love it. And him.

One of my shortest, sweetest memories:

I am climbing up on his lap to kiss him goodnight. Before I get to his face, I smell him, I smell a man for the first time: cigarettes and leather. Both smells are very sharp in my nostrils, and not unpleasant. I wonder if I'll ever smell like that.

I kiss him on the left cheek—I can't remember if we ever kissed on the lips—and I feel the roughness of his black razor stubble. It reminds me of sandpaper, and I wonder how any woman could ever put up with that. Maybe this is why my mother and father are divorced.

He acquires a Siberian Husky pup and brings it to our house one Thanksgiving when he's come to pick me up for a weekend. I curl up on the living-room couch while he and mom talk in the dining room. I am tired and drag the pup over to sleep with me, and she does, willingly. I fall asleep with her wrapped around my feet, keeping them warm in the cool dark parlor. When I wake, it's time to go. I have the aching feeling my parents have been watching me, that they've smiled together for the first time in years.

Years later, again at Cricket Dell. A cool season, probably late summer. There is an overpowering sting of tear gas in the kitchen, where he must be doing the experiments he is always doing. I go to bed hungry more than once because the stench keeps me away from the refrigerator.

I have a hankering to go fishing, so he buys me a cheap fishing pole. The flimsiness of the pole bothers me: I know it's going to fall apart just as I'm about to land The Big One. I already prize durability in everything.

We try the stream that is adjacent to his Colonial stone house. There is a small bridge over the deepest pool, and he stands on the bridge while I wade into the water below. I am wearing only underpants, which frightens and humiliates me when things start going wrong, which is immediately. The line keeps getting tangled in overhanging trees and surrounding bushes. He has to come down and untangle it while I stand there useless, holding my cheap pole. I cast again, and it snags on a rotten log. Finally he gets disgusted and tells me to quit, it's over, no more fishing for today. Maybe no more fishing *ever*, I think, and start to cry. I'm hot and cold all over, feeling much too naked, chilled by my own sweat, raging inside with despair over my inability to conquer such a tame environment, to make him feel that time spent with me is time well spent, that I am well on my way to becoming a man.

Later I'll direct my anger at everything and everyone but him: at myself, my mother, my cats, my tropical fish. I'll catch beautiful butterflies and kill them in seconds by pinching them in the middle of their bodies, when I really only want to spend a few hours each week with my beloved father. I'll shoot paper clips with rubber bands at my cats, when all I really want is someone to ask me how the world is treating me. I'll discover solar energy and torture crickets and grasshoppers, I'll set fires in fields, when all I need is a pat on the back at the end of the day, when all I want is to kiss that rough leathery face goodnight every night.

I call out so many nights for that miracle to touch our lives and bring my parents back together again.

I wonder if I'll ever be in control.

I learn to defend myself against my mother's incessant rages against him, her attempts to poison my feelings for him, my need for him.

I ache with the knowledge that I am powerless.

In my tenth August he sends me the biggest package I have ever received in the mail. I take it out to the backyard, to the six-foot by three-foot by four-foot foxhole I have been digging all summer. I hunker down there, my back pressed against the hard dirt wall of my own private sanctum. I open it slowly, religiously, unsealing the huge manila envelope inch by savory inch.

At first I don't know what it is, but I am patient. I know my father well enough to know he would not send me something less than fascinating. I am much too proud to ask mom what it is, so I keep prodding it, unfolding it, trying to picture it in my mind's eye. After several hours of serious Saturday afternoon contemplation and reflection, I realize what it is: a solar still.

First you dig a small hole. You put a cup at the bottom of the hole. Over the top you stretch the sheet of plastic. The hole has to be small enough so you can push the plastic down in the center so it almost touches the cup. You put a small pebble in the center of the plastic, so it's now forming a V, with the bottom of the V pointed straight into the bottom of the cup. You seal the plastic by piling dirt (or sand, if you're in a desert) around the outside edge of the plastic. If you leave this arrangement over-night, water will collect in the cup after it condenses on the underside of the plastic. As it condenses, it rolls down the sheet, forms droplets, and falls into the cup. The water will be fairly pure because the earth will have purified it.

This device will save my life seven years later while I'm hitchhiking across the Utah desert.

He sends me pocketknives that, he says, have been recovered from sunken Spanish galleons. Spanish galleons! Spanish galleons are alive and well in the American suburbs! They're shaped like tiny crescent moons, each one small enough to fit in the palm of my hand. There are intricate designs carved into the gold-plated handles. Sometimes they arrive slightly rusty, but I chalk this up to the fact that they've been under the sea for centuries. He suggests I soak them in Coca-Cola if I want to get rid of the rust, and I do, and it works. If you want to find out what soda does to your teeth, he says, put one of your baby teeth in the Coke with the knife for two days. See what's left of it after the second day.

I stop drinking Coke at the age of nine and a half.

The day after being released from ninth grade at High Cliffs Junior High, at the age of fourteen, I write my first poem. I am about to embark on my longest journey away from home alone: a friend's father owns land in Maine and has given me permission to camp there for all or part of the summer. Transportation is up to me. I'm short of funds, as usual, so I intend to hitchhike, as usual. I'll do anything not to be stuck in New Jersey for the summer.

The night before my departure, I call him from the phone booth around the corner. I recite my poem entirely from memory, and I'm amazed when my voice doesn't crack, when I don't choke on

my words. He loves it, and for the first time tells me he is also
a poet.

Also a poet!

"I would expect the son of a Rothman to be a poet," he says,
"but a *virgin* poet? Where did I go wrong?"

Zapcap is a toy firework that he invented in the early 1970s.
It looks exactly like the federally illegal M-80, which was said to
be as powerful as a quarter of a stick of dynamite. Zapcaps are
not nearly as loud as M-80s, but they can be detonated in the
palm of a child's hand and are completely harmless. He hopes
Zapcap will enjoy wide appeal among the Probation Generation.
He has been telling me for months that he hopes to set up a
Zapcap factory in Puerto Rico within the year. I warn him to
make sure he knows how to recognize Latin-American feminine
endings.

22 February 1975

Son of Kong:

Rec'd your sonnet (excellent!) and letter today. Things
(ZAPCAPS (Trademark reg'd US PATENT OFF, Property
B. Rothman) are steam rollering: they sold a ¼ million $
worth of ZAPCAPS at the N.Y. Toy Buyer's Fair. We are in
business, I do believe. I expect to make first, relatively short
trip to P.R. ca. the 2nd week in March. I will return, then
soar off for more-or-less prolonged stay (weeks? months?)
soon after. I will have to stay there until the factory is
well-established. If all goes well, I will make quite substantial $ out of this for the next few years. . . .

Now then: I will certainly find out if I can export a
puertorriqueña to the wilds of Minnesota. I will pick a
suitably young, supple, vigorous specimen that will survive
the transplant. You will, of course, have to nurture, keep
warm, etc, this piece. Being a Rothman you do not, I know,
need further instruction. You will also note that I will make
GREAT effort to share the wealth, unlike certain unthinking
siblings that I know of who selfishly keep miniskirted maids

all to themselves & do not make any effort to share same with aging, lecherous father who certainly deserves better treatment, etc., ad nauseam.

I will also have you know that, if little else, I am singular expert in recognizing feminine endings in *any* language. (Color, flavor or shape, for that matter.) I have begun memorizing useful phrases that I will need, e.g.:

"Do not stir the acide with your piñada, por favor."
"I didn't know she was your sister."
"Where are the women?"
"   ″   ″   ″   rest rooms?"
"   ″   ″   ″   girls?"
"   ″   ″   the resuscitator?"
"   ″   the penicillin?"
"Is SPIC 'N SPAN a Spanish detergent?"
. . . and other ingratiating phrases.

Must get some sleep. I'm getting martyred in the morning. (An old Hymn.)

LOVE!
dad

There is now a local post-office box instead of his home address.

14 May 75

Dear David:
A hurried note to bring you up to date on the latest chapters of Payout Place. . . .

With relatively little acrimony, and for the better of both, Dawn and I have separated. This has been brewing for some considerable period, as I think you sensed long ago. We both feel better. Dawn & kids are living at Hill House on Wood Mill Road, and I've been a gypsy of sorts, by choice.

Nothing in my life has ever arrived in tolerable, small increments. It's always been stop or violent. So it is now, what with marital, business and all other problems of survival. However, it seems to all be working toward a better condition and, surprisingly enough, I feel rather good.

Business has carried me to 8 major cities in the past few

weeks, so I've really been mobile. And motile. I will either be shortly quite wealthy or dirt poor. The next few weeks will tell. Is there no middle ground, he asks plaintively . . .

When I settle somewhere, I will send complaint up/down there: I am sore tired of not being control of the Great Script.
Write.
Love,
Dad

Is he afraid I will turn on him, that I will someday demand back pay for all the years he abandoned me and my mother? I just don't know how to tell him: I love you because you're my father, you don't have to prove anything to me. I am bold, but not that bold. I feel him getting more and more naked, even through letters that arrive in my college mailbox in Minnesota, but I have no way to tell him I love him more for his nakedness, I love him more and more and more for his nakedness. I love him.

23 May 75

Got your note of the 19th yesterday.

By now you know about the poetry contest, independent study in Pakistan, etc. I hope you've had better luck than I this week. I am hanging by financial thumbs waiting for legal shit & Etc. so I can collect many $. I am living day to day, fending off bill collectors, sundry associated aggravations and potentially lethal anxiety. I hear that all great (grate?) inventors have to go thru this sort of trial. I am beginning to wonder if it's all worth it . . .

You see, I've found a splendid woman who brings out the best I've got, and that seems to be mutual. Now for the plot twists: She is married, in agonizing process of trying to separate from husband. He is aware of my role. She wants to leave. I want her to leave. She can't. Why? We have no place to go. With no fucking money there is no place to live. (I am submitting this scenario to one of the soap operas: they will no doubt reject it as too corny.) Something's got to give soon, and I hope it isn't one of my main arteries . . .

The poems you sent, in my uneducated opinion, are among the best you've written.

Perhaps you'll get down this way to celebrate spring rites?

Have to move again. They're coming through the wall to get me . . .

Love,
Dad

I am eighteen and I am just beginning to discover my father, as he is discovering me. We have always been able to talk, as long as I can remember, but he has never seemed as interested in me as he does now. I get the feeling that now I can give him something mature and intelligent, witty and creative on his level —he has never been able to come down to a boy's level. Now we can talk, really talk. About anything.

Never before has he expressed such a desire to keep track of my plans and ambitions. By now I know he isn't capable of most typical fatherly actions, such as paying for all or part of my education (I feel better paying for it anyway), but that doesn't matter to me. I don't know if he has ever understood why I've never asked him why he left us. I always get the feeling that he's amazed I'm not bitter. I'm not interested in such poisons. I want most to understand him, to hear about his joys and troubles, to ask for advice on Girls & Grades, to cry over the phone just because I'm talking with him, just because I'm with him, even at such a distance, any distance.

Again at Hill House. I ask him if he can sit with me in the living room for a few minutes before going up to bed with Dawn. He says sure, and turns around and sits across from me on the sofa. I am nervous just asking for his time so directly—I'm afraid to show him how much I need him—maybe I'm just in awe of him.

My voice catches in my throat, I have so much to say in so little time. The words don't come, but the tears do, and finally, choking:

"I'll bet you think I'm a jerk for crying like this in front of you."

"No," he says, not rattled a bit. "I envy your ability to cry. They stomped that out of me when I was twelve. I haven't been able to cry since."

I want to hug him, I want to say more, I want to share more, I want him to move across the sofa and put his arms around me. But neither of us moves.

My first year at college ends with a whimper and I return to the New Jersey suburbs to try to find a lover and make money painting houses, in that order.

The next missive arrives handwritten on Holiday Inn stationery. He is now living outside of Crystal Springs, Massachusetts—just a few miles from Hill House—200 miles west of Boston. The middle of Colonial Revolutionary Nowhere.

June 1 '75

Happy Intergalactic Ennui Day!

I am imprisoned in this sterile room feeling downright shitty, suffering from that most dreadful of combined psychomaladies: boredom, frustration, loneliness and depression.

Business, it seems, is dragging interminably but (seemingly) toward success. Nonetheless, I am infernally broke. My health is good, by some weird chance.

Mostly I am gloom-doom as result of falling in love at obscene age of 40. How can I, one who has survived being shot, stabbed, poisoned, blown up, attacks from my own heart and kidneys etc, ad absurdum, how, I ask you, can I be mooning about like this? Eh? I have not seen my woman for a week (she is with her "lawful" husband on vacation) and I am—well—desolate. I haven't been interested in screwing anyone else. Lunacy. I *am* very ill. Love/need/ desire is/are hazardous to your health.

Lesson for Son: Even aging fathers are frequently fools.

I regret that you did not win poetry contest. Pakistan beckons? I will supply you with a liter of penicillin and scimitar-proof Jockey shorts in case you unwisely lift a veil.

Do not know what is happening for Glorious 4th. I am

unable to plan more than a day or two ahead, need $ and a place to call home, first and foremost. I miss my dog, cats, snakes, alligators, lizards, tarantulas and books.

May have housepainting job for you here, right away. Can you do repair-installation type work? (Like, installing kitchen cabinets/counter??) Let me know.

Love, Dad

Nothing goes right. Not the "Glorious 4th" ((the first time in a decade that we don't have some sort of celebration, which tells me in an untranslatable language that something is slipping); not the painting job, which I try to get but somehow it disappears; not the business with Zapcap that he has been living for. I hope this new lady works out, but I never hear about her again.

I have a batch of red-hot new poems, and I want my best reader to read them. I haven't had any contact with him all summer, not even a firecracker in his backyard. I have no idea what turns his life is taking. For some inexplicable reason, I feel compelled to see him before leaving High Cliffs for St. Cloud, before beginning my sophomore year.

I can see him now, ambling out the back door, taking his time because of the heat. He's wearing a sleeveless white T-shirt and his usual black pants. His bald spot gleams with sweat. I am walking up the driveway, within twenty-five feet of him, after taking a long, slow walk through the woods. I left the poems with him because I wanted him to have time alone with them, with me. I am vaguely afraid he didn't like them, but I have a stronger feeling that he loved them, that he loves me. My stomach is jumping like the bullfrog I just saw down at the reservoir, but I am trying to look cool on this scorching August afternoon in 1975.

"I wish I'd written it."

A shudder goes through my entire body. I'm sure I look like I've just been hit.

I ask if we can take a walk down Wood Mill Road, and he says sure. It's only the third or fourth such walk we've ever taken, but somehow it seems so familiar. I feel awkward at first, but not for long: One of his gifts is being able to make me feel at ease. I don't have to perform, pretend, or be anything or anyone other than what and who I am. He doesn't need proof of my manhood. I don't have to measure up. I am simply free to be. He goes back into the house and gets his favorite piece, his .22 Walther PPKS. I stuff my pockets full of .22 long rifle shells, trying not to be too obvious. I want this walk to last long. I want plenty of ammunition.

We're walking down the long gravel driveway, about to cross the threshold from gravel to dirt to worse dirt road, his gun in my right hand and his heart in my left. He jokes about how I will support him when he's old and horny and broke and I am young and horny and a famous writer. I want nothing more in this world, nothing more out of this life, want nothing more from him than the privilege of growing old with him. But I know it will never happen, I know he can't let it happen. I can't admit it out loud, but I can feel his death hovering somewhere over him, around him, emanating from somewhere deep inside. It's no secret, it's right up front, all out in the open, there for anyone with eyes to see. Someday I will learn to love him for this courage, this beautiful primitive ability to look death in the face and fuck it in the ass. He's fucking death just by taking this walk with me, by enjoying the crazy buzz of the grasshoppers and the blue jays cackling like insane old ladies and the box turtle basking in the sun and this dust rising out of the earth and hanging in the air, catching the light, the stuff from which all fathers are made and to which this father will soon return. I can feel it clanking around inside his bones, beneath his armor, waiting waiting waiting for its moment to claim him. He has one last chance on this orange August afternoon and he's taking it, he's sharing his last hours with me, he's letting me touch his death the way he's always let me touch his life. Only now it's not from a distance, it's not from a telephone booth in the dead of winter, it's not through letters, it's not through poems, it's not through solar stills or gold-plated penknives from sunken Spanish galleons. It's here right now, gleaming in the sun, ambling down the lane, shooting the shit like nothing extraordinary is ever going to happen, like everything incredible is of course going to happen. Maybe he figures if he didn't have the guts to share his life with me when I really needed him, at least he can share his death with me, up close, within the shelter of his aura, within hurting range; he's letting me feel it he's letting me touch he's opening to me a solemn Death Flower in its last day on fire. Of course I can't possibly know all of this now, but he's letting the bullet lodge for removal at a later date, no pain-killers necessary, doc, just gimme a shot o' the old red-eye and yank it. He's letting it sink deep, he's letting it tear through meat and bone, he's not trying to stop the bleeding, he's teaching me something without my knowledge and maybe even he doesn't really know what's happening. But he's letting each slug find its own true resting place. He knows I can take it even if I don't. Yet. That's what counts.

He appears to be in the prime of life, and maybe he is. There is a concentration of energy in his eyes I have never seen before, as if his soul is right there beneath the surface, as if I can reach out and touch him that deeply with the slightest effort, as if intimacy can come to him now with an immediacy that he has never experienced. I have always thought of him as one of those men who get more handsome every year: His skin has a deeper tone, his hair is thicker, his glow more radiant. I have always thought he looks better with long hair, and now his hair falls over his collar in rich black curls. His Manchu moustache is as thick and crooked as ever, giving him that rakish look he loves so much. And he's dressing more hip, too. He's wearing a pair of black bell-bottoms with red threads in all the seams.

Can it be true? In his fortieth autumn he looks younger than I have ever seen him. And it isn't just on the surface, it isn't on the surface at all. *It* is inside him, radiating an unmistakable warmth and gentleness. I feel it in his voice. I feel it when we shake hands. It is as if he has cut himself loose from some heavy baggage that has been with him all his life and now he is living in the open, naked, finally free.

In a kind of knowledge beyond words or feeling, in a corner of my heart I have not yet explored, I know he will not live to see where my life will take me, what it will become, and I will never have the chance to hear him say where he has been, what he did while he was there, what he has become. So for the first time I ask him about his childhood. And he tells me.

He tells me about his first love, and the death of that love; of his first death. He tells me about making homemade firecrackers

out of toilet-paper rolls and homemade gunpowder out of whatever he could get his paws on. Inevitably, he tells me about his
adolescent troubles with the law. He tells me secrets about
women.

"There are an awful lot of unhappily married women out
there." I don't say that's not nice, thou shalt not covet thy
neighbor's wife, even if she is unhappy. I listen and smile, a
solemn son.

He tells me how to keep them hot on your trail, how to juggle
more than one. He tells me about the era between marriages
when he decided it would be a neat challenge to have a different
woman every night of the week. Somehow he managed this
Herculean, suicidal task for the better part of a year. He goofed
one Fourth of July when they were all invited to a fireworks show
he was shooting for a wealthy private client. He said hello to the
first, and then the second, and then the third, and so on, until he
realized his ass was going to get cooked and the safest place to
play was as close to the fireworks as he could get without becoming smoke and ash.

At the end of the walk, I am satisfied, I feel full, I've heard
some great stories that will stay with me for a lifetime. I want to
sleep at least twelve hours in the peace and shelter of his Hill
House, breathing that rich magical air. I now know enough about
my father. I am well on my way to becoming a man. I can fly
away.

We fall out of touch in late autumn. Again I have no idea
where his life is leading, what it has become. We don't even
talk by phone at Christmas. One more letter arrives at the end of
the first week of January, just as I'm about to begin the second
semester of my sophomore year. I have a few questions to ask
him about it; but by the time I put them on paper, it's too late.

If he were here now, if I could only dial his number and call
him collect, or drop him a line, or put it in a poem and send it
special delivery so he'd have to sign for it . . . I would tell, I would
tell him everything, I would tell him he had nothing to fear from
me, absolutely nothing, nothing to fear from me but love.

2

His Black Dawn

Thanksgiving weekend, 1968. I am twelve, he is thirty-three, and we are riding in his leased Buick Riviera on the back country roads of rural Massachusetts. Technicolor trees are rushing by on all sides. A chill is in the air that says early snow. The wind is kicking up, cranking up for the first siege of winter. I'm happy. I'm with my dad, away from the accursed New Jersey suburbs. I'm with my dad, I'm feeling slightly awkward, as I usually do when I first see him after a long absence, but I'm beginning to unwind. I'm with my dad, and my happiness is rising just as fast as the temperature is dropping. I can't imagine a better way to spend Thanksgiving.

We have been making small talk for the past half-hour or so. There is a lull in the conversation, and then he says, in his calm, casual voice: "How would you feel if I married a black woman?"

I'm stunned, of course, but not because of the black woman. I'm stunned because he's asking me, *really* asking, for my twelve-year-old opinion on this very delicate, important matter. After a powerful silence, I answer as honestly as my prepubescent heart and soul can answer.

"I wouldn't mind. As long as you love her and she loves you."

We are on a mission—probably to pick up one or more of the following: snakes from some backwoods snake collector, fireworks from some fellow pyro freak, or dirty books from Sam the

Dirty Book Dealer. My father is not strange to me—we have the same interests, and, besides, he is the only father I will ever have.

I am thinking he is driving a little too fast and a little too close to the overhanging trees on my side of the road, but even his driving can't shock me. I think he drives great. Just the way I'd like to drive when I get my license: a little out of control. I love the way he doesn't seem to care how close he comes to hitting parked cars or pedestrians or trees, and since I never actually see him hit anything, I think he never does.

We talk, as usual, about school and girls and my escalating juvenile-delinquent behavior. I always wonder why he doesn't scream at me, like mom does, for getting busted for walking around town with a brown paper bag full of homemade grenades. I always wonder why he never acts surprised when I tell him about breaking into an abandoned drugstore and cracking the safe with nitric acid and a few other goodies I stole from his basement. I am always a bit confused when, instead of trying to discourage me from carrying a weapon, he shows me how to choose the right one for the right occasion, how to conceal it, how to use it safely. He gives me a book called *Kill or Get Killed* when I ask him about knife fighting, and he doesn't seem to notice when I sneak off to a corner to plan more JD escapades.

Two years after this cruise down a country lane, at the age of fourteen, I will call him collect from a phone booth in fear and trembling. I'll tell him, in a voice cracking seemingly beyond repair, that I just had a bad trip. Instead of asking me where I went that was so unpleasant, he suggests drinking lots of orange juice because it will help get the LSD out of my system. I am still drinking lots of orange juice, trying to get that acid out of my system.

Back at Hill House the main course for Thanksgiving dinner is pheasant he shot with a shotgun in the backyard. To be exact: a Number 10 Riot Gun, the kind police use to tear-gas antiwar and antipoverty and antinuclear demonstrators. The pheasant made the mistake of wandering within range of the kitchen window, and he shot it *through* the closed window. We laugh

about that while spitting out pellets every other bite. *We:* my
father, me, his black Dawn, and her three young children.

All right.
I'll confess.
It's love at first sight.

I remember I was mostly angry then; and now, as I summon
these past lives, the anger returns.

I am angry because I can't be with my father more, because
I have to live with my mother in the boring suburbs instead of
in the country with him and his foxy new lady.

I am angry because I am just beginning to feel the lean hard
rock of young manhood in my belly. I am too shy and too awkward and too self-conscious to go out and get laid.

I can recall no time when Dawn went out of her way to flirt
or tease, but there was a feeling—I'm struggling for the words,
and this is the best I can offer—a feeling that she would eventually become one of them, that I would be one of hers. Lovers,
that is.

Fuck it. Here is how it was exactly, in black and white: She
didn't have to flirt or tease; she was a walking talking breathing
tease to a near-maniacal sex-starved teen-ager.

I can recall only one time when we even came close to talking
about it, stepmother to stepson. It is another holiday, maybe a
year or two after my problems with The Law, and I am visiting
Hill House. It is late and I am going to bed. I sleep in the laundry
room, and as I open my door, Dawn appears and is about to
slink into theirs. She is wearing a tight, thin, shiny green mini-
dress with nothing on underneath. She has a drink in her right
hand and is trying to open their door with her left. We bump
shoulders halfway between our respective doors, and I don't
remember exactly what I said, but it must have been some
wisecrack about my father's legendary sexuality.

"Nobody's better than your father," she says with a slightly
drunken slur and a laugh.

I laugh along, and smile. What else can I do?
I'll tell you what else I can do, because I did.
I tear into that dress in my dreams.

I don't remember another time when we talked so intimately
about sex or anything else, but I know I devoted more time to
secretly studying her than to any other subject in my life at that
time. I am amazed even now how clearly all those well-developed
mental negatives still hold the original tints, shadings, and color
intensity. I love her almond-shaped brown eyes, how the brown
itself seems deeper, more mysterious, than the brown in white
women's eyes. I notice the broad facial structure, the fine thin
lips, the angles of her head when she is involved in a conversation
and when she is barely listening—there's a difference. I study
her laugh, how rich and deep and downright dirty it can be. She
isn't squeamish like most women about the important things in
life: *Playboy,* porno, guns, fireworks, snakes and other exotic
animals. *She* is an exotic animal. I know she carries a .25-caliber
Baretta and knows how to use it, and I love this about her.

I study her so well I can tell if she is wearing panties and a bra
without even letting her know I have glanced in her direction.

I listen to the silent language they speak, and try and try to
translate that special look they give each other. I hear hard
rhythmic thumping upstairs, but it's an embarrassingly long time
before I realize what it means.

I watch so carefully as she walks down the driveway that I am
able to predict her walk. I can tell you which quadrant of her
ass is in motion at any given time. I am always surprised when
she goes along with my father's crude jokes and awful puns, and
even adds to them. I am amazed that a woman can be so much
fun.

I especially take note whenever I see them touch or kiss or
dance slow or hold hands. For example: When we all watch TV
together, she lies down with her head in his crotch. Sometimes
they lie down together on the couch, and neither is inhibited
about where they touch or stroke each other. Of course I stare at
"Star Trek" or "Ultraman" in rapt wonder, working very hard to
hide my boyish supersexed agony.

. . .

Three and a half years later. The early-morning hours of January 14, 1976, to be exact. I am sleeping soundly on the floor of my single dorm room while a blizzard is on the rampage outside. Even though I am in a deep sleep, I wake suddenly shortly before eight o'clock. I don't know why, but all of a sudden I am wide awake. It is as if something from the beyond tapped me awake, gently but firmly, and there I am, waiting for a sign.

It is not long in coming. There is a knock and a voice at my door, which I recognize to be Anne, one of the girls from the room down the hall. A face peeks around the door, and she says quietly that there is a long-distance phone call for me. I thank her and even before I'm up I know what it's about. This is the only time I've gotten an unexpected long-distance call, and I have no doubt what awaits me in the hall.

"David, I called to tell you that your father passed away last night at around eight o'clock from a severe heart attack. I was with him and it was very sudden, very quick. Almost no pain. Amazingly quick. Thank God."

I don't feel anything, but I make a sudden outburst because I don't want Dawn to get the wrong idea.

This is the first time in my life that someone dear to me has died. I don't know how to react, what to think and feel, what to say and what not to say. No one, no thing, has prepared me for this moment.

I stumble out into the streets, into the blizzard. I don't care where I go, I want to lose all that college-boy baggage something fierce, I want to be the eye in the eye of the hurricane. I say to the wind, snow, ice: Hurt me, hurt me, make me feel this moment, don't let me forget. . . . I walk for hours, senseless. At first I don't feel anything, then it comes in a tidal wave, and I ride it. Then another and another and another. *Why? Why?* I say to no one. Nothing. I am in one of his poems, the one where he says: *Time warp, a knowing calm.* I know something is happening but have no idea what it is. Cars lose their colors, houses blur and become one with the trees, everything is getting lost in the snow, everything, the little town of St. Cloud is getting blown away. What comes after is raw as a mauled buffalo. I hardly know which way is up, but I know one thing for sure: I'll be leaving this place forever. If I ever come back, it will be for entirely different reasons and I will no longer be the boy I am today.

The next few days are a blur. I remember carrying the casket to the burial site on my shoulder with five other men. I remember wishing that we could have trudged through snowmelt for miles and miles, could have burned our grief halfway across the state through every storm imaginable. I remember feeling robbed of the chance to really feel the impact of his death—to burn it into my soul by engraving it into my body. I had seen photographs of Irish funeral processions that wound through rainy hills for miles and miles, whole villages walking across the countryside releasing their grief to the clouds and grasses and mud and rain and sleet, and I remember feeling a helpless anger at our way of burial. *It's too quick.* We shouldn't want to get rid of our loved ones so fast, with barely a kiss or a tear goodbye. When the casket was open, I kissed him on the lips, possibly the only time I was ever allowed to do that, but even that was improvised, my invention. No one told me you can touch the dead, let alone kiss them. If I hadn't done it then, I never would have had another chance. His lips were hard, and cold, and waxy, and I found out later that they looked so strange because the embalmer did a sloppy job of sewing them shut. I didn't even know we sewed shut the lips of our dead. Why? Are we afraid of what they might say about us, now that they are free?

I spend most of the year at Hill House. How can I possibly go back to a college where everyone pretends that death doesn't exist, people don't make wars, fathers don't leave behind huge messes to be cleaned up by dutiful sons?

A voice tells me I will have only one chance and, if I let it get away now, I'll never have another—a chance to dip my hands and feet into the debris he left behind, to clean up his act, to get my paws dirty with the stuff I've always wondered about: everything I didn't know about my father. I've always liked rummaging in his closets. Now I have a chance to do it for a whole year. *Stay,* the voice says. *Stay. You won't regret it.*

So I stay. I rip rusty gutters off the roof, paint the kitchen and dining and living rooms, put new doors on new hinges—all the maintenance he never did. I clean out the basement, attic, and closets—more garbage than I ever want to see again under one roof. There is one room in the basement that is ankle-deep in cat shit. I use a pick and shovel to get through to the concrete floor.

Dawn is busy preparing the legal papers, keeping her kids out of trouble, getting a new job, and working toward the day when we can pay his debts and sell the house and land. When that day comes, we'll move out. She'll go her way with her kids and broken dreams, and I'll go mine with my memories and an army foot-locker full of his papers and $100 hard cold cash.

3

Ode to Pandora

I floated for a couple of years. Went back to live with my mother in High Cliffs. Where else could I crash? Where else could I sort things out, plot the next step, and be reasonably well taken care of? The rent was cheap and the food decent. I knew the town. My mother wouldn't ask too many questions, wouldn't pry. I could work as a housepainter and carpenter while pursuing my writing. I set myself a goal, the only one I could think of that made any sense: to become a professional, published, free-lance magazine writer. Within two years, I told myself, I would save enough money to be able to move to New York City and rent my own apartment. I didn't need a psychic to tell me my chances of success would be far greater if I lived and worked in the media capital of the world.

I met my goal. Moved to Brooklyn because I couldn't find a cheap apartment in Manhattan. Wrote for the skin mags—*Oui, Chic, Club*—because they were the only magazines that would listen to a twenty-three-year-old unpublished nobody. I wrote about the dangers of nuclear energy, the controversy over genetic engineering, protection of privacy rights. I wrote about impotence, interviewed rock and movie stars. Most of my rock stars died after talking to *Oui* through me. Rock 'n' Roll, Sex and Death, Fame and Megadeath.

I never earned enough money to meet the minimum poverty level established by the United States Department of Health, Education and Welfare, but I was too proud to take welfare or food stamps. Orwell and Steinbeck never had food stamps. Henry Miller never went on welfare. I scribbled and starved.

I can still remember the day. The air was close, humid, muggy, riddled with a biting chemical stench. The hydrocarbon mists blanketed Brooklyn. It was almost noon in late spring 1979. My street was usually alive with Hispanic curses and jests, with black bop and jazz, but the kids were at school and the workmen hadn't broken yet for lunch, so all was quiet. I was on my way home from the library, where I'd been researching nuclear waste, trying to make the subject attractive to a girlie mag. Wouldn't I be better off writing smut? I'd make more money and would probably live longer. I'd certainly have more fun. At least I wouldn't get ulcers from the pressure. My phone would never be tapped. Even if I woke up with secret agents pounding down my door, they wouldn't be the same secret agents.

Just as I placed my right foot on the first steps of my stoop, I was shaken out of my cranial cloud. Could that be tear gas I smelled? How long had it been? Ten years? The last time I'd caught a whiff of this fun stuff had been in my dad's kitchen, when he was busy making tear-gas bullets. Could it really be that old familiar CS—the technical name for that specie of gas my dad (and Uncle Sam) played with years ago?

I made my way up the stairs, past the perennially stoned Haitian family, past the karate freak, past the college computer whiz kid, past the Shooting Gallery. The gas—for I was sure that's what it was—came wafting out of my apartment door, curling out from all four sides. How the hell did it get inside my apartment? Were the burglars getting weird? Were my roaches so fierce that my junkie neighbors in the Shooting Gallery had to put down a rebellion just to rifle my bureau and other shabby possessions?

There was no damage, at least none that I could see, because I couldn't see. Tear gas had unmistakably found its way into my apartment. Had crept along the lead-painted walls in great gray plumes, hanging just about at eye level.

I pulled out my handkerchief, wet it with water, and tried to breathe through it. The smoke seemed to be coming from

his army footlocker in the corner of the living room. There was
no sign of a struggle, forced entry, or intrusion of any kind. Everything was as I had left it. My papers were still on my now-
fumigated desk, untouched.

I had salvaged this trunk from Hill House, and had never
opened it—had taken Dawn's word that it was just full of his
papers and old junk. Figured I'd get to it someday. During that
year at Hill House, I had satisfied my curiosity more than I'd
ever dreamed possible, and felt no more compulsion to try to
know him by knowing his things. Let it wait. I've got more
important things to do now. Like make a living and forge a life
for myself. I'd almost forgotten about it after making it into a
coffee table by draping a dirty sheet over it. But there I was,
banging on the padlock with a hammer, weeping and howling
with laughter. The fucker found a way to mess up my life even
from the grave!

The cloud layer was too thick to see to the bottom, but I could
tell there'd been an explosion within the cask, probably just an
hour or two earlier, because it was still hot. Chunks of metal
were lodged in the walls of the trunk, sharp and red. There was
one big chunk of metallic substance that seemed unharmed, so
I picked it up, very gingerly, and slammed the lid back down.
After a few minutes, I was able to see what I already knew I held:
a grenade. This one still had the pin intact. It weighed about a
pound and a half.

FEDERAL GRENADE

#121

"NO FIRE"   "AIR FLOAT"

TEAR GAS GRENADE
(blast dispersion type)

TO ASSEMBLE: Screw firing mechanism AF2 into top center
hole.

TO DISCHARGE: Grasp in throwing hand with fingers holding
firing lever against grenade body—withdraw safety cotter
—throw.

CAUTION: Do not relax grip on firing lever after pulling until grenade is thrown. DO NOT CARRY GRENADE BY SAFETY COTTER RING.

DANGEROUS IF DISCHARGED WHILE HOLDING IN HAND!

There was an expiration date at the bottom: USE BEFORE AUG 1959. There was also the name of the manufacturer, but the label was so worn I couldn't read it.

I wondered briefly what you were supposed to do with this artifact—this *device*—if you weren't able to "use" it before August 1959, which happened to have been the month my parents divorced. I wondered if Pandora ever had this problem, and released a quick laugh, whereupon the dirty handkerchief fell out of my mouth, and I commenced to cry.

I recovered enough to open all the windows. My eyes, nose, and throat were burning beyond belief. I had to know what other "papers" might be in that trunk. The stench was still too fierce to leisurely rummage through its contents, so I opened it once more and made a quick, blind grab. My eyes were streaming, but I *had* to know. Through the tears I managed to make out the following message, typed on his typewriter:

The subject of this interview is an explosive expert who worked for 20 years designing assassination devices for the CIA while holding various cover jobs in military research and development. While still in high school, he was regularly approached by CIA contacts with requests for poisons, explosives, gun silencers and specially designed gadgets for killing or incapacitating people. He worked his way through a number of employers during this period and finally ended up director of research at a large, well-known firearms manufacturer, where he continued to do work for the CIA as well as implement projects for the gun company, which, in turn, sold its work to the military.

His career began in the early Fifties. In the late Sixties, he had two heart attacks in as many years. His absence from work due to illness finally forced him to quit and in 1970 he had his last official contact with the CIA. At this meeting, he said he did not want to do any more work for the agency. For a number of months, they followed him, thinking that he was running guns to radicals or showing them how to build terrorist weapons. They finally left him alone, as far as he was able to tell.

To establish his credibility, I verified that he did hold the jobs he claims to have held. In addition to this, I saw extensive documentation of the type of work he was doing. He also showed me several devices that he had built for the CIA, including a modified butane cigarette lighter that fired a tiny poisoned dart capable of penetrating a heavy coat. He brought out an explosive .22-caliber bullet, which I tested in the presence of a firearms expert. It did explode. His activities were also verified by others in the intelligence community who are involved in similar fields. And, finally, he was given a series of lie-detector tests, which indicated that he was telling the truth.

The subject wanted to remain anonymous to protect his family. Chemical and material names have been deleted in some cases to avoid providing a "cookbook" of weapons and tactics.

No doubt this was my father. No doubt at least two of those employers were the Lincoln Institute in Boston and Western Weapons, a major firearms manufacturer whose lab was, at least in 1968 when I last visited there, located in the rural countryside of western Massachusetts. No doubt some of those blobs in the backyard, those gadgets on the bookshelves, those weird-caliber handguns and rifles in the closets . . .

No doubt about those heart attacks. They were distant from me, *he* was distant from me, those summers when his heart attacked, but how many fathers have hearts that attack twice in as many years? How many fathers quit working for gun companies in 1970 and became free-lance pyrotechnists—free-lance fireworks designers and shooters? How many fathers enlist their sons on the Fourth of July to shoot fireworks shows for country doctors on huge estates? Some of my happiest memories . . .

I'd seen that modified butane cigarette lighter. I'd found it (could there have been more than one?) in the basement in one of his junk boxes. I'd asked him what it was, and he had told me, point-blank, no extra emphasis, nothing startling in this revelation. And I had accepted it and moved on. What boy questions his father when his father drops a bomb like *that?* Its a privilege just to have the guy for a father. You want to prove to him that you can be cool, you can be trusted, he can tell you anything and it won't go anywhere.

And he had told me things, things I'd never repeated to anyone. He told me he *shot nine men with nine bullets from my metric Mauser on a fetid nightmare road in Venezuela.* He told me that at the time he was *a bright and aggressive arm of The Group.* He never said exactly when, but I gathered it was in the late Fifties, when I was two or three years young and he was twenty-two or twenty-three.

My mother and I were extra baggage to him then. My memories of him rarely went back before I was six or seven— he was so vague, so invisible yet omnipresent. But I could never hate him. Never. When I heard these tales, I loved him even more, his myth grew ever larger. It grew so large I was compelled to keep it secret, absolutely secret, dead secret. Not that he made me feel I would be punished if I told anyone, quite the opposite. He made it sound as if he were leaving it up to me. If I wanted to tell someone, well, that must be okay, because you're smart enough to know whom to talk to. But who in my life was good enough to enjoy this intimacy, who could be trusted that much? Not even my first girl, not even my second girl, not even my third. No one.

He never came out and said who The Group was, but more to the point: Who else could it be?

I'd found an unusual box of .22 shells one visit, found them on the living-room bookcase, and asked if I could use them to go out plinking on the target range behind the house, up in the woods.

"Yeah, I guess so," he said. His voice was tentative, almost shy. It had always been yes before, unless there was a very obvious reason not to, like the neighbors had been complaining a lot lately about the noise, so maybe it would be better to wait till next visit. But now it was a little yes and a little no.

"Are you sure? Is there something special about these? You wanna save 'em for a happy occasion?"

He laughed. "No. Go ahead. Just be careful. Don't shoot anything metal or glass or even plastic with 'em. You're liable to send out a lotta shrapnel."

I snickered. I'd been shooting .22s since I could walk. They'll travel up to two miles, but *shrapnel?* This was bizarre.

"They explode on impact. They're made for taking out heads of state and other undesirables. Literally. Each one of those slugs'll pop a human head like it's a gourd being hit by a .45 at close range. Be careful. Have fun."

I had fun. Lots of it.

It had never occurred to me that I had been traveling an incredibly paradoxical career path. I'd put my father and his death toys so far behind me, I thought that was all there was to it. Sure, these were not the toys upon which poets are usually raised, but so what? My father was my father. He wasn't a killer, he wasn't a destroyer, he wasn't an assassin, he wasn't a man who steals innocent souls in the middle of the night, he wasn't anyone's fool, he wasn't a vicious human weapon who dealt terror at the touch of a button, he wasn't a pawn, he was too smart to be used by anyone. He was my father. I loved him, I loved his paraphernalia, his trappings. I loved the suspense of not knowing what I'd find in his basement this visit, or what he'd tell me on a walk down a country lane, or what little bomb he'd let me detonate out on the range. I never made the connection. My father was my father, I loved him and he loved me.

He was dead now, and so were his mysteries, so was his magic, so was his charm. My father was dead now, had been dead for two or three years too many. He was gone and he'd never be back, we'd never walk down Wood Mill Road again. I'd never have another chance to ask him to his face, to test his voice when he answered me, to search his eyes for answers, answers to questions like "Is there a God?" and "What is life?" and "Why is there always a war?" and "Why do we have to die?"

Once I asked him: What is death? Asked him over sausage and eggs in a Kountry Kitchen in that last August of his prime, our last meal together, one of my highest highs, sharing an unhealthy meal in a grimy diner on a side road to nowhere important, nowhere spectacular, no great temples, no holy shrines erected along these asphalt paths.

"It's just like changing your clothes," he said, eyeing the waitress, who was always named Candy. "People make a big deal about it, but I can't figure out why."

I'd never have another chance to search his eyes for answers, to learn about writing from his poems and letters, to learn about life and death from his lives and deaths.

But I'd have to try.

PLAYBOY INTERVIEW

January 1977

MR. DEATH: I had a lot of strange ideas and talents. I was apprenticed to an Italian fireworks designer when I was about fourteen. I remember he used to eat garlic and sardine sandwiches and I'd kid him that he'd set off the whole place just by breathing on the fireworks. And actually, maybe that's what he did, because one day it was snowing hard and I couldn't get a ride to his place. When I finally got there, his business had spread laterally and him with it. Something went wrong, the shed went up, and he died.

My first experience with chemical warfare came even before that. When I was about eleven, I was always getting beaten up because I was small and couldn't see. Somebody'd hit me and I'd lose my glasses and walk into a telephone pole. So I started carrying a handkerchief full of cayenne pepper. Snap it in the face of a kid any size and you've won the fight.

PLAYBOY: How were you at defending yourself?

MR. DEATH: I was absolutely terrible at fighting. First of all, I was not very athletic or healthy or robust. Second, my eyesight was terrible, so if I lost my glasses *I* lost. And that's the first thing they go for when somebody slugs you. I was blind.

PLAYBOY: When were you first interested in fireworks and other odd . . .

MR. DEATH: I can remember being interested and reading about fireworks—popular articles and books—when I was seven or eight. I'd always look at pictures of them and try to go to displays. The first time I tried to make gunpowder was when I was eight.

PLAYBOY: How did it work?

MR. DEATH: Terribly, of course. But it was a start in the right direction.

PLAYBOY: Are you essentially self-taught?

MR. DEATH: More or less. Mostly more.

PLAYBOY: How were you first contacted by the Central Intelligence Agency?

MR. DEATH: At the age of seventeen or thereabouts, I met M., who was going to high school at the same time as me. Since I had a consuming interest in things explosive and in firearms, we got along well together. He had an encyclopedic knowledge of guns, particularly Nazi weaponry. M. was a fascist basically. He had a deep-seated, violent prejudice against anything that wasn't Aryan.

PLAYBOY: You mean like you?

MR. DEATH: Well, I never could explain that. One day I asked him, because he professed hatred for Jews constantly. I said, "How come we're such good buddies if you hate Jews?" He said, "You know, you're not really a Jew." I said, "Because I don't follow any religion?" He said, "Yeah, that's part of it. But *you* don't have the Jewish outlook." I never did discover what that was, so I let it slide. At that tender age I knew that M. was very much involved with gun-selling and all that jazz. I never knew precisely what else he was involved in, but it was one calm day that he announced to me—and I didn't believe him, I must tell you—that he was doing some work for the CIA.

PLAYBOY: Wasn't that a violation of his secrecy oath?

MR. DEATH: No. It was a recruitment effort. He said, "You're a pretty bright guy and have all kinds of ideas that could be handy. Why don't you work with me? We'll send a couple bucks your way." At that stage I wasn't interested in money, so I said, "How about guns?" He said, "Oh, yeah." So I designed things in order to get guns. At seventeen I owned the most incredible arsenal, shit that you can't imagine: a 3.5 rocket launcher, a .57 recoilless rifle, complete with ammunition. An array of heavy machine guns that you just wouldn't believe. My basement was jammed with—

PLAYBOY: Did your parents know?

MR. DEATH: My parents didn't know what I was or what the hell I was doing and didn't care.

PLAYBOY: You were still in high school?

MR. DEATH: That's correct. My senior year.

PLAYBOY: You're saying the CIA recruited you when you were seventeen years old?

MR. DEATH: Around that time.

PLAYBOY: Is that common practice?

MR. DEATH: I have no idea. M. was working for them even before that. It's not so young if you consider that a lot of seventeen-year-old kids fought in Vietnam and World War Two. People always think of spooks as forty-year-old seasoned James Bond types. Hey, that kid riding by on that bicycle may be carrying an automatic pistol in his belt—with National Security as his excuse.

PLAYBOY: I would like to go through the recruiting process in detail, simply because I don't think anyone has brought out the fact that they actually recruit kids so young.

MR. DEATH: That's a very bad thing to go digging into at the moment. I don't know what M. is doing. I don't know what his position is. He's an ominously dangerous man, and I'd just as soon not get him peeved, angry, or anything else. Not that I live in mortal fear, I don't. I haven't had contact with him for quite a while. But I see no reason to stir that up.

PLAYBOY: What came after the recruitment pitch?

MR. DEATH: It was a very simple setup, in which the Sunday School–type indoctrination sessions were taught in a small cell, in which assorted characters like myself had access to basic instruction in firearms, explosives, and so on. We used a church as a front.

PLAYBOY: How did this come about? The guy just came to you and asked you to do some stuff and you did some stuff?

MR. DEATH: Mostly it was with my good friend M. They were like seminars.

PLAYBOY: He'd just say come along?

MR. DEATH: Yeah. We're going to have a meeting and we'll be talking about this machine gun or demolition tactics or that kind of thing.

PLAYBOY: Were you rewarded for attending these meetings or was it just a kind of social gathering of brilliant minds?

MR. DEATH: It was more instructional than social.

PLAYBOY: And who did the instructing?

MR. DEATH: I don't know who they were, but they were certainly well prepared with slides, charts, literature and so on. Documents. Stuff to read.

PLAYBOY: Was it or is it your impression that the practice of recruiting kids was just run-of-the-mill? Was it well organized?

MR. DEATH: It was fairly well organized, but my impression was that it was experimental at that time, that they were trying to see if it was a good way to train crack troops, if you will.

PLAYBOY: Do you have any notion of the success or failure?

MR. DEATH: None at all. I would have no way of knowing.

PLAYBOY: It strikes me as odd that someone like you—namely smart and curious and inventive—that you weren't constantly asking what was going on. Why didn't you ask? Why weren't you more forcefully curious about what was happening? Everything seems weird to me now. Maybe it didn't seem weird to you then.

MR. DEATH: It didn't seem weird to me then.

PLAYBOY: Secret stuff, government spy.

MR. DEATH: Yeah, but see, that had it's own appeal. It would appeal to many levels, especially to a kid. I was a big kid making bombs and doing it under government license. It was a macho thing to a certain extent.

PLAYBOY: But you couldn't take advantage of the macho thing, could you?

MR. DEATH: Oh, in my own head I could.

PLAYBOY: Didn't you ever tell your girlfriend, "Hey, I'm—"

MR. DEATH: No, for the simple reason that I knew I'd be jeopardizing a good thing. I'd lose it. Number two, I was satisfied with my own rewards, of knowing that I was part of an elite. I think they had me psyched out pretty well. I don't think it was an uneducated guess on their part at all. Besides, who the hell would believe you in 1952? I'm making silencers in the basement for the CIA. Come on.

PLAYBOY: Exactly what did they want you to do?

MR. DEATH: Nonsophistication. It was slanted so a guy could improvise systems, methods, weapons, techniques. Mostly what they used my brains for, what I was good at, was coming up with whacked-out solutions to difficult problems.

PLAYBOY: Can you be more specific?

MR. DEATH: Mostly silencers. Fooling around, developing them, making some. I'd turn out a model and screw around with it. Now, I don't precisely know what happened with those things.

PLAYBOY: But you'd give them to M.?

MR. DEATH: Yeah. He'd say, "We need one for a 9mm Mauser pistol," just to give you an example. So I would load the ammunition so that it was subsonic. Most bullets are so loud when they're fired because they're breaking the sound barrier. I would load the powder so they'd be firing below the speed of sound. He'd want two or three hundred of that. Then I would build a Maxim-type silencer for that gun. A Maxim silencer works basically the same way that an automobile muffler works. Series of baffles, that's all.

PLAYBOY: And you would make a metal tube?

MR. DEATH: Check. And line it up. Little metal washers stacked on each other with holes for the bullet to go through. Once I made one where the parts were strung on a piece of jewelry chain so it looked like some kind of modernistic jewelry. It was actually rather attractive. I made another one with Japanese coins, some of which are manufactured with holes already in them. I packed some of them with glass wool for additional silencing. Most of them were throwaways. One-time, two-time use, and then you threw it the hell away. I remember now that every single one that I made was a disassembly type. In other words, you could strip it into pieces and dispose of the pieces, without having to throw away a whole hunk of metal, which would be pretty obvious. Most of them were for .22 automatics.

This was the physical work. Later, a good portion of what I did was just talk. Brainstorm. He would say, "Suppose we had this situation . . . " It was like a chess game. It was a long time before he openly recorded the sessions. In fact, it was so long ago they were using wire recorders.

Then I got heavily into experimenting with pyrotechnics, which I had always liked. I loaded small-arms ammunition with white phosphorous; .38s and .45s in a neat, sealed shell, so that at close range you could really zonk somebody. A very small charge, a sealed cup, and a slog of WP in a plastic capsule to keep it away from the powder. At close range it was a pretty nasty incendiary weapon.

PLAYBOY: How did you and M. avoid getting caught?

MR. DEATH: Except for the firearms jobs, which were certainly illegal, I never knew M. to do anything specifically illegal. He stored explosives, though, which wasn't as illegal then as it is today. He had shit that was mindbending. A case of grenades would come in and go out in a day or two. Where's that going? It's not going to the Mafia. He was very good at it. Really amazing. I could see why he was very useful to them.

PLAYBOY: How long did you work exclusively through M.?

MR. DEATH: I knew M. on and off continuously through high school. I don't remember exactly when I met him, but from roughly late high school and more or less continuously through my first marriage, which lasted from the time I was nineteen till I was twenty-five. That would have been roughly 1952 to 1960. We had a very steady liaison, in the sense that I would see him once or twice a week. The turning point in my relationship with M. came when I joined the [deleted] Institute and went to work in their laboratories when I was nineteen.

I have no formal education, by the way. I was thrown out of high school. Once we had a science fair. I was a shitty student, but I was good in science classes naturally, and they—poor fellas—gave us free rein and said, "Do your number." You've heard the normally apocryphal story of the kid who blew up the chem lab? Well, I did. I set up a TNT nitrator that ran by itself. You know, the complete system. Very neat. Beautiful model. It metered toluene, nitric acid and sulfuric acid automatically. Metered the drops and measured the temperatures and the whole smear. Beautiful little system. Unfortunately I let it run over one whole weekend. About two o'clock Sunday morning that mother blew up, and boy oh boy.

PLAYBOY: How much TNT went up?

MR. DEATH: Not a lot. But enough to do considerable damage to the lab. It took out a lot of windows. Nobody got hurt. And there were other things I did in high school.

Even then I was screwing around with chemical warfare. A friend and I synthesized alphachloracetophenone. The old CN tear gas. It's a solid, sugarlike substance and it's very potent. We snuck up to the lab with a box of condoms, inflated them with hydrogen, dumped half a teaspoon full of CN into each one, and then ran down the back stairway and released them in the girl's gym. At the class break the girls go in with their teacher, and the teacher comes out red-faced a few minutes later. You can hear the girls laughing because these rubbers are floating around on the ceiling. The teacher comes back with one of those janitor poles with a nail taped to the end of it. OK, are you ready for this picture? And of course, when she bursts the condoms, the tear gas is released and this delightful exodus of scantily clad nymphets runs out into the hall.

PLAYBOY: There is a distinct problem with that story and I don't know whether you recognize it or not. Maybe you are the origin of that story, but every high school kid in the country has a story that goes something like, "I didn't know the guy, but my brother who's a year older than me had a friend who . . ." But you're claiming you actually did this.

MR. DEATH: Yes indeed. How do I explain it?

PLAYBOY: I don't know.

MR. DEATH: [silent]

PLAYBOY: Did you do it?

MR. DEATH: Sure. Unfortunately there was one flaw in the plan. We were the only males in the hall, and we were rolling on our asses and laughing and drinking in the scenery and they caught us. For which I was forthwith expelled for several weeks plus the . . . anytime something exploded, it was my fault. My father came and got me and I never did graduate from high school until I was twenty-six. By then I was working at the [deleted] Institute. My boss finally said, "God damn it, you can't do this kind of work without some kind of paper." So I went and got my general degree.

4

Siss-Boom-Bah

Buffett High is still on the corner of Bingham and Bly.

Buffett High. Siss-boom-bah.

The football field (where he never scored) is still here, and on this bright windy September morning it is full of little heroes wearing plastic shields and shoulder pads. There are still bright squads of blond cheerleaders (that he never got his hands on) prancing to the beat.

There is a man with no legs on the sidelines, walking on his hands with his wife at his side. He's still smiling and saying, "I remember when . . ." I'm not smiling. I'm thinking: Who designed and built that land mine that took your legs? Who sent you to the front, for what cause? Whose side were you on? Does it matter anymore? Are you proud of your sacrifice? When you played on this field, did you ever dream that someone or something could and would take your legs, and try to take much more?

These thoughts come all at once: How long would it take to dismantle this prison brick by brick? Who laid these bricks before he starved, and who took his place when he slumped to the ground?

What went through my father's mind as he walked up and down these steps? Did he ever try to count them, as I am now, or did he have more important things on his mind?

How often did he turn his head at what just walked by in skirts?

I say to no one: I am coming to collect the pieces you left behind.

Marvin J. Cribbins, the archetypal high-school principal. If you saw him walking down the street, you'd know he was a high-school principal. If you were eating dinner at his table and he said, "Please pass the gravy," it would sound like a principal's decree. His voice has little or no modulation: It is loud and deep, or very loud and very deep. He is big. His shoulders, arms, hands, neck, chest, and thighs are big. Some paunch, but he is not fat. Just big. In the first five minutes of conversation, he finds a hundred ways to make you feel small, but he does it so well you hardly notice.

I think: *What kind of woman* . . .

I ask him how to find my father's page in the June 1952 yearbook, and he shouts, "Don't ask me! How should I know? I don't sit around here all day looking at yearbooks! I've got work to do!" He is truly indignant. "Not that this job is important or anything, but . . . five thousand people live here! It's a city!" Then he reaches over his desk, takes the yearbook out of my hands, finds Barry's page, and, instead of handing it back so I can treasure that first delicious shock of discovery, he says, "Isn't this interesting . . ." and reads the goodbye blurb beneath my father's picture.

Glee Club, School Paper ("Freelance"), Literary Magazine.

"Snake" . . . appropriate name for guy who used to carry snakes in his shirt . . . known for movie "criticisms" in Paper . . . unique sense of humor . . . going places . . . listen to his dissertations on life, love . . . a true intellectual.

Reads in a voice so thick, so crude and downright mediocre that I realize this is a fitting reawakening of the ghost in that senior-class picture. Later I will see a sharp edge in that picture, a hint of future hardness.

"You sure are lucky I looked through this for you," Marvin blurts, puffed and pleased.

Marv says he came here in 1949 as a substitute teacher and never knew my father. I suddenly know how he got to be top dog. He'd probably love to spill his version, but I don't ask and he doesn't think of it. He pulls out Barry's "pocket"—an envelope that contains all of his school records. Yes, he can show me these records, but first he'll have to explain what they mean. He can't let me copy them without a letter from my mother or one of my father's parents.

"I'm twenty-two years old," I say, "and he's *dead*. What am I gonna do, blackmail a ghost?"

He grins like a buddy. Shrugs stupidly, but very sincere. "Yeah, I know. But it's the law. And I have to obey the law."

He calls a week later.

"I think we may have found a gold mine. I talked with Mrs. Joffy, one of our English teachers, and she says she remembers your dad. Did you know your father wrote poetry for her?"

"No."

"Didn't know that, didja?"

"No. Was it any goo—"

"Don't ask *me!* Ask *her!*"

I am walking into someone else's home movie. I have a camera whirring on my shoulder and a notepad and pen in my hands. Scene after scene unfolds before me. It is all so strange and yet all so familiar.

Clara Joffy meets me in the hall. "You're so lucky I'm still here," she says. "You're so lucky I have this hour and a half free to chat. Today is Conference Day. All the parents come in to talk with us about their precious little ones."

"Yes," I say, somewhat disoriented. "I am very lucky." Later I will realize just how lucky—that so much of his past is still alive and kicking.

"To me he was Barry, and I'm stunned." She is referring to brief details I told Mr. Cribbins about my father's career and early death.

We make small talk while she leads me to an empty classroom on the third floor, where we will be able to talk without interruption. I have no idea where we're going. Only when we are deep into the interview will she tell me, oh so casually, that this was his classroom. He sat back there in the second-to-last seat in the second row. He wrote his compositions on these chalkboards. He hung his little coat in this cloakroom. His pranks once tore this class apart.

Walking into his past: a musty classroom with creaking old pine floorboards and chalk dust in the air and tired sunlight filtering through yellowed shades. One hundred thousand children have passed through these halls, have walked these floorboards, have sat in these chairs, and some have left their signatures, but these walls still stand. If anyone ever came close to tearing them down, I'm sure it would have been you, dad. How much high explosive would it have taken? Are you listening? Which brand would you have selected for this type of demolition? Would the device have fit in your lunchbox, or would you have had to smuggle it in brick by brick? Would you have gone for damage to property or damage to bodies, or both? How many souls would you have taken? None? All? Are you listening?

I look back there over my left shoulder and I swear I see the little man with the smooth black hair and deep brown eyes. I can't believe it. I can't believe it's coming to me so easily, so clearly, this entire chapter, *right here*. All I have to do is record it with my tape recorder and my eyes and ears. So much, I want to believe, like it must have been for him.

On this particular morning, I don't want to spar with anyone, don't want to prove anything to anyone. Don't *have* to. But she is appraising me, sizing me up the way a man measures another man. She radiates the feeling that she is the fountain of wisdom and I have come to sit at her feet. Whatever she doesn't know about him obviously isn't worth knowing. Just how much do *you* know about your father? On this particular morning, I'd rather sleep late than win points with a tenth-grade English teacher.

She seats herself behind her desk. There aren't any other chairs, so I pull up one of the armchairs that the kids use. (Later in my research, I will discover the odd fact that Benjamin Franklin invented this kind of chair as well as the first American detonator.) Clara is wearing a knee-length pinkish dress. Her body is thick—like Cribbins—but obviously well cared for. Her hair is clipped short to fit her face, and has been dyed black but not offensively so. Her bifocals are large and magnify her owlish eyes, making them even more intense. They dart back and forth, always afraid they're missing something. Eyes of the fairly intelligent that must prove their intelligence.

It doesn't take long to get her going. Pretty soon she's talking with incredible intensity and accuracy about things that happened thirty years ago. She only stops to cross-examine the interviewer.

"You didn't go to school here? Did you go to college? No? Probably thought it was a waste of time. Like your father. . . .

"He was rather diffident. Your manner is something like his. And he looked something like you. Same skin tone. Same color eyes. . . .

"He must have been hard to live with. Are you, too? . . .

"You really never knew what he did? Well, how could you if it was CIA? That's secret, isn't it?"

There's a pause after each of her questions. When I'm just about ready to chew on an answer, she saves me the trouble by doing it herself.

Her body language is succinct: arms crossed now and then, legs crossed now and then. She doesn't look her age, but is not as sure of that as I. She speaks in theatrical, exaggerated, snobbish tones, with all sorts of untranslatable inflections. Soon I'm taking notes so quickly I lose track of myself, of her, this school, this age. And I fall into him, his age, his world.

Let's say he's walking into his favorite class, an English class. Clara Joffy is his favorite teacher, and today he wants to impress her. He has brought a surprise for her, a little special something from his private kingdom. He brings a snake. A five-foot boa constrictor named Boris. Boris is big and fat and hot and thick underneath his shirt, pressed against his belly, wrapped around his waist. He doesn't know it—or maybe he does—but he's trying out his mask, the mask he will wear for the rest of his life. He's got a secret, he's got power, and he's going to make sure everyone knows it.

"Wanna see my friend?" he says to Mrs. Joffy quite innocently.

"Yes," she says, going along with the game.

He lets this huge thing slither out his sleeve and up the aisle. Of course the whole class goes wild. She's usually scared to death of snakes, but when Barry holds them it's all right. She thinks it's funny. She thinks he's marvelous. He is.

Clara realizes very quickly that snakes are not just playthings for Barry. He's serious. He shows her plaster casts he has made of several of his "pets," and tells her he has sold similar casts for $250 each. They are correct in every detail, he says.

He is also selling antivenom to scientific laboratories. Antivenom is made from the actual venom of poisonous snakes. Somehow, in a conversation, he lets her know he is milking his own rattlesnakes for their venom. He tells her he catches them during school vacations by hitchhiking down to South Carolina and Georgia.

She believes him. She believes everything he says. She has no reason to think he lies.

They are reading *Ivanhoe,* and Clara asks the class what it means. A tense, scrawny kid in the back raises his hand slowly, as if he is doing the class quite a favor.

"Ivanhoe . . . is a cardboard character . . . one-dimensional . . . who two women are crazy about . . . for some reason I'll never understand."

"He always gave answers like that," Clara says. "It was like: Wellll, I'll give you a little answer to your little question. Then I'll be on my way.

"I always gave him A's because he was so unusual."

He's already a marvelous cartoonist—as well as an expert with snakes and literature—in her eyes, at least. Barry makes a newspaper for Clara. Hand-prints, hand-letters a complete newspaper. Has himself down as editor, treasurer, vice-president, chairman of the board, etc. He includes an advertisement:

FOR SALE. THREE MONGEESE.
No. Cross that out.
FOR SALE. THREE MONGOOSES.
No. Oh, the heck with it.
FOR SALE. ONE MONGOOSE
AND ANOTHER AND ANOTHER.

He also includes a little subscription blank on the back, and Clara fills it out for the next issue. Or at least she thinks she filled it out. She can't remember. "I'm sorry I didn't save these things," she says, and I want to wring her neck. "Especially since I had the feeling we would all hear from him again. But, you know, one can't hold on to every scrap of paper."

There are bound to be disciplinary problems with a student like Barry. One day Clara runs into him in the hall.

"What are you doing here when you're supposed to be in German?"

"This is a waste of my time," he says very seriously. "I have important things to do. I don't have time to listen to this garbage."

And he won't go. And he's right. It *is* a waste of time. It *is* garbage. But he needs the credits to graduate, so Clara gets him switched over to a music class. Then they fill him up with music courses. Glee Club, A Cappella, Boys Choir.

The slow students are mixed in with the regular students. The slow students have come from several classes and don't know who is slow and who is average. Barry has some fun.

They're studying Wordsworth's poem "The World Is Too Much With Us." It talks about what a mess the world is and how only the rich are admired. Clara asks the class what it means. This young man in the second-to-last seat in the second row raises his hand, and in this sloooowwwww voice, says: "Thisssss . . . poem . . . is . . . about . . . a . . . rat. . . ." And he stops. Even the slow students turn their heads to look at this exceptionally slow student who is now apparently nodding out at his desk. They begin to snicker. Until he finishes the sentence, with his head completely bowed: ". . . race that all of us run every day of our lives."

He hands in a composition to another teacher. A nice maidenly lady who believes in correctness. She fails him. She says he's a smart aleck. Clara is stunned. How can you fail this marvelous kid? But then, she'd have failed him for saying Ivanhoe was a cardboard character. The composition goes like this:

There was a man who told tall tales. He always exaggerated. When he heard that somebody had done something, he would always say that he had done it better. One day when he was exaggerating a story, he felt hot breath on his neck, and the Devil appeared and said, "We don't like this. Next time you do something like this, we're going to make you go through the experience you claim you had."

So he was good for a while. Then one day he was sitting in a bar, listening to some guy say he nearly froze to death the last time he was up north. So this man who always exaggerated had to say, "That puts me in mind of the time when I was all alone up in Alaska in an igloo—" And just then he felt the hot breath on his neck again. He was suddenly transported to Alaska. The Devil appeared and said, "This is just to show you what we can do. Don't you go around telling tall tales again!"

The man was properly chastened, and he was very good for a while. Then, again, one day he was sitting down at the bar. He heard somebody talking about how he had once been stranded on a desert island, and he just had to say, "That puts me in mind of the time when I was stranded on a desert island—" And he felt that hot breath, and he said, "Just a second—with only Jane Russell and Betty Grable as companions—" Then he turned to the Devil and said, "If you don't mind, I'll go get my toothbrush."

Another one of his compositions begins like this:

"In the Beginning, the Lord made Americans. Then He made just ordinary people. . . ."

He is flunked for that one, too. His teacher says he is still being a smart aleck. (He took the name of the Lord in vain.)

He gives her correct compositions thereafter.

"You could twinkle your eye with him. You could look back there when somebody made a stupid comment, and you'd know you were going to get a *lit-tle* twinkle."

He is always turning posters around. But then, Clara thinks, his taste is good. He sees that this thing is claptrap, this one is shoddy, this one is nonsense. He shows you he knows you understand, too.

The name Rothman always sounded Jewish to Clara, but she understood from him that it wasn't. If anybody ever mentioned it (and they did, often), she would say, "No, I don't think he's

Jewish. I think he belongs to that Rothman family with the drugs or something. They're German or something."

His Civil War guns are the beginning of the end. He brings one in to school, supposedly to trade with somebody, but he gets caught. Clara believes that if he says he brought it to school to trade, that's exactly what he's going to do with it. The kid is marvelous.

But there are others who say he is going to end up in jail or an asylum. Clara claims he's an authentic genius. They can't understand this *individual* who goes against laws. So they throw him out.

"You're right," they say to Clara. "He's a great kid. He's a smart kid. But he doesn't belong in a public school. He should be in a place where he can have the kinds of things he's interested in."

They believe that because he has a gun—even a gun that is muzzle-loaded and can only fire one shot at a time, with much difficulty and nonexistent accuracy—he's automatically bad. He's dangerous. He might shoot somebody.

"Not *Barry*," Clara tells the administration. "For one thing, I really think he's a pacifist. I doubt very much that he'd fight. Secondly, he *collects* guns. If Barry told you . . ."

She has no reason to think he lies, but it's no use.

Eventually she cools it. Stops communicating with him. He has been out of school for a while and she has recently married—to an attorney. She has her own problems. Her new husband becomes seriously ill.

Barry sends her samples of his poetry. "Again, the poems were superb. But he must have just discovered sex, because they were very graphic . . . I showed them to my new husband, and he got suspicious."

Barry calls and asks if she has gotten the poems.

"Yes," she says nervously, "but I haven't had time to read them." She thinks: Why am I dragging this thing on? I have so many other things to worry about! She feels bad about it, but what else can she do?

One day she's in the teachers' lounge, and someone tells her that Barry is waiting in the hall for her. She's fearful of how to handle that poetry—you know, what to do.

"I was a little cool and he was very sensitive. . . . Mind you,

I would not consider those poems to have been *porno*graphic, just graphic. Somehow he started writing the stuff and wanted me to see it. It's only—I was naïve. I was a young teacher, you know, thinner. It's only *now* that they tell me some of the boys had crushes on me. I had no such feeling about Barry. Here was this unusual kid that I enjoyed. That's it. I probably gave him more enthusiasm than knowledge anyway. That's as far as it should go. Who needed to handle that anyway? I said to myself: Let someone else take it from here."

Where did he get all these talents? These tastes? From his family? From within? She doesn't know now and didn't know then.

"When I heard he married young, I was surprised and glad. I hoped he'd find himself. But the snakes would be hard for any woman to take care of. It takes great love to want your husband's snakes around the house.

"When I heard he went to work at the Cancer Research Institute and then the Lincoln Institute, I was glad again but not surprised. With his talents, he could have worked miracles. I hoped he'd find himself there, too."

Thirty years later, and Clara still remembers.

"He was able to do these kinds of things with me. These are the precious memories a teacher savors. You don't get too many of them. By the way, this isn't the first time I've told these stories, and it won't be the last."

Thirty years later, and she quotes the Bible in Barry's memory: "He did not suffer fools gladly."

So this is the boy I conjure, the boy who, six years later, will give me life. The boy who became the man who became Mr. Death.

He gets thrown out of Buffett High because of the gun, but makes up the credits by taking night classes in chemistry and physics at the Standard Evening High School for the next six months.

Twenty-five years later, he'll tell me—and *Playboy*—that he was thrown out of high school for designing and building a machine that produced TNT automatically. He'll tell me the exact same story that he told *Playboy,* and I'll love every word of it: One weekend he left the machine on as part of a science project, and something went wrong and blew out all the windows in the east wing.

Early in my search, I discover they weren't even teaching chemistry or physics in the main building at Buffett High until 1960. It would have been impossible for him to have done scientific experiments for a chemistry class that did not exist in 1952, when he was seventeen—for an assignment that was never given. Standard Evening High was also quickly eliminated as the possible scene of these alleged early crimes. The classes were held in an old American Legion hall. There was no room for beakers or test tubes or shelves full of chemicals, let alone a machine that produced TNT automatically. There wasn't enough money in the school budget to buy these materials, even if the assignment had been given.

It therefore comes as no surprise when I interview Samuel McBain, the principal of Buffett during those years, and he does not recall any explosion or fire—not even a minor one. McBain is ninety-eight and spry as ever in a suburban nursing home. Any doubt of his ability to think clearly is quickly erased. He wrinkles his well-worn brow and says: "How far have you thought beyond your explorations?"

"Not very."

"Did you see that bust of Mr. Whitman while you were visiting my school?"

"No, I didn't. Why, should I have?"

"Well, yes. It is relevant to your story. I'm sure your father knew of it. It's in the hall outside the principal's office. Nine of his immortal words are cast in bronze beneath that lusty mug. Do you have any idea what words they might be?"

"No, Mr. McBain, I'm sorry, I don't."

"No need to be sorry. Just remember this: *I say nourish a great intellect, a great brain.* Got that down in your little notebook?"

"Yes. I've got it. I've got it."

5

How to Be a Jewish Grandmother

These are stories that he passed on to me on a last afternoon in his last August.

I was named after Uncle Dave. Dave was a wild guy, an outlaw, a gangster who gambled and hung out in pool halls where *duh guys talk like dis* and wear black gangster hats and pinstripe suits with white ties and smoke huge Cuban cigars. Uncle Dave would come over to the house for Sunday dinner, with Martin, my grandfather; Hilda, my stepgrandmother; and Barry's two younger sisters. Dave would always try to say something outrageous to upset Hilda, who was an uptight Catholic.

"There's two kindsa women," Dave would say to Barry, leaning across the table, talking into his face. "Those that can *cook* and those that can *fuck*. Try to find one who can do both."

Hilda would freak out, Martin would mumble something about that's enough, Dave, and Barry would try his best not to laugh, but it never worked. He always cracked up so bad he'd get sent away from the table. His sisters would just stare at their plates.

Dave was a cabbie during the Depression, and had to drive fourteen to sixteen hours a day just to stay alive. One winter was so cold that Dave got frostbite while driving and had to have his legs amputated. But that didn't stop him. Martin designed a car that he could drive with his hands—the first such car in all of Massachusetts.

My grandparents separated when Barry was very young, and the kids stayed with their mother—my paternal grandmother,

Seena, whose name he didn't even want to say. She was a religious fanatic who gave all their food money to a different church every week. Barry could remember nights when he stole a roll from the bakery around the corner just to have something to fill his empty stomach.

When he was twelve and his two sisters were eight and four, she just up and left them one day. She was a "whore" and ran off with some drunk—he didn't even know where she went, nor did he care to find out. She brought Barry with her to the train station and, just before she got on a train headed west, gave Barry her purse full of coins and told him to call his father. He was so angry he decided to take care of the household himself. He succeeded for almost a year, forging his mother's signature on the monthly support checks that his father sent. Eventually he was caught forging the checks, his father was called, and the household was once again under his rule.

Martin wasn't a violent man, but Barry could remember two instances when he was provoked into violence.

The first was when Jackie was born. Martin was Jewish and Hilda was Catholic, which in those days caused real problems. They were living in a poor neighborhood in Boston—a neighborhood full of poor Irish, poor Jews, poor Puerto Ricans, poor blacks, "mostly grays," as my father once wrote in a poem. Jackie was born retarded, with serious neurological impairment, and Hilda was near hysterics even two weeks after his birth. In an attempt to calm her down, Martin said it would be okay for the Catholic priest to come over and bless the baby.

Martin is sitting in the living room reading the paper. The priest knocks on the front door, and Hilda lets him in. Jackie is in a cradle in the middle of the room, and Hilda and the priest are standing over him, very tender. Nobody says anything. Finally the priest speaks.

"Well, I guess this is God's punishment."

Martin, who is behind the priest, quietly folds his paper, gets up, lays the paper down on the coffee table, and walks over to the priest, who still has his back to him. Without saying a word— Hilda is in tears—Martin grabs the priest by the back of the neck and the crotch, lifts him straight off the ground, carries him across the room, and throws him *through* the glass door. The priest tumbles down the concrete stoop. Still silent, Martin goes back to reading his paper.

Barry, who is fourteen now, runs down the stoop to see if the priest is still alive. He's bloody and unconscious. *"Dad!"* Barry screams, *"I think you killed him!"*

There are now about thirty people crowded around the bloody, broken priest. They carry him away.

Martin doesn't look up.

Barry could not communicate with his father, not because he didn't try, but because Martin was so isolated, almost nonverbal. He rarely talked except to give orders, and never touched. From a very early age, Barry rebelled by wanting to be extremely verbal. He sharpened his tongue and started writing poems, short stories, filmscripts, anything just to write, to communicate.

Martin has been dead for almost ten years. Hilda and my aunts refuse to talk. That leaves Seena, my other grandmother, the one I've never met.

Obsolete towns have a way of being full of poetry. There are the prayers of cleaning ladies echoing up and down all these empty halls; there's a psalm going out from Akron Sheet & Tube that can be heard around the world; there's a hymn rising out of these eviscerated hills that can be heard in the wheezing, the grinding, the screeching, the humming of every Pontiac and Chevy that ever drew breath, that was ever baptized by radioactive rain.

Stuff comes out of these hills to put bones into the world's buildings, cars, trains, and planes—there's a sign outside one of the foundries that says, in tortured scrawl: NO REGRETS.

Full-grown men kneel down in the halls of Akron Hospital long past midnight and say: "Our Father who art in Heaven, we pray to You to thank You for the doctors and nurses who are trained to heal our physical bodies. We know that You are the Creator and that You know all things. . . . We pray that tomorrow morning the doctors will restore our sight. . . . We pray that You will lift this fog so George's wife and family can come to be with George in his hour of need. We pray to You with thanks because we know You are so good. . . ." Others wear

tattoos that say: "Not This Pig," "Born to Lose," "Don't Tread
on Me," "Once More with Feeling." And, of course, "Mom." The
women pack their skins in fat: It's a privilege to see one who can
walk and talk without some kind of wound becoming obvious.

Camus once said that we are responsible for our fates from
twenty-five on. If he had been born and raised in Akron, Ohio,
or just passed through for a couple of hours, you can bet he would
have released a much more conservative estimate. The drinking
age is eleven, you marry at fifteen; anything else that comes along
is considered manna from heaven and is eaten real quick before
it has a chance to go bad. There are seventeen-year-olds who are
over the hill.

I came out here for a story, and it was three days after a
twenty-year-old waitress said the following that I realized I'd just
got it, both barrels: "Don't expect anything and be surprised at
what you get."

In the summer of 1976, while I was living at Hill House, a
letter arrived from my grandmother, asking about me. I wrote
back, and we started getting to know each other.

At first I accepted every word she said as true. How could I
not? Here was this beautiful, wise, compassionate, warm, loving,
and *psychic* grandmother tucked away in a poverty hotel in the
armpit of the greatest nation on this side of the earth—with a
simple story to tell. A tale of ignorance, narrow-mindedness, and
injustice.

Then I began to question. Could it be possible that she *had*
been a whore and had really run off? Could it be possible that
she *had* been a religious fanatic and *had* given their food money
to a different church every week? Could it be possible that she
abandoned him out of greed and lust, and that that crime led to
much of my father's tragedy? Could she be lying just to keep my
love?

She had been struggling alone to raise two young daughters
and one impossible young son while Martin, my grandfather, was
running around with everything in skirts. Seena, being an ortho-
dox Jew by birth and upbringing, was shattered by his infidelity.
She started having seizures, "fainting dead away" on the kitchen

floor. Young Barry knew about them and would often splash water on her face, as she had instructed him, to revive her. Sometimes that didn't work and he had to run to the doctor up the street, who would use smelling salts to bring her back. There was no cure because there was no diagnosis (she claims) for *petit mal,* a dramatic though relatively minor form of epilepsy. Its cause has sometimes been proven to be a severe physical or emotional shock.

My grandmother has said hundreds of times over these few years that she only left the children so they could have a better life with their father. The only way to get him to take care of them was to abandon them. What good was a crippled mother who kept falling down in the middle of her duties?

"You'd think we could inherit money, but, no, we inherit genes. I was born with one bad arm and two broken legs, and he was born with rickets. So there's a deficiency on your side. I useta give'm so much cod liver oil the poor kid almost croaked.

"I was very tiny, very petite, very neat about myself. Didn't weigh more than ninety-two pounds until I was well into my fifties. I was very sexy—see I'm honest with you, my grandson— but I never discussed sex with him. You ever hear of Bette Midler? I saw her on TV today. I love her. She reminded me of me when I was young.

"Poor Barry was my firstborn. Boy, was he an experiment. But I'll tell ya one thing, I cooked him all fresh vegetables, fresh lamb, mashed vegetables with my one arm. Half would go on the floor and half on his plate. I wanted him to have a good body. When he was very young, he had beautiful black hair.

"He didn't have confidence, his father didn't take him out. So I hadda tell'm to stay away from the *shiksas.* 'Why, mama?' he'd say. 'Because they're lousy cooks,' I'd say. 'And another thing: You'll be better off stayin' with your own kind. And you better go to Hebrew School, or I'll kill ya!'

"I was very strict with him—I hadda be. His father was never around when we needed him. Always out paradin' with that Uncle Dave, who was really crazy. He'd spend one-third of his time makin' those little ribbons they give out at football games and another third tryin' to do nasty things to me and another third out drinkin' his pennies and Marty's, too. One time he grabbed me when I was standin' up on a footstool tryin' to fix a shade, an' I was so innocent I had no idea what he was up to. When I figured it out, you can bet I stayed the hell out of his reach! Makes me sick even to say his name.

"Barry's father was a true genius. He could build with steel, with iron, with anything metal. He could repair the whole house. And build! He was really a brilliant young man. It was Uncle David that made him immoral. Honest to God, because up until he met'm, he was a very nice, beautiful man to be married to.

"I useta say to him: 'You know, Moishe'—his name was Martin, but I called'm Moishe—and he'd say: 'What, Seen?'—he called me Seen, he didn't call me Seena. I'd say: 'You have two golden hands. Thank God every day that you are a genius.'

"But he had a lotta quirks. If he could make a fast buck, he made it. I always told him: If you don't work honest, it won't stick with ya, babe. It'll float.

"Marty had jet-black hair, gray eyes, his skin was golden like grandma's. Gold. And he had high cheekbones like me. Fact is, people thought I was his sister, not his wife, because we looked alike, except that Marty had gray eyes and my hair was between an auburn and brown. No dye stuff—I never dye my hair—but it was very long. He was tall, not quite as tall as you, but a few inches less. I'd say he was five ten and a half. But he appeared taller, because when I was married to him, he was not fat. He was *built*, and I mean B U I L D T T T. That's what attracted me to'm first. And he was slender! He had firmness, muscles, legs perfect.

"He was very quiet and I was vivacious. I would sing and laugh. I was fulla fun. In the beginning we had a perfect marriage. I was the happiest girl alive, young girl of seventeen that I was. I deeply with all my heart and soul loved that man, David. But one thing you'll note, even in my voice: I am not bitter over what happened between us. I don't blame me, I don't blame him. I believe in fate, Dave. What's supposed to be'll be. I was brought up on that concept of life. I just skip over it now and I say, Well, there were good days, there were beautiful days, I had a beautiful life with him for a while. Hey, some women don't have

even that in life, honey. Real love. Whether he really loved me,
I don't know. Not the way I loved him, apparently.

"But I can't blame him. That's the way he felt. If he really
loved me, he never would've married his second wife, right? Run
away with her while he was still married to me? When I found
that out, I just packed his things and told'm to leave. He could
have his divorce. I said I don't want anybody sleepin' with me
that don't love me. And I'm not jealous, 'cause there's a *lotttttaaa*
men out there. My time'll come. I'm not worried. Wouldn't it be
useless to live with someone you don't love? I think that's the
most horrible situation, for a man or woman to force themselves
to live with someone they don't love. And I don't mean love the
way the kids today take it. I mean the love I like. And I guess you
do, too. You'll meet a nice girl someday, you'll know what I
mean. You'll meet a verrry, verrry nice girl, really you will, Dave.

"Your father was very secretive when he was a young boy.
He'd say, 'Mama, I'm goin' for a walk.' Then he would go
walkin' and hikin' miles away, into caves or somethin', lookin' for
bats and critters, and he wouldn't come back till late, till six
o'clock. I called it late because we said our prayers at five and
ate dinner at six.

"Ohhh, I useta call his daddy: 'Where's that roving boy of
ours? Where *is* he?' Marty worried, too. He went out lookin' and
couldn't find'm. He'd say: 'Didn't he tell you where he was going?' I said: 'No. I only asked if he was goin' with anyone, and
he said no.' Which was true. He almost always went out alone.
But he came back with rocks and minerals, and Marty made a
display case where he could mount every one of the rocks. That
kid, at the age of ten, knew every name of those rocks and the
names of every mineral it contained.

"Then he would have the most *horrible* animals in my house—
that I threw them out! Almost threw my son out with 'em! It
wasn't funny, Dave. A Jewish home never had frogs for friends!
And a Jewish mother never went into the pockets of her son's
pants and pulled out gooey bird's eggs! And no birds flyin' out!

"Then he useta catch monarch butterflies. He would have their
cocoons and wait for them to hatch. He didn't tell me—and I,
being not acquainted with those things—when it opened its

wings, I thought the damn thing was a bat. And I called Big
Daddy, the man next door—grandma adored him, he was six
four to my four eleven—and I hollered: 'Big Daddy! Get in here!
There's an animal downstairs that's flyin' around and I don't know
what it is!'

"He went downstairs—and no Jewish man from the yeshiva
knew what it was either, so he tried to catch it. But we couldn't
catch'm. He went way up. When Barry come home, he got the
first lickin' that I ever gave him in his life with my hands. At
that time, my good arm was so strong I coulda broke his neck
if I hit'm wrong, so I hit'm only on the *tuckus* 'cause I was afraid
a hurtin' him, you know, really injurin' him. He didn't sit for a
long while, kitten.

" 'But it's a *monarch!*' he said.

" 'I don't care! I don't want the king of anything flyin' around
in my basement, especially it has to migrate when I have to go
down for the potatoes—and I come up lookin' in the eyes of
somethin' I don't know what is!'

"He also had a habit of carrying worms in his pockets. You
ever try washin' clothes with worms in it?

"Ooohhhh, his father didn't know what to do with'm, honest
to God. He warned'm, though.

"He loved trains, anything with a motor. He got the first real
electric train when he was between eight and nine. Marty got
large tracks and made a table from one end of the playroom—
we had an entire playroom for him—we spoiled him—honest
to God, he was a spoiled kid, and if he said he wasn't, he was
lyin'! He would play with that train for hours and hours. And it
taught him about machinery and that's what taught him how to
make things with his hands.

"We bought him an Erector set. He used to build. He loved to
do that. But he was such a lousy brat that he was jealous of any
other kid who came near his toys or anything else that was his.
When he was just comin' outta babyhood, he beat one of his
sister's boyfriends to a pulp. That's when I went on him. I told
him if he ever hit anybody ever again, I'd kill him. And I think
I would've. I took holda my baby and told'm, 'You're nothin' but
a tramp, you get the hell out and let me cool off before I kill you.'

"He said, 'Mama, I didn't mean to be so mean.'

"I said, 'You better do it or I'm gonna take you to the nut-house.'

"I'll tell ya one thing Barry never done as long as I known'm, and that was gamble. He never shoot dice, he never played pool. He never run around with young men that were, you know, nothin' but nice kids. The only trouble with'm was he had an inferior complex.

"Did you ever see your father's face where he had a scar on his nose, close to his eye? They removed a tumor there with radium years and years ago. And they removed one at the back of his head. And I think he was conscious of it, honey. I think he felt that because, you know, because of the scar—but it was better than what it was when he was very young—when it was growing—it was growing very rapid, and that's when I knew I hadda do something about it, 'cause his father sure wasn't gonna take care of it.

"At first it was flat. Then it started growin'. And it turned purplelike. I took him to Dr. Roth at the Jewish Hospital. All my children were born there. Dr. Roth was the head surgeon and the head therapist, whatever you call it, for tumors.

"'I do not know if I can cure your son,' he told me. Then he said, 'How old are you?' And I said, 'Sixteen goin' on seventeen.' He said, 'My God, little girl! With all those diapers, do you nurse him?' 'Yes,' I said. 'Don't nurse him now,' he said. I said, 'But he'll starve to death!' He said, 'Yeah, I know, I got a Jewish wife. He won't starve to death, Seena. I'll give him back to you.'

"And meanwhile I'm sufferin' up on top because I had enough milk for him and it hurt me.

"I had to take him back for two and a half years. Once a week. But Dr. Roth was very good. The nurse hadda hold his little head still so they could do what they had to do.

"Then Dr. Roth come in one day with smiles. 'He's cured,' he said. 'And here's your little boy.' He looked at me and—see, there's only two years between Barry and his oldest sister, and then another three with his other sister . . . they were all good kids, really. It was only when I divorced'm that the whole trouble started. I think that's what started my son. He was in shock. It's

really hard on kids when their parents divorce, but I felt that was
better than havin' two people argue and not be happy. 'Cause
sooner or later they're gonna find the farce out.

"You probably think I just disappeared into the woodwork and
forgot about my babies after moving. I thought about 'em constantly, I prayed that someday we would be reunited and I could
tell my side of the story. I knew their father would try to poison
'em, but what could I do? I was fallin' apart myself, what with
takin' sick with *petit mal*. I hadda find a way to make a living,
first and foremost, and that's when I started usin' my gift and
readin' for people, psychically. People would come to me without a penny to their name and a broken heart and a broken home,
and I would try to help them. I would, David, honest. Some of
'em I wouldn't even take a penny from. I'd just say, 'No, thank
you, it's enough that I could be of service to you. You take your
pennies home and save 'em, you're gonna need 'em, times are
hard and gettin' harder.' One lady once offered me diamonds
'cause she didn't have anything else of value, but I didn't want it.
I figgered she might have to sell them diamonds to pay her rent
or buy groceries, so I just very quietly said no thank you, and
walked out.

"But all the while I was prayin' that God would tell me how to
get in touch with my babies, so I could at least find out if they
had enough food to eat and were they out of trouble and did
they have a roof over their poor little *keppelehs*. Oh, Dave, you
don't know the heartbreak a Jewish mother feels when her children are taken from her. It must be terrible for all mothers, but
especially for Jewish mothers, 'cause they feel things so much
closer, they feel so much more love than *goyishe* women.

"I got people from here to search for my children. They found
Barry and talked to him. That's when he got in touch with me.
But it took a lotta prayers, a looonnngg time. I don't feel sad
about it, if you'll note. I take life as it comes. You take people
just the way they are. You realize there is nothing you can do
about certain circumstances. Gotta leave 'em alone. Besides, life
is more interesting that way. Wouldn't it be boring if everybody
was the same?

"My son tried to make up for his inferior complex by conquering women. He really wasn't lookin' for a nice person. Because your mother was a nice person in the beginning, honey. I had their wedding pictures—she looked like a livin' doll. Really. And he was married by a clergyman, a Lutheran clergyman. He explained to me: 'Mama, I married a Christian girl.' I simply said to him: 'So what? That don't make no difference to me. As long as you love her, Barry. Be good to her. Try to get along with her. No marriage is perfect.' Marriage you have to work at, Dave. And it's a long, long job.

"See, when you first meet a girl, you notice all the good points. Boy, she's built nice, she's gorgeous, she got a good brain. You like the beautiful things about her. Then when you marry her, you see the other side of her. Some things that might irk you. But then again, if you sit and think, maybe you, too, have disappointed her a little. You, too, have not been up to par. So you talk it out. Love will conquer a lotta things, Dave.

"You ever see a real beautiful girl married to a real ugly man? And you often wondered how the blazes she could marry that man and find that she was the happiest woman alive? Because there was somethin' in that man that she saw that other women could never perceive.

"There's more to marriage than physical attributes, in a woman and a man. I'm givin' you good advice, honey. Believe me. I read an awful lot about it, I thought about it, and I gleaned the parts from all of it which is true. That will be the kinda marriage that you'll be lookin' for, sweetheart.

"You could be married to the most beautiful Chinese girl, and people would say, 'How could you love a Chinese girl?' But to you, she's kind, she's gentle, she's intelligent, and you really love her from your heart. And you won't give a damn what the world will think as long as you love that girl and she loves you back. But it has to be even stevens, babe.

"And don't marry an uneducated girl, honey. You'll be miserable. I don't want you to marry an intellectual who's a snob, either, 'cause then you'll also be miserable. But you don't have to be macho, my little grandson. Women who look for macho get what they're lookin' for—a buncha bums. But a man with quality and tenderness and really loves . . . I know what grandma really wants; all her life she looked for it . . . *that* is important in your life, Dave. Don't make the mistakes I made. Okay?

> "I'll never walk alone again
> Because a young man walks by my side,
> My little grandson number one.
> So, my grandson number one,
> Let us cherish each moment we have
> And I pray to God to keep you by my side.

"How's that for a little spontaneous combustion from your grandma? It just came to me over the wire.

"You think it didn't hurt me when he divorced your mother? Oh, did it hurt me! 'Cause she was so sweet to me. She sent me nice letters, and beautiful pictures of you kids, and then—when that happened—nothin'. She wouldn't answer my letters. It ain't my fault they got divorced. When I called, she'd hang up on me. I just wanted to see your cute little mugs. But I guess she had to give someone the front of her heartache.

"If only I could have had a chance, I would have helped her raise you kids. I would have loved you all. Her life hasn't been no apples in the orchard, so I don't blame her. I love her.

"If I had a mother who was a streetwalker—God forbid—and she had to leave me to have a better life with other people, I would search heaven and hell to find out why she was in that condition, and I wouldn't stop loving her for a minute. Not one minute. And I just can't understand why God has not answered my prayers for my other children and grandchildren to come and ask me *why*. Just my side of the story. *Why.*

"Barry never shoulda been the way he was with you. He was loved by me, a great deal of it. Fact was I spoiled him rotten. So that's a paradox there. I'll never understand it.

"He wasn't as bad as they said. He only had one serious problem—his sex problem. Sure, I knew he had it. Even as a little boy. And not because he was funny-funny. Because he liked women. Too much.

"I saw evil in my son when he was just a boy—but I don't like to talk about that."

P L A Y B O Y   I N T E R V I E W

MR. DEATH: Right out of high school I went to work at a place called the Cancer Research Institute. I was hired to perform the noble duties of a dishwasher. Then they put me onto the exalted throne of lab tech, after a few weeks. I very quickly realized that I was not put on this earth to observe the mating habits of fruit flies through a microscope. One day my boss said, "Hey, I hear there's jobs down at the [deleted] Institute," so I went down for an interview.

So I went to work at the [deleted] Institute for less than four thousand a year. I didn't care. I was happy with that. I went to work in the Applied Physics Section, which was starting to develop and test miniature detonators for artillery and missile fuses. These were miniature blasting caps to set off the main charges in artillery and missile warheads. They were very sophisticated little electric gadgets. My initial assignment was to implement a program to test their reliability and output, and all kinds of jazz like that there. The first year I was there I fired close to half a million of 'em, one at a time in test chambers. Our section rapidly acquired a rep for reliability and imagination. The number of employees tripled and quadrupled. Remarkably enough, the only one in that group of scientists and engineers who had any knowledge of explosives and pyrotechnics was me. I was therefore very useful. As time went on I was exposed to a vast variety of things and I absorbed it like a sponge and I loved it.

They had a great big vault where they locked all the confidential reports. I used to go in there and close the door and read reports on everything imaginable, just because I was fascinated. Nuclear stuff, cannon technology. This was from 1952 to 1959. They were very heavy into the study of flame fuels, called thixotropes. It behaves like a solid if you don't disturb it. But if you pump it, it behaves like a liquid. All kinds of goofiness went on there. Some of it totally unrelated to ordnance. Hell, they'd test anything from the strength of Kleenex for Kimberly-Clark to new methods of making toilet paper. You name it, they got into it. But ninety percent of the work was military. In that vault, for instance, I found reports discussing the reality of building a death ray with laser beams. That's something the Defense Department won't even mention these days. It's a breakthrough in technology equal to the atomic bomb.

They soon discovered I had a great flair for writing technical shit. I could do that in my sleep. Original research proposals, editing stuff, handling any kind of—how might we say—literary work? I sold one hell of a lot of research for them. That's when M. became very interested in what I was doing and said, "You'll be a contact. We'll get some work your way." I think those were his exact words.

PLAYBOY: Would he come to you while you were working at the Institute—before he asked you to be a contact—and say: "We need such and such done"?

MR. DEATH: Yes.

PLAYBOY: And he was still paying you in guns or money?

MR. DEATH: A little of both. A lot of the time I accepted work because it was kind of like a hobby by that time.

We were branching out by then. I built a number of gadgets for demolition that were basically miniaturized timers, electric and otherwise, for unknown-strength demolition devices. In other words, if you wanted to plant a satchel of explosives somewhere, all you'd have to do was plug in this little thingy and you had a detonating system. Some arsenal was manufacturing a regular wristwatch and giving them to certain select individuals. The only thing different about it was that it had terminals on it, to which you could connect wires. It became an automatic timer system for which I designed little detonators. I tried to get one of the watches for myself but couldn't.

I remember the Marlboro box was the best disguise for my little demo specials. Marlboro was the first to come out in a hardpack, I believe. You could slip it out and plug it into a charge of explosives, turn the timer, and you're on your way. There weren't many of them made, you know.

PLAYBOY: When did M. drop out of the picture?

MR. DEATH: M. dropped out of the picture when I was contacted for the first time. I think by then M. was traveling out of the country. I remember what my new contact looked like. This guy looked like the villain known as the Penguin in the Batman comics. I think he had been hurt at some point in his life, because he spoke out of the side of his mouth. He told me that my talents were unique and all that flattering bullshit and would I be willing to do some miniature design work, little gadgetry. There would be some bread in it for me. I had started to generate a family and was really scraping hard to make a living, so I took the offer. I designed and/or built what I call onezie twozies, you know, one or two of a thing or half a dozen sometimes, maybe even more. Stuff that I could fabricate or have fabricated *in sub rosa*, you know, pieces and parts out of the machine shop. I became very friendly with the machinist there, and he did some of that work for me. I'd slip him some money and he'd build a tube or gadget or a hunk for me.

PLAYBOY: Anything else?

MR. DEATH: There was some silencer work there, too.

PLAYBOY: What do you suppose they wanted all these goddamn silencers for?

MR. DEATH: Most anything I built was an assassination device. Almost exclusively.

PLAYBOY: How do you know that?

MR. DEATH: Because they were designed for single-kill operations, that's why.

PLAYBOY: Guessing roughly, how many assassination devices came off your production line in all that time?

MR. DEATH: You mean in individual number, the number of pieces?

PLAYBOY: How many assassinations could we count in your career?

MR. DEATH: That's a rough one, because a silencer can be used a number of times.

PLAYBOY: All right, but say each one. Say each single device was used once to kill one person, just to make a minimum. In the tens? In the hundreds?

MR. DEATH: OK . . . probably . . . I'd guess now . . . I'm trying to give you an educated guess . . . would be about a hundred and fifty. Something like that. . . . Silencers are pretty conventional. And again, the designs were mostly throwaways. There was a lot of accent on stuff that could be thrown into luggage and wouldn't be very obvious if it was opened for inspection. They can be made out of anything—rubber or metal. Metal is better. And then you just have to line up the baffles so the bullet goes through the hole. It's a muffler, and very easy to make.

PLAYBOY: What other types of assassination devices did you invent?

MR. DEATH: I started to get into special ammunition, like six rounds of something that did something unusual. Bullets that contained poison, and so on. Since I have some expertise in animal venoms, there was a lot of concentration on that.

PLAYBOY: When did you get into animal venoms?

MR. DEATH: From the time I was a kid, because of my interest in snakes and reptiles. My talents were also still being used for brainstorming sessions. The Penguin would say, "If you were in a room and you had eighteen nasty gooks coming at you with scimitars, how would you put them down?" Or: "If you were on an airplane and wanted to—" I can't remember the exact words he used—it wasn't liquidate, it was something much more euphemistic than that. *Extract!* Extract, yes, that was a lovely term. If you wanted to extract a guy on an airplane and you had to do it while the plane was in flight, obviously even the best silencer wouldn't do you much good. How would you do it? Poison dart, this, that, and the other. Again, the accent was on low-profile methods, relatively unsophisticated so it wouldn't leave a signature that said U.S. TECHNOLOGY. Maybe even a kook could have done this. I was a kook, so I was very good at that. The very simplest way would be to use a contact poison. Have an eye-dropper full, sit behind the guy on the plane, and put a drop on his neck or on his clothes or in his shoes—someplace that he wouldn't notice. By the time he would, it wouldn't matter.

PLAYBOY: What type of poison would you use?

MR. DEATH: Lyophilized (freeze-dried) tiger-snake venom, mixed with [deleted], which is a liquid that penetrates your tissues on contact. Sodium cyanide in [deleted] is a liquid, but it feels dry when you touch it, because it's already inside you, carrying whatever was mixed in with it. Very simple.

PLAYBOY: The Penguin would come to your lab?

MR. DEATH: No. During lunch breaks, we had a system set up where I would get calls from home.

PLAYBOY: Why and when would they do it? Emergency?

MR. DEATH: On a sunny day we'd sit out in the park and talk.

The airplane scenario is a specific project I worked on for a long time. What finally evolved from that was a contact poison using boomslang venom, which is another very poisonous snake. Its poison is very subtle, causing internal bleeding. I mixed [deleted] and the venom, and then made a gadget that looked like a felt-tip pen, and actually *was* a felt-tip pen. You could really write with it if you had to. You'd just pull it apart and she'd write, touch, period. That's it. And throw the thing away, dump it.

PLAYBOY: The victim was touched with this?

MR. DEATH: That's all you'd need. Don't forget, it's a tissue penetrant. The pen was larger than a fine point. There was some quantity of spread there.

PLAYBOY: How long was the delay?

MR. DEATH: Depend on the human being, the size of him.

PLAYBOY: Say a big Russian.

MR. DEATH: About three days. The symptoms are very subtle. The snake that you saw at my place that I said was venomous is actually second cousin to the boomslang. That was a mangrove snake.

PLAYBOY: Where did you get boomslang venom back then?

MR. DEATH: It used to be easy to get exotic pets from pet stores, back in the early Fifties. Now it's a bit harder if they're dangerous. Incidentally, never try to milk a boomslang. A bad snake. They're damn dangerous, hard to get, not very cooperative, and because their fangs are in the rear of their mouths, it is hell on wheels extracting venom.

PLAYBOY: Did you have to get approval to build the gadget?

MR. DEATH: As I remember it, I went back to my contact with the idea after I thought about the problem for a while. He said, "Will it work?" I said, "Well, I don't have any volunteers to test it on; are you interested?" Like all the other spook types I've met, he had no sense of humor. I mean zero, zilch. He just gave me a very calm, "No. We'll take care of the testing. You make one."

The snake pens apparently worked, because later he seemed very pleased. I remember making some comment like, "I hope you tested them in-house." No reaction.

PLAYBOY: You invented the felt-tip pen, in other words?

MR. DEATH: Yes.

PLAYBOY: You missed your calling. Think of all the money you could have made.

MR. DEATH: See, I goofed again. Like some of my songs that were smash flops. "We're with you all the way, General Custer." The thermonuclear dildo. All things that never went.

PLAYBOY: So what else did the Penguin ask you to do after that?

MR. DEATH: The only time he had to get specific was when they wanted to kill a man in a certain way. He drove a Jaguar, I think, and he had to die at a certain point in the ride he was to take, say eight minutes after he started—for what reason, I don't know, perhaps to keep him from crashing into a schoolhouse or to get him to a remote area. I had to know a lot in order to get it to work in a foolproof way. Body weight, was he right-handed, that sort of thing. They eventually had to actually bring me the steering wheel from a similar car and a photograph of the man driving, which was just his hands on the wheel. That's how I knew he was black. This was somewhere between 1954 and 1959. It could have been for use anywhere, Jamaica, Ghana. I mixed up a batch of [deleted] and good old sodium cyanide, which I told them to paint onto his steering wheel where he was going to put his hands. I adjusted the dosage so that knockdown time would be the eight minutes or whatever the figure was. Apparently they were pleased with that.

PLAYBOY: How could you tell they were pleased?

MR. DEATH: Well, a guy I knew pretty well invited me to my first outside job then and I got the impression that it was being offered as a bonus for work well done.

PLAYBOY: What do you mean by outside?

MR. DEATH: Out of the country.

PLAYBOY: What sort of job was it?

MR. DEATH: I was picked up in a car. My friend was there. We were driven to an airplane. Then we flew all night, it seemed like. We landed somewhere. Another car picked us up. We were driven out into the countryside. Some guy had an antitank weapon and said, "Do you know how to use this thing?" I said, "Yes." He said, "Well, use it." I asked what he wanted it used on and he pointed to a convoy of military trucks over the rise on a little road. So I blew away a couple of trucks.

PLAYBOY: Do you know what that was all about?

MR. DEATH: Well, evidently they didn't like some of our South American neighbors. No, really I don't. I just know it was in Caracas. As soon as I had blown away the trucks, my friend sent me back to the car and he went over to "finish them off," as he put it.

PLAYBOY: Meaning what?

MR. DEATH: He just took his pistol and put a bullet through each guy's head to make sure he was dead. It was my impression that this was my reward for doing a good job with the poison systems. It wasn't my idea of a reward. Later, I asked the guy who had invited me what it was all about. He just looked at me with a stunned expression and said, "But didn't you enjoy it?"

6

Lengthened Shadows

One week after my twenty-third birthday. The day is unusually warm for late October. I am rocking gently across the city of Boston in one of those ancient trolley cars I used to dream of riding to escape out, out, out to the country where he lived. Boston is one of the few cities in America—indeed, in the world —that still have a functioning trolley system. Or, I should say, barely functioning trolley system. One of the maxims of living in Boston is you don't take the trolley if you want to get somewhere on time. You walk.

But today I am quite happy to take my time, because I know that I am about to open another chapter in his life, a chapter he kept closed from me all the years I knew him—which, oddly enough, were not all the years he was technically my father. I did not start to get to know my father until I was in my early teens and in trouble with the law. And then it was not as a father and son that we became friends. It was simply friends.

I've always known my father worked for the Lincoln Institute during the 1950s—the years before, during, and after I was born. There was never, as far as I knew, any attempt to hide that fact, either by my mother or my father. I've always known he worked for *the Institute*. That's all. The only times I heard it discussed were as reference points in my family's history: thus-and-such must have happened before, during, or after he worked for *the Institute*. I always liked the sound of the words. I respected them long before I knew what "professional" meant.

It's just that I never knew what he did there or with whom he worked or what visions he had in those dark rooms. Dark, that's the only image I have of him and his work those years. I don't know why. But was it really so dark for him? Maybe it was a time when he did exactly what he wanted to do. Maybe he really did find himself. Maybe it was a time when things like wives and children just got in the way. What kept him there so long?

Imagine an American Gothic museum of science and technology overlooking one of the city's largest, most beautiful parks. A major traffic circle winds around the museum and through the park. In front of the museum, the circle forms a small island on which has been constructed a huge fountain. There is a light spray of mist in the air; the sun catches there, brilliant, rainbowed, lovely. Two swans glide across the surface of the small reflecting pool at the base of the fountains. A few children are feeding them bread, while their mothers talk quietly in the shade of an ancient maple. Maybe they're talking mortgage rates and husbands, maybe they're talking their last good piece of tail. The universe is unfolding as it should, I think, as I get off the trolley and take in this scene. The museum, with its giant white pillars and hundred or two hundred granite steps, is absolutely magnificent. Who could afford to build a mansion like this today? Thank God somebody had the vision to do it *then*. What if they hadn't bothered?

When I called the Institute's personnel department last week and asked to speak with anyone who might have known my father, I was put in touch with a Mr. Todd Barnes. This Mr. Barnes seemed delighted to hear from me. Told me to look for a "newish-looking building just to the right of the museum." That's the new research-and-development building, he said. They moved out of the basement of the museum, oh, musta been fifteen years ago if it was a day. Mr. Barnes actually talked like that, used clichés like that, spoke them in a basic friendly American voice. He sounded like a man who has been a father for a couple of decades, and maybe even a grandfather.

Walking through the swinging glass doors, I could be entering the main office of a real-estate agency, or an electronics firm, or an insurance company, or a public-relations outfit. There's a full-

body cast of Abe Lincoln on my right, cast in bronze like Mr.
Whitman. He's smiling. I smile back.

There is a small switchboardlike desk in the center of the
lobby. A blond, middle-aged woman is perched on a stool,
answering calls from the outside and connecting these callers
with unseen phones on the inside. It is also her job to "call up"
when a visitor arrives. I tell her my name, that I'm here to see
Mr. Barnes, and she pushes a few buttons, speaks with someone,
and then tells me to just have a seat, he'll be down in a minute.

Along the far wall, before the elevators, there are a series of
glass display cases, like those you might see in an electronics
company's headquarters, advertising their newest, neatest devices
and doodads. These cases are different. Some of them contain
prototypes for the first telegraph, with succeeding models in an
evolutionary chain. The last link appears to be a tiny radio, but is
actually a transmitter. A little sign underneath says it is for under-
sea research, the kind of transmitter that can be plugged into a
shark's belly and run for a year without a recharge. There are
other nifty items, but electronics is not my bag, so I plunk down
next to Abe with my satchel full of spy tools.

I imagine how simple things must have been when my father
was twenty-three and doing what he did best. There's the simple
pleasant anticipation that, no matter how much of my past has
been annihilated, it can still come alive through a voice on the
telephone, a grandfatherly voice welcoming me to my task.

"Yeah," Mr. Barnes had said, "last time I saw your dad he told
me he was gonna design a pornographic fireworks display for
Hugh Hefner over the skies of Chicago. Can you imagine that?"
He chuckled. "Yeah, I'll bet *he* could have imagined that. Bet he
coulda found a way to do it. Yessirree bob. Quite a guy, your
dad. I'd be glad to talk with ya about him. I'm sure some of the
other boys round here would, too. Gee, there's Jack, he knew your
dad. And Fats, I'm sure he knew him. And there's . . ." This
friendly American grandfatherly voice rattled off half a dozen
names faster than I could write them down, so I gave up. If I
were meant to meet them, I would have the chance.

And now, ruminating in Abe Lincoln's shadow on this warm
October afternoon, I have the feeling that I really am going to

have that chance. I'm digging now, dad, but I'm getting farther and farther from the shoe boxes at the bottom of your closet. I'm getting to the bottom of the boxes in you.

A hand is outstretched. A ruddy, reddish, puffy face is beaming. A barrel-shaped man is walking toward me, grinning. I had been concerned that my casual dress (also known as sloppy, also known as poor) would offend my father's professional colleagues, and therefore make my job even harder. But there is no need to worry. Mr. Barnes is so tickled that I get the feeling I could have appeared in swim trunks and sandals and he wouldn't have noticed. I contemplate the strategic advantage of dressing down for these suits-and-ties. If I look like a bum but talk and listen well, they'll give me the time of day but won't take me too seriously.

"Did you know that Emerson said 'An institution is the lengthened shadow of one man'?" Mr. Barnes is not trying to intimidate me with erudition. He simply wants to know if I have heard this beautiful line.

"No, I didn't know that, but it sounds like something I should know about, Mr. Barnes."

"Call me Todd. I'm glad you're here. This oughtta be a lotta fun. I been rackin' my memory ever since you called, just to make sure we make the best of this time. I'm at that age when my memory takes long vacations and most of my friends are retired or dead. So you might have to make way for a few momentary lapses."

There is no need for small talk. Even before we're in the elevator, he's off and telling me how highly he thought of my father, how he used to get such kicks out of having him around, how everyone here remembers him as the guy who was always blowing things up. I am often flustered in new surroundings, and now I am more flustered than usual. I never thought it could be this easy to reach back thirty years and more, never thought all it would take to open the door would be a phone call and a short walk through a swinging glass door and a request to see a certain gentleman in the Applied Physics Section who once knew my dad.

In less than a minute we are several stories above sea level. The doors open into a typical institutional hallway. A typewriter is clackety-clack-clacking somewhere. All the while Todd is talking, telling stories, great stories for which I'm trying to find storage space because I haven't even had a chance to pull out my notebook and pen. Soon we're in his office—a basic boring office with a desk and a telephone with more buttons than I've ever seen, a safe, an electric typewriter, and all the usual junk—and then I am being offered a seat, and I put down my satchel, and I'm listening with every pore.

Todd was always up in his ivory tower on the third floor, so he rarely caught a prank in progress. News of them always got to him a little late, and some he didn't hear about till years later, usually with good reason. For him it was vicarious, voyeuristic; he knew something was going on, but never knew exactly what. Besides, he couldn't do anything about it. That would have ruined the game. And the important thing to remember about the game is everybody plays. Even the captain, *especially* the captain, wants someone to rock the boat once in a while. That's probably what he misses most with Barry gone. There isn't anybody to stir things up, and probably never will be again. "The business has changed," he sighs. "Things were looser then. It's a different age."

He has a deep respect for the dead. It shows in the way he cares for Barry's files and gives me reports, memos, and documents from them. "These are dead files anyway," he says. "You can take these."

He rummages through a stack of reports, and finally pulls one out. "Here. Your dad worked on this."

He hands me an army technical manual dated 20 May 1962. Perfect: *Unconventional Warfare Devices and Techniques: Incendiaries*. Chapter 1 introduces incendiary systems, definitions, tools and techniques. Chapter 2 covers initiators: improved fuses using concentrated sulfuric acid and water. Chapter 3 moves me into igniters: sugar chlorate, fire fudge, sugar, match heads, potassium permanganate, white phosphorous, subigniters for thermite. Chapter 4 explores materials: napalm, gelled gasoline (exotic and improvised thickeners), fire bottles (impact and delay ignition), more thermite, flammable liquids, incendiary bricks. Chapter 5 incorporates delay mechanisms: cigarettes, gelatin capsules, rubber diaphragms, paper diaphragms, candles, tipping delays (filled tube or corrosive or dissolving action), stretched rubber bands, alarm clocks. Chapter 6 is, of course, the climax: spontaneous combustion. On page 143, the Index.

He has a hold on part of a past that is my future, and he wants to pass on every fragment, everything that is not classified. Everything that has been downgraded.

He describes the procedure. When a report has been downgraded, usually after twelve years, they have to go through every page and icky-out the CONFIDENTIAL or SECRET with black Magic Marker. If it's being downgraded from SECRET, they must write in by hand CONFIDENTIAL at the top and bottom of every page. Twelve years after that, they might declassify the CONFIDENTIAL report to DISCREET ACCESS. So a report usually drops down one rung on the ladder of security every twelve years. But they don't even bother doing it most of the time because it's such a pain in the ass—unless someone petitions for Freedom of Information, or Freedom of Misinformation, as Todd likes to call it. Then they'll check the date it was released, and if it's okay, they'll just hand it over. Sometimes they check with the security office first, but not very often, unless it's something real heavy-duty, like a nuclear grenade. Usually they'll just icky-out the SECRET or CONFIDENTIAL at the top and bottom of each page, without even bothering to write in the new classification.

He swears in the same breath he must be allergic to this place, blowing his nose and dabbing the corners of his eyes. That's not it at all, I say to myself. Not at all.

He leans back in his chair and chuckles like a schoolboy at my father's pranks, his face going red and holding back the tears.

"Lady says, 'Excuse me, sir, but your bag is moving.'

"Barry says, 'Yeah, I know. That's just my snake. He's sick and I have to take him to the vet.'

"Riot on trolley."

While he's rooting furiously through another dead file, he tells me that when Barry got tired of stamping SECRET and CONFIDEN-

TIAL on everything, he had his own stamp made up, and used it: DESTROY BEFORE READING.

Todd takes a breather for the first time, and we both lean back in our chairs, ruminating. I am still scribbling, still trying to catch up, when there's a knock at the door and a very fat man peers in. Todd introduces him as "Fats" MacNamara, "another guy who knew your dad, isn't that right, Fats?"

"That's right. I knew'im I guess just as much as anybody else round here."

I suddenly get the feeling that that might not have been very well, not nearly as well as they thought.

Fats informs Todd that he's needed "over in Storage for some reason or other." Todd excuses himself, says, "Make yourself at home. I'll be back as soon as I get these nitwits straightened out."

Fine. I'm good at that. How can I *really* make myself at home? That safe would be a good place to start. It looks at me and I look at it, determined. I've cracked more than one safe in my time—one of the many cute tricks I learned from dad—and this one is just your basic clunker, as he would have called it. No alarms, just a basic combo lock.

In approximately two minutes I am able to reach in and get a grip on *Unconventional Warfare Devices and Techniques: References.* Looks sort of like a companion tome to *Unconventional Warfare Devices and Techniques: Incendiaries,* so I stuff it into my satchel and resume my ruminations. Approximately fifty seconds later, Todd walks back in, grumbling about "those sonsabitches who're wastin' tax money and keep everything in disorder just to stay on the payroll. Why do I have to do everything around here?"

One of Todd's favorite words is "waffle." Not the noun you eat for breakfast, but the verb he invented, oh, gosh, many years ago. When he's telling me about his stay at the Ambassador Hotel in L.A., he identifies it as the place where Bobby Kennedy got waffled. Or his wife waffled the steering on his new Pontiac by hitting a bad pothole. Or a piece of artillery machinery got "waffled" when engineers at the arsenal exploded sixty-five pounds of Pennelite, a high explosive, in the powder-packing room. It was a test, only a test, but the roof of the building—a thirteen-by-thirteen-by-thirteen slab of reinforced concrete more than a foot thick—flipped off like someone had flipped a giant coin. It landed on the instrumentation wires, which got "waffled." Wires that transmit data from the test site to the engineers huddled 300 yards away on top of a concrete bunker. But that wasn't what brought the boys down. They were sad because, even though the machinery withstood the blast with only some banana-peeling around the edges—and even though a $5-million contract was about to come because of the test results—the government was closing the arsenal. These men were old enough to know General Douglas MacArthur's famous lament: "Old soldiers never die. They just fade away."

Most out-of-work war engineers don't die, one of them might have said. They just go to work somewhere else.

Todd got this letter the other day from the Department of Defense, and he's more than willing to share it with me, because it's "just another rip-off by those so-called civil-service bastards. They're not civil and they don't serve anybody but themselves." The letter is a request for data on "destructive devices, concepts, and technologies for individual and small unit combat operations." I suggest that the Department of Defense is supposed to have all the secrets, and Todd just fumes. I get the feeling he has been in this job so long because he has a genuine desire to serve his country and its people, he is a true patriot—a vanishing species— but he is now a casualty of his own ideals. He has seen too much waste, too much stupidity, too much self-serving in the name of something else. There is a carelessness about him, a feeling of wrecklessness. "Patriotism" is almost a dirty word. In a year or two it might be filthy.

The Department of Defense has undertaken a project to improve the capabilities of the Armed Forces to employ destructive devices at the individual soldier and small unit levels (team, crew, squad) in a variety of conventional and special purpose missions.

Primary objectives are the adoption or application of

lightweight, man-portable destructive devices, concepts, technologies to perform the following functions:

- Blast (hard/soft structures, military equipment)
- Cut (trees, concrete, rails, girders)
- Breach (walls, bunkers, doors, fences, shields)
- Mine (surface, sub-surface, underwater)
- Burn (facilities, POL, ammunition)
- Booby-trap (military equipment, structures)
- Launch (explosives, penetrators, incendiaries)
- Crater (soil, concrete, rock, asphalt)

The US Army Armament Research and Development Command (ARRADCOM), as the lead service for this DOD task, has contracted with Management Technology Corporation (ManTech) and McLean Research Center, Inc. (MRC) to help identify and evaluate practical destructive devices, concepts, and technologies available. Selected agencies within the US Government, foreign governments, and private industry are being asked to participate in this project.

Your organization is being approached to assist in this search and can help speed this step in the study effort by sharing your pertinent knowledge and ideas. Several copies of a data sheet are enclosed to indicate the data needed and to facilitate your response. If you prefer, however, the information may be provided in any form convenient to you: brochures, drawings, photographs, specifications, etc. Please indicate *proprietary* portions of the data; any dissemination restrictions you may specify will be followed strictly. Please send information to: [DELETED]

ManTech, Inc., and MRC, Inc., under contract with ARRADCOM, have no competitive hardware interests in this field and will be bound by the restrictions regarding the safeguarding of proprietary and military security information.

Copies of the resulting descriptive catalog of destructive devices, concepts, and technologies will be provided to all appropriate Department of Defense organizations and laboratories.

Your assistance in this project is appreciated. To meet the analysis and publication schedules, your prompt response— within 30 days—will be necessary. . . .

Does this request have anything to do with Iranian rescue missions?

"Oooohh," Todd whispers. "That would strike a nerve. Yeah, send one to Jimmy Carter. . . . Actually, I think this is a smoke screen. When the press comes to 'em and asks 'em what they're doin', they can say, "Well, we've sent this letter out, and it's not our fault if we don't get anything back." Speakin' of screwin' up, I didn't even change my calendar. Shows you how screwed up I am. . . ."

His secretary, who worked behind the same desk thirty years ago, when my father was here, takes this moment of levity to chime in.

"Do you, uh—have the same, uh—*interests* as your father?"

"What interests did he have?"

"Oh, you know, playing with bombs and—and—blowin' things up."

I don't exercise those interests quite as often as I'd like, no. I ask her if she'd like to tell me anything she remembers about him from those days, and she says, quite simply, that she doesn't remember anything about him. Then:

"Has anybody come after you because of anything your father did?"

"What exactly did he do?"

"Oh. I don't really know, but . . ." But nothing. She doesn't finish the sentence. I am being forced into this conversation, which is really a guessing game. Who, then, would want to "come after me" because of what my father did?

"Oh, maybe the FBI or the CIA or some of those people."

No, I say. To my knowledge I have not yet been investigated or interrogated.

"If they tried," Todd chuckles, "hell, he'd interview 'em!"

I wander out into the hall, looking for Fats MacNamara.

I already feel like I live here.

Fats looks the part: arms and shoulders like he once wrestled and played college football, good tan, low center of gravity. He exudes the aura of the hardworking, righteous, play-it-by-the-rules middle American. He's not too smart, but he's got plenty of substance. Don't put graffiti on his garage door, or snap off his car antenna, or damage his property down at the shore, or go after his daughter with a joint in your paws or a coke spoon up your nose. He'll tear you in half.

He is suspicious of me—maybe he's pretty smart after all—or maybe wary would be more like it. He doesn't make any assumptions about my mission, at least none that he puts up front. He listens to my explanation of why I'm here, and he's not exactly waiting for me to hang myself, but he's not gonna ignore it if I do. We shake hands and I have a seat after I apparently pass the preliminaries.

There was the time Barry tied a screaming yellow zonker to the sparkplug in Fats's brand-new '53 Chevy. Damn thing wouldn't start, so Fats gets out to take a look. Sure enough, there it is. Uh-oh, I know who did that. Only he shoulda tied it to the starter, not the sparkplug. Not enough juice there to get the thing lit.

"You should know better'n 'at, Bar." (Givin'm heck with thick Boston accent. The dummy.)

"Who, me? I dunno what you're talkin' about." (My young father slinks away.)

But everyone knew who did it, and everyone knew how Fats felt about it. He wasn't mad that Barry did it. He was mad that he did it wrong.

"Very few people would have questioned what he was doing if he was working for one person.

"I wouldn't put him anywhere near electricity, but he was a good chemistry guy.

"I remember him dragging around, being very tired. I don't think he was getting enough sleep at night. If he got interested in something, he'd work on it till he dropped. Five minutes can be worth a day if you can work like that. Forget about eating, forget about sleeping. It's a great way to be. Not all of us can do that. . . . Whaddaya do? Walk in there and say, 'Hey, you dummy, get outta here an' go get somethin' to eat'?

"His technical reports—you didn't have to touch 'em. They said it all. Everything you needed to know. It was right there. Kinda made you wish you could do that."

Fats claims it's possible Barry was doing "extracurricular" stuff at the Institute.

"I never saw it or heard about it, but that doesn't mean it didn't happen. Some of the stuff in the *Playboy* interview is entirely plausible. I'd rather not go into details, but I know for a fact that we never *made* detonators here. We designed *machines* that made detonators, but we never built the actual product. They were always complete by the time they got here."

Was it common for someone to come in on weekends or late at night?

"No, but that doesn't mean it didn't happen. Doesn't mean it couldn't have happened. I never did. I wanted to get away from here as fast as I could. Still do. But while I'm here, I work my butt off."

Fats likes making money. "Nothin' wrong with making a lot of money."

One thing I saw when I opened Todd's safe was a report dated 1959 that obviously had a lot to do with Vietnam. It had Fats's name on it as author, so I ask him about it. He doesn't ask me how I found out about it, but he does look puzzled. He frowns, chews on his cigar, then ruffles through a thick notebooklike folder. He looks up the report, which I have simply walked around, not actually naming it, because I saw the SECRET imprint.

"I can't show you that report," he says, shaking his head. "Nope. That's still a hot report. Sorry, but I can't show you that." Shakes his head and frowns. Jowls wobble. "I can't even tell you the *title*. Even that's secret."

As he walks me to the elevator, he declares: "I've been here going on thirty years. I'm one of the survivors."

It's not hard to see why.

We could be walking through the basement of your old high school, or a hospital, or a chemical supply house. There are rooms and rooms full of old research equipment, empty acetylene tanks, reels and reels of wire, ancient sinks, even a bathtub on lion's paws. The light is bad and it looks like the place hasn't been swept corner to corner for at least a year. Was that a rat I just saw out of the corner of my eye? I don't wanna know, just keep walking.

Finally we come to what looks like an office in all this subterranean disorder. And this is the *new* basement? I'm sort of glad they moved out of the old one. I see more than one spider web in this man's "office." It is as if the upstairs order and cleanliness and efficiency is directly offset by this nightmarish, Draculesque cavern upon which the entire Institute rests, both physically and metaphysically, for this is where all their original research is conducted. Granted, they don't do much of that stuff anymore— the fun stuff, as Fats calls it—but once in a while they get something cookin' down here. "Like what?" I ask Fats just before we cross the threshhold.

"Like the EEDs that'll keep the MX from blowing to kingdom come in all those underground silos."

"Have you guys worked on any other missile systems?" I inquire as innocently as possible.

"Oh, sure. We've worked on all of 'em, haven't we, Tim? Mr. Timothy Schmitt, meet Mr. David B. Rothman."

There is a painful sensitivity about this Mr. Schmitt, as if anything I might say could hurt him. I reach out my hand, and he shakes it suddenly, awkwardly. He offers me a seat with a gesture of his right arm, and I take it. He's fiddling with this and that on what looks like a huge HO train set, but, he tells me, is actually a prototype for the mobile underground transport system for the MX. The idea is to load all these missiles on huge trucks, build an enormous underground roadway underneath the deserts of Utah, Nevada, and a couple other western and southwestern states. The missiles will constantly be rotating from one silo to another, with lots of false silos—in other words, silos without missiles in them. If the Russians launch an attack, they might knock out some of ours, but not before we've had a good solid chance to wipe out a few tens of millions of them.

"Do you think the Russians will ever fight a serious war with us?" I ask Mr. Schmitt.

The question registers with a large amount of pain. I can see it in the sharp edges around his eyes and mouth. He stands as if his feet barely touch the ground. He leans into this and all my questions, tilts his head, looks far away, and then comes back with an answer that is well thought out, considered, considerate, serious, tight.

"They're already fighting a serious war with us. Have been for years. Problem is we still don't recognize it, because they're not actually shooting at us. They're shooting at everything *around* us. Knocking off our allies left and right. Hitting us in the flanks where we're too dumb to feel it."

He offers to show me parts of the lab that were here when my father was here. "But I thought they moved the lab from the basement of the museum next door to this brand-new building fifteen or so years ago," I say.

Yes, Mr. Schmitt says, but they liked the old one so much they actually moved parts of it over here. We walk over to the far end of the lab, where there is a huge steel door painted black. Must be five feet by six feet. On the outside, in thick black Magic Marker, someone has scrawled: SHERWODE FOREST. The handwriting is very familiar.

"Open it," Mr. Schmitt commands, and I do. Inside, it looks like a meat locker. You could set off quite a device in here and nobody would hear it. I walk around in it, picking up all the old vibes. As I turn to leave, I see more hieroglyphics in the same hand on the inside of the door. It's a very simple line drawing, quite good, in fact, depicting an Old English countryside, complete with castle, turrets, rolling hills, and a few jousting knights.

I can tell that my presence is upsetting his day, so I try to drink in as much as I can as quickly as I can swallow and scribble. I note: *Eyes, clear green. Well defined features, hair parted oh so straight down the middle, old fashioned. Painfully precise. Wonder how he copes with such a sloppy world. Reminds me of a deer, medium height and build.*

He shows me another, smaller, vaultlike room.

"Here's the Iron Maiden," he says, grinning quick and turning his face from me. "Your dad, I think, helped build 'er. We used to test explosives on her."

This hunk of rusted iron is comparable to an incubator, complete with glove box and small window through which you can watch your little blast.

"Push that little shield over the window."

I obey. Again, scribbled in the same Magic Marker: CLOSE COVER BEFORE STRIKING.

"He had no fear, absolutely no fear. Detonator blew up in his face as he was looking over this shield. That was the one and only accident we ever had. Had he taken the proper precautions, like we were told to, it probably wouldn't have happened. He could have been blinded. He wore thick glasses, and then safety glasses on top of them. He could have been blinded. But he healed."

There was always the feeling he had something going on somewhere else that was much more important than all of this, something much more dangerous. He was a great worker—when you could find him. Sometimes he'd disappear for days at a time, no explanations for where he'd been. Didn't really matter, because nobody asked anyway. Sometimes they'd find him in the museum library, researching something or other. When he wasn't out wandering somewhere, and wasn't at his desk, and wasn't home with the flu, he was on the phone. Sometimes he'd get up to ten calls a day, every day, men and women, not always the same callers either. It was weird, but nobody got into anybody else's business. They'd just try to go find him. If they couldn't find him, they'd ask if the party wanted to leave a message, but they never did.

During lunch periods, Barry and Mr. Schmitt would work on designs and prototypes for what eventually became Barry's teargas pengun. Mr. Schmitt built the first model. In fact, he built all the models; Barry couldn't handle a lathe if you paid him solid gold. For six months they toyed around every night. Make one that doesn't look right, one that doesn't work right. Too bulky. He wanted them slimmer, smaller. Design talk. They were pretty crude.

It is known that Barry spent a lot of time in the Institute's library. It is not known what he researched or discovered or thought while he was there. It is reasonable to assume, however, that he read the following words at least once, because they are inscribed on a bronze plaque in the elevator that takes employees up to the library. (It's not open to the public, meaning me.) Mr. Schmitt dictates this speech, on behalf of Benjamin Franklin, who happens to be his hero.

> The rapid progress which *true* science now makes, occasions my regretting sometimes that I was born so soon. It is impossible to imagine the heights to which may be carried, in a thousand years, the power of man over matter. We may perhaps learn to deprive large masses of their gravity, and give them absolute levity, for the sake of easy transport. Agriculture may diminish its labor and double its produce; all diseases may by sure means be prevented or cured, not excepting even that of old age, and our lives lengthened at pleasure even beyond the antediluvian standard. O that moral science were in a fair way of improvement, that men would cease to be wolves to one another, and that human beings would at length learn what they now improperly call humanity.

Mr. Schmitt can share one more anecdote before he really must get back to work.

Barry brought in all kinds of snakes and kept them on the firing range in the basement of the old museum, next to the labs. It must have been beautiful, really tender. I can hear it even in Mr. Schmitt's voice: respect and sadness and even loss. Yes, loss for pet snakes down on the range. None of that "he was so bizarre" stuff. They all learned what and how snakes eat, how to keep them clean, how they like to be held, how to keep them healthy, how to feed them when they're sick, and mate them and hatch their eggs and raise their young. Learned how they live in the wild, how to catch them without hurting them.

"So what if they bite?" he'd say. "Just let 'em chew on you a little while. They'll get bored and let go. That way you don't tear out any of their teeth."

Those snakes were the only living things, aside from themselves, down on that range. No one but Barry would have done that. No one.

. . .

Todd dictates a few more reminiscences on his secretary's Dictaphone.

Another thing I think everyone should know about Barry: he was practically a genius when it came to the verbal side of the intellect. We sent him to Atlas Research Personnel, an outfit where they test employees to find out what their potentials are and how well they've made use of them. He was practically off the scale. I think this explains why he was able to handle the chemistry and explosives and all the other things that he got into without really having any advanced formal education. He was basically self-taught, a fast reader, and he remembered what he read. He really knew his stuff. He was also a good writer, although he didn't write very much for us because he was a technician and we kept him pretty busy.

Another interesting story that just came to mind about Barry concerns some of his exploits as a blaster. He had a blaster's license sometime in his career and was frequently called upon for specialty jobs. One involved opening a safe that was in a building that had been destroyed by fire. The safe was badly burned and they couldn't get it opened. They hoped the valuables had survived the fire, but they didn't know how to open the darn thing. So they asked Barry if he could do it.

Now, as Barry explained to me, he didn't know what the heck to do, but he took part of a Coca-Cola bottle and used that as a cast to mold some explosive material around. In other words, he improvised a shaped charge, the kind you might use to blow a hole in a tank if you only had a few scrap explosives layin' around. He placed the charge on the door of the safe, and I suppose aimed it at the combination dial. Stuck a blasting cap in it, retreated behind a barricade, and fired the fool thing. When the smoke cleared, they approached the safe. It sat there, apparently undamaged, and as they walked up to it, the door quietly fell off. [Laughs heartily] Just a perfect choice of charge, and that's Barry for ya.

Which reminds me of another one that he told me. He had

been hired to clear stumps or excavate a ditch somewhere out in the rural area, and since it was a wide-open space, I guess he really, really put in a bunch of big charges and then fired 'em all at once. It's now mandatory to use a delay technique—fire your charges with a rippling effect—so the noise level and shock waves are reduced. But in those days I don't think it was mandatory, and even if it was, I doubt Barry obeyed it.

Through some strange phenomena, the shock wave traveled over the nearby hills and shattered all the windows in the houses in the surrounding area. Fortunately, I understand his blaster's insurance covered the damages, otherwise he'd probably still be payin' it off.

In 1956, a photograph was taken by the Institute's staff photographer of the entire Applied Physics Section. Everyone that I have profiled in this chapter made it a priority to be photographed that day. More than three dozen men and women lined up or sat down on bleachers in the assembly hall. It is a standard Fifties photo, in the sense that most of the men are wearing dark suits and ties, while the women are wearing dresses or skirts and blouses that all came out of the same mold: Basic Boring. It is not surprising that my father is the only man in that photo who is not wearing a suit, or a tie, or even a starched white shirt. He is the radical of the group, and he is wearing a simple gray flannel shirt, unbuttoned at the collar, and his usual black chinos. He is also wearing a huge watermelon grin. Why?

Todd managed to get a blowup of this photo for me, and it is now very clear to me why he is smiling so broadly, and why so many of his colleagues seem to be happy, too. Smack-dab in the middle of his twenty-one-year-old forehead, there is a solid, shiny black eye. It was extracted from the skull of a Barbie doll earlier that morning, and transplanted—with epoxy glue—to my father's forehead.

This photograph has become legend, and has passed on to the level of secret lore among the "survivors" of that era. None of my interviewees will reveal the secrets of that prank—how it was orchestrated, who conceived the idea in the first place—but

Jonathan Woodcock, a "refugee" of the Institute, is at least willing to admit he was a "coconspirator."

Woodcock exudes au aura of energy, straightforwardness, clarity. It has developed into a very manly force that emanates from every pound of him. One imagines many women watching him walk into rooms. Not that he's beautiful, because he isn't. He's solid, full of deep rich earth and muscle, a country woman's man, chock-full of good clean fun. In his own words, he is "a corny romantic intellectual ex-engineer who now drives a blue pickup like a pro." Now he works more with his hands than his brain. He feels a little guilty about that. When he switched from explosives engineering to contracting and renovations, he had a hard time dealing with it. Thought it might be a waste. Then someone told him he would be improving people's living conditions. That straightened him out. He's too old to get back into that game anyway.

He picks me up and we drive around for forty minutes looking for a place to eat and talk, and the whole time I hold on to anything that doesn't move. Finally it's a Pizza Palace on the boulevard. We talk for about two hours. He remembers one thing more clearly than any other, and it has nothing to do with the Institute: My mother and my father were great lovers.

"What do you mean by great?"

"Well," Jonathan recalls between bites of his fourth slice, "I remember Barry telling me that sometimes they would't get out of bed for *days*. They'd keep a jar of orange juice by the bed to keep their energy up. They'd get so sore they'd hardly be able to walk for a week. Sounds great to me. What do you think?"

Rick Bolinski has done pretty well for himself as an aerospace engineer at Westinghouse's Re-entry and Environmental Systems Division. He's got the house in Chestnut Hill, one of the most luxurious suburbs of Boston. He's got the Chevy on company lease. He's got a willing wife and a willing kid and a dog that my father would have called Snake Food.

He's now working on the *Voyager* satellite, which recently orbited Jupiter and sent back fantastic photos. He may be working on something else, too, or not on *Voyager* at all (even though several huge color glossies of Jupiter adorn his Tupperware kitchen). He's got Westinghouse's brand of top-secret security clearance: I couldn't even go up to his office to retrieve something of Barry's that has been in Rick's files since they were kids. So he photocopies it, folds the copy in half, staples it with one staple, and leaves it with the receptionist/guard at the front desk, near the front door, with my name scribbled on the back. So much for security.

DEPARTMENT OF COMMERCE
National Inventors
Council
Washington 25, D.C.

January 13, 1955

Mr. Barry M. Rothman
Technical Director
Explosives Engineering
507 Robbins Avenue
Boston, Mass.

Dear Mr. Rothman:

We have your letter of December 6, 1954, and should like to thank you for submitting your proposal to us.

The preliminary study of your material by our technical staff suggests that it is worthy of further investigation to determine its possible value to the defense program. We are accordingly forwarding it to further technical personnel for additional examination. We will advise you of their findings as soon as they are available.

We assure you that we appreciated the opportunity of examining your idea. If you should have any further suggestions that might aid in the defense effort, we shall be glad to hear from you again.

Very truly yours,

L. S. Hardland
Assistant Chief Engineer

When I'm sitting at his kitchen table, I get the feeling that, yes, he'll sit and talk with me as long as I like, just as long as it doesn't take more than ninety minutes. He smokes a lot of cigars and cigarettes, and his arrogance shows even in the way he holds the filter away from his lips, in the way he flicks his ash. This Sunday he's wearing a gray high-school gym sweatshirt and jeans.

His twenty-two-year-old daughter, whom he introduces as Sharon Boles, is not too bright but is very well trained. Does everything just so. Just the way daddy wants t. She worked in the city last year at something I can't remember, and she's looking to get a similar job in the same field.

She comes downstairs to the kitchen where we're sitting and plops herself down between us. It's time for her afternoon Coke and candy bars. She's wearing skintight jeans (no panty line), heels, tight sweater. A great body. I try real hard not to look. (Later, when I'm about to go, she'll be out on the patio with a book, another Coke, and more candy bars. I'll stand at the screen door, saying things like, "How long will you be here before you move back to the city? . . . Uh, well, it was really nice meeting you. Maybe . . ." Maybe nothing. Maybe vomit. She doesn't offer anything, and not because she's not interested. She wants to make me work with no promise at all.)

There is also the fact that daddy wants me the hell out of there so he can watch the game or do whatever top-secret homework he does on Sunday afternoons. First he gives answers that have beginnings, middles, and ends. Then they just have middles and ends. Then you're lucky just to get the ends. He doesn't offer anything either.

Before I leave, Rick tells me about Barry's early tear-gas pen-guns. He regrets mentioning he still has one of the big old ones, because now he has to go get it. He comes back with this cigar-size pengun. He doesn't hand it to me—he puts it on the table. He probably thinks I'm too young to handle it properly. He's sure to remind me they're very illegal.

I thought I'd seen all the models, but this must be one of the first. All the ones I've seen have .38 shells, and this is a .410 shotgun shell. Nasty! He keeps it with the shell screwed all the way in, so the firing pin is pressing real hard against the primer. I sort of mention the possibilities, that all it takes to fire the bugger is a jolt or a drop from a very low height. Or maybe, after all these years, no help at all. Right, his grin says as he tilts back in his chair, flicking his ash and taking half a puff. Yeah, he says silently, as he crosses his arms and grins again.

Just then I notice it's pointed at me.

PLAYBOY INTERVIEW

PLAYBOY: So far, we're talking about chemical systems. Did you also design gadgets like that dart gun?

MR. DEATH: Not quite like that, but quite a number of other things. After the automobile episode, my contact came to me with another hypothetical problem: Suppose you're in a situation in which it is impossible to bring into a room any firearms or unconventional things that would be suspect. How would you take care of a roomful of guys? Well, next question is: How taken care of? I mean, do you want them extracted, do you want them blinded temporarily? Biological assault?—always loved that term. It sounds obscene. Well, in this particular instance my contact said, "We want them extracted for sure. A fair number of them, in a moderate-sized room." And I wound up with one of the nastiest nasties that I came up with. That, incidentally, was the jargon for those gadgets: Assorted Nasties. This one was a sub-miniature bomb, roughly the size of a .45-caliber cartridge. You threw it and it exploded. It was loaded with hardened steel shot, like bird shot, which was coated with poison. Eventually, I replaced that with small pellets of [deleted]. If you get hit with an incandescent fragment of it, you go into anaphylactic shock almost instantly. It kills you faster than you can believe. I've seen films of tests on monkeys. The knockdown is truly remarkable. Load it into a shell, fire it at someone, and his whole central nervous system goes berserk.

PLAYBOY: Wasn't that a bit dangerous for the person throwing it?

MR. DEATH: It certainly was. It would kill him outright.

PLAYBOY: Didn't the agency object to that drawback?

MR. DEATH: No. And I found that interesting. They did ask that I make two versions, the second being one that would give the guy a chance to survive. It has what amounted to a fuse you could light with a cigarette or something. Another version lit like a road flare. You could remove a piece of tape that covered a material similar to what's on the tip of wooden kitchen matches. Strike it and throw it. In a third version, I mixed red phosphorus with [deleted]. When you wet this down with chloroform, it will not explode. But if you let it dry, it becomes highly explosive. You could just plop it into the middle of a room and it would explode. You could put it on the top of a door, put it under a toilet seat, or anyplace where it would get bashed. Once it was armed, it was not easy to disarm, either.

PLAYBOY: How many of those did you make?

MR. DEATH: Maybe fifteen or twenty. I also loaded a lot of small-arms ammunition with incendiary bullets made of [deleted]— .22s, 9mm, shot shells. Those were for rapid kill. And there were strange requests. I made some ammunition that was loaded with an explosive called tetryl, so that when you fired it, it blew you and the gun all over the ceiling. The .22 Walther PPKS was a fairly standard firearm with the CIA people I knew. I was issued one that had a barrel threaded to accept a silencer. And I was once asked to modify one so that the slide would blow back and take the guy's head off. I assume that was for one of our own people.

PLAYBOY: Do you mean to say that they were assassinating their own people?

MR. DEATH: I have no idea what they did with that device—or any of the devices, for that matter. I was only building them. But others within the agency had given me the distinct impression that they would kill their own people if it suited them to do so. And, at that time, it seemed odd that they wanted that particular gun modified in that particular way. It's certainly not standard equipment for any army or government I can think of.

PLAYBOY: When you say you were issued that weapon, in what sense do you mean that?

MR. DEATH: Well, again, it was given as a kind of reward. I did some job that pleased them. Then a friend of mine—the same one who took me to Caracas—took me to lunch one day. He indicated they were pleased. Then he gave me a package. At the time, I was working at the [deleted] Institute. So I took the package back and fluoroscoped it to see what was inside—

PLAYBOY: Why didn't you just open it?

MR. DEATH: Well, I thought if they were so pleased, they might want to send me to heaven. Seriously, it was just a standard precaution. And, lo, there was a brand-new Walther with a nice new silencer custom-fitted to it.

PLAYBOY: So far, is the work you've described representative of what you were doing throughout the mid- and late Fifties?

MR. DEATH: Yes, but, of course, I had a regular job as well. I was doing research for the [deleted] Institute, which was involved in everything imaginable. One of my first projects for them was to design and test miniature detonators. I knew they had a vault where they locked secret reports, and I used to go in and read reports on everything imaginable, just because I was fascinated. Nuclear stuff, cannon technology. They were very heavily into the study of flame fuels. Thixotropes, for instance. A thixotrope is a gel that turns into a liquid when you move it; for example, if you pump it. There were reports discussing the reality of building a death ray with laser beams—that was in the Fifties. Of course, they have now actually developed it and it's something the Defense Department won't even mention. It is a breakthrough in technology equal to the atomic bomb. When I worked there, the laboratories were in the basement and included a fully equipped range for firing anything up to and including 20mm cannon shells. I felt like a mole. Especially in the winter. I'd go down in the early morning and it was dark and I'd come up at night and it was dark again. I never saw daylight.

PLAYBOY: Was this institute a secret operation?

MR. DEATH: No, not the institute itself. Most of the work I did was classified, but parts of the place were open to the public. There were public exhibits upstairs from us. And the institute did a lot of unclassified work, stuff that had nothing to do with the military, like testing the strength of a certain kind of toilet tissue or something equally strange. But the fact that people were allowed into the place and that we were obviously working for the military had some funny results, because we got a reputation for being able to handle strange objects. If somebody found an old pineapple grenade in his attic, he'd bring it down to the institute and ask us if it was safe or to dispose of it.

PLAYBOY: Did you personally have to deal with people's leftover war souvenirs?

MR. DEATH: Yes, for a while, anyway, until one day, when my boss called me up and said that some little old lady had brought in this thing her son got in the war. He didn't recognize it and neither did I. It was about the size of a frozen-juice can, plain metal, and had a T-shaped handle. No markings. So I took it down to our range, taped a blasting cap to it, and, as I was wrapping the wires, I accidentally hit the handle and heard this clickety, clickety, clickety—a timer going—whereupon, being very brave, I dropped it, ran like hell, and slammed the armored doors. Nothing happened. So I told the range attendant to leave the doors barred, put up a sign, and I'd be back after lunch. I had a very long lunch that day, but when I went back, nothing had happened. Then, as I was opening the doors, that mother went off. It caused the first miniature quake in town and scared the shit out of me. The blast took a big hunk out of the concrete floor and scored the walls.

PLAYBOY: What was it?

MR. DEATH: It took me two years to find out. It was a very rare Italian World War Two demolition device. They were made with variable-time fuses ranging from—get this—two seconds to several hours. After that, I flat-out refused to accept any unknown devices and sent a memo to my director, saying, FUCK YOU; STRONG MESSAGE FOLLOWS.

PLAYBOY: Was all of your work there oriented toward ordnance?

MR. DEATH: No. I worked on methods of applying gold to the edges of Bibles. Some company wanted to find a way to do this by machine, because, at the time, it was all handwork done by old craftsmen who were dying out. I was up to my asshole in Bibles for a long time. I found that kind of ironic, working with one hand on that and with the other making miniature land mines or something.

PLAYBOY: You mentioned miniature detonators. Were they for the CIA or part of your official work for the institute?

MR. DEATH: Both. Officially, I was developing detonators to be used in the warheads of missiles and artillery shells. Unofficially, I was making miniaturized timers and detonators for setting off high explosives. All you do is take a battery-operated wristwatch or a penlight cell to provide power to run that little thing I had made; plug the two together and that's your detonating system. Some arsenal was manufacturing a wristwatch that looked normal except it had terminals on it to which you could connect the detonators I was building. I tried to get one of the watches for myself but couldn't.

PLAYBOY: What, then, was the difference between the detonators made for the institute and the ones for the CIA?

MR. DEATH: Basically, just looks. The CIA models were most commonly disguised as Marlboro boxes. They had asked that I make them so that they could be disguised as a package of cigarettes, and the handiest thing was the Marlboro hardpack. After that, there were some other strange requests. Later, toward the last part of my stay at the institute, the Gravel mine was being developed. "Gravel" was the code name for a land mine about the size of a tea bag that contained no metal or moving parts. They were dropped from airplanes and armed themselves by evaporation after they hit the ground. Their purpose was to be sown by air in vast quantities as an area-denial system. They didn't kill. When stepped on, they detonated and would shatter every bone in your foot. Actually, my task was to develop a disarm system, because of a meeting in which I had asked a casual question, like, "Hey, if you sow thirty-jillion-trillion Gravel mines and you go to take the territory again, what is everybody going to do, walk on stilts?"

PLAYBOY: Was this work for the institute or for the CIA?

MR. DEATH: Again, it was both. My job was to develop a disarm system. I made some Gravel mines that were conventional

in the sense that they functioned as they were supposed to. I
also made some for the CIA that contained poisoned glass fragments. I made others that would appear to be disarmed but were
not. With one system, the Gravel mine would change color if it
was disarmed. So I made some that would change color but not
really be disarmed. I made them by hand and delivered them
to my contact in Maxwell House coffee cans. For some strange
reason, that was specified. Sealed in the cans. The institute had
no knowledge of it. I had to buy the Maxwell House coffee, open
the cans, resolder them, sand them and repaint them so they
looked as if they hadn't been tampered with. Why, I don't know.
I understand that in Guam, where Gravel mines are still stored
in great Quonset huts, some of them have become armed in the
magazines. They're manufactured wet and if they dry out, then
they are armed. Apparently, that happened there. Makes for an
interesting problem. I think what you do is push the island away
with a big stick.

PLAYBOY: Was the mine ever used?

MR. DEATH: Jesus Christ, yes. Vietnam must be one large Gravel
mine. It wasn't a lethal thing. It just pulverized every bone in
your foot. I mean to jelly. A nasty bastard. I know because I saw
them tested, which was truly horrible.

PLAYBOY: How did you test them?

MR. DEATH: We had to take severed legs from cadavers—which
were, incidentally, legs stolen from guys killed in Vietnam. Their
families were told the legs were lost in combat. Anyway, we'd
put a foot in a regulation army sock, insert that in a combat
boot, and then rig it to a machine that applied it to the Gravel
mine with the force of a one-hundred-and-seventy-pound man
stepping on it. We were so disgusted when we finished that job
that we mixed up a batch of straight two-hundred-proof ethanol
with Coca-Cola. I got stoned blind and so did my buddy. We
took a forklift truck, went into the janitor's supply area, and took
out a fifty-five-gallon drum of concentrated detergent. Outside,
there were huge fountains. In the summertime, they were turned
off in the wee hours of the morning and then turned on again
about five-thirty or six o'clock. They were off, so we took the
drum out and dumped the entire contents into the biggest fountain, right in the middle of the road. Then we waited for the

sun to come up while we were singing and dancing and carrying on. When those fountains came on, the Great Amoeba Caper started. A wall of foam twelve feet high erupted and began creeping across the road. It was absolutely impenetrable. Traffic stopped. It was magnificent to behold.

7

Bomblets

Picatinny Arsenal is a very real arsenal located in Dover, New Jersey. It is a major research-and-development installation of the United States Army. When I called Picatinny's public-affairs office and asked to speak with anyone who worked on the Gravel mine, I was eventually connected with several men who all said they had belonged to the Gravel project team. "The infamous Gravel mine," one of them said, waxing nostalgic on the phone with a writer who, for all he knew, could have been a foreign national.

All of those men—including the gentleman who claims to have been the real inventor of the mine back in 1959—said they would talk with me about the mine and release any declassified information regarding its invention, design studies, production, and eventual "application." One of them told me it went through all the necessary stages of development, including "extensive" use in Vietnam in the late Sixties and early Seventies. Problems arose when we discovered that it was killing more of us than them. For example, this chap said, when one planeload of Gravel mines was being shipped by plane from Eglin Air Force Base in Florida to Vietnam, the bomb-bay doors accidentally opened over the west coast of Florida, scattering thousands of armed Gravel mines on a certain undisclosed, though very popular, resort beach. The beach was declared off-limits by the governor while National Guard troops went to work gathering up the fruits of military labor. Area Denied Very Long Time.

I obeyed standard operating procedure and submitted a formal, written request to interview these men on this subject. The reply, two weeks later, via the chief public-affairs officer:

"We don't seem to have any luck finding anyone who worked on the Gravel Mine or related projects. Will put your request in the Employee Magazine."

But all was not lost to the shredding machine and the secret file. Before submitting my request, I spoke on the phone with one man who worked on the project and seemed more sympathetic to my search than any of the others. I asked this gentleman if he would inquire into a certain report that was "generated" by the crew at the Lincoln Institute in the early Sixties. My research, I told this man, had led me to believe that my father played a very important role in the conception and execution of that report. All my efforts through the Institute to acquire the report had failed. It would hold a great amount of sentimental value for me, etc., etc.

This gentleman said he would be glad to help. He meant what he said, because three weeks later I received a letter on official stationery which stated that if I sent them $6.35 to cover postage and handling and copying costs, they would send me the report. This man got the report declassified in three weeks—after it had been SECRET for twenty years—and all by picking up the phone and pushing a couple of buttons and talking nice for a few minutes and sending the required amount of hard cold cash.

I have the report, called *Gravel "A": Preliminary Design Studies*, before me now, and I can hardly believe it.

The title page would be ordinary if it weren't for the half-dozen stamps of approval, disapproval, classification, and declassification. One of them, so faint that it is almost unreadable, states: DOWNGRADED AT 12 YEAR INTERVALS; NOT AUTOMATICALLY DECLASSIFIED. DOD DIR 5200.10.

Another: EXCLUDED FROM GENERAL DECLASSIFICATION SCHEDULE. EXECUTIVE ORDER 11652.

Another: REVIEWED 1967 PICATINNY ARSENAL. There are three blanks for the security officer to choose among: *Retain Present Classification; Downgrade; Destroy.* There is a handwritten X next to the first choice.

This is stamped in bold black letters at the bottom of the title page. I wonder what it takes to be declared a foreign national. I wonder what prevents such creatures from infiltrating the United Kingdom and our northern neighbor.

At the top and bottom of this and every page of the report, the word SECRET has been ickied-out with black Magic Marker. UNCLASSIFIED has been stamped at the top of the first few pages, but then it is as if the security officer gave up and went back to his beer.

This document contains information affecting the national defense of the United States within the meaning of the Espionage Laws, Title 18, U.S.C., Sections 793 and 794. The transmission or the revelation of its contents in any manner to an unauthorized person is prohibited by law.

By Authority of A. A. Titch—23 Feb. 60
DD254, 9 June 1959

(1) INTRODUCTION

The Lincoln Institute on March 18, 1960, entered into a contract with Picatinny Arsenal to study the feasibility of disarming Gravel mines.

Gravel is an antipersonnel mine designed to deliver a disabling wound when initiated by foot pressure.

The Gravel mine in its present state of development consists of a fabric envelope that forms a 90 degree sector of a 5-inch diameter circle. Within the envelope is a perforated fiber stiffener. The envelope contains a mixture of RD 1333 lead azide, RDX, ground glass and colloidal silica. This mixture is kept inactive prior to field use by impregnation with 1,1,1 trichlorethane. In this state the mines are insensitive to bullet impact and to normal handling. When the mines are sown the 1,1,1 trichlorethane evaporates and arms the mine. This unique arming system and the low cost are attractive features of the Gravel mine.

Since the present Gravel unit is designed primarily for use by infantry, tactical requirements necessitate a method of disarming or disposing of armed mines to permit area access by friendly forces. Gravel is totally chemical; it contains no fuses or mechanical safety devices and cannot be disarmed in any conventional manner. In combat, Gravel mines will probably be sown in large numbers. Hence, it is apparent that the mine must contain an integral self-sterilizing feature.

A sterile mine is defined as a mine that has been rendered inert by decomposition of the explosive.

The following basic considerations are requisite for a suitable self-sterilizing system:

1. The system must be low in cost.
2. The system must be reliable and fail safe.
3. The mine must sterilize a reasonable time after arming and over the temperature range of 0 to 125 F.
4. The system must not interfere with the arming or affect the sensitivity of the mine.

A major consideration is the arming-sterilization cycle. The mine is armed by solvent evaporation, which is dependent on environmental considerations such as atmospheric diffusion, temperature and humidity. Arming time is therefore variable. In an optimum system, sterilization should be coordinated with arming delays to prevent a mine from being sterilized before it has armed or undergone reasonable tactical exposure. A compromise based on fixed sterilization action for an average arming time may be necessary. Environmental conditions affecting arming may also affect sterilization. For example, a cold mine may arm slowly with a corresponding delay in the sterilization action.

Another consideration is the size limit imposed on the

sterilization system. The Gravel mine is half the size of a pack of cigarettes—must necessarily be small and unobtrusive.

Chemical action appears to be the most practical way of sterilizing the Gravel mine (mechanical or electrical systems would be either too bulky or too expensive). The sterilizing chemical must be effective in small amounts because of size limitations. It must render the mine insensitive and at a predictable rate. It should have storage and handling characteristics at least equal to the mine itself.

(2) EXPERIMENTAL PROGRAMS

. . . Means were sought whereby the sterilizer would react with the explosive only after a given period of time following the arming of the mines. This could be done by activating a delay unit at the time the mines are sown that would allow the release of the sterilizing fluid at some desired time thereafter. Two ways of achieving this delay were investigated. One technique depended on forcing a viscous fluid from a chamber through a small orifice by applying pressure. At the end of the delay period the chamber would be emptied and the pressure would then be utilized to drive the disarming agent into contact with the explosive.

The other system depended on a chemical reaction, allowing a liquid to act on a barrier. At the time the mine is sown the reaction would start and at the end of the predetermined delay the fluid would have eaten through the barrier. There it would react with a gas generating reagent to build up the pressure that would then drive the sterilizer into contact with the explosive.

Both systems would be simplified if the sterilizing fluid could be used to provide the delay. The chemical system would probably be much simpler but might be more temperature sensitive. Both methods were pursued simultaneously. . . . The aim was a six hour delay at any temperature between 0 and 125 F. . . .

Since hydrochloric acid (but not sulfuric acid) is a suitable sterilizer for lead azide it would be desirable to use hydrochloric acid also as part of any chemical delay system and therefore limit the entire disarming unit to one liquid component. For this reason the aluminum–hydrochloric acid combination appeared most attractive. . . . When held horizontally serious difficulties were encountered. The hydrogen evolved in the reaction insulated the metal from further attack by the acid. For such a system to be feasible provisions would have to be made that permit the hydrogen to escape from the metal-acid interface. This was the case when the test units were vertical. In Gravel mines, however, the delay device could not be kept in that position since it would make the units too big. Ideally the disarming component should function independently of attitude since the mines may be oriented in any position after being sown, the most likely attitude, though, being a horizontal one. . . .

. . . Again the disarming system would be greatly simplified if hydrochloric acid could be used as the solvent. The reaction at room temperature between hydrochloric acid and Saran was found to be too slow to be practical. . . .

. . . More than six hours were required to penetrate 0.0075 inch barriers. A barrier thinner than this would be required to give a six hour delay at room temperature or colder environment. Since such thin discs would be fragile and probably difficult to reproduce, this system does not appear attractive. . . .

. . . At 125 F, however, twelve 0.010 inch discs were penetrated in an average time of 69 minutes, indicating an 0.05 inch barrier for a six hour delay. . . .

Once it was established that hydrochloric acid was a suitable reagent for destroying lead azide and that it could also be used to react with cellulose acetate to give the required delay before disarming, means were sought to store the liquid and expel it into the mine. . . . To activate the device the vial was crushed by exerting finger pressure on the Tygon tube. This caused the ampule to shatter into many small fragments and allowed acid to contact the delay barrier. At the end of the delay period acid had penetrated through the remnants of the disc and reacted with the sodium bicarbonate to generate carbon dioxide. The pressure developed blew off the polyethylene film and ejected the acid. . . .

. . . After activation, delays on these models ranged from 8 to 24 hours, rather than the expected six hours. Several possible causes for these long delays came to mind. . . .

Once it had been established that twenty milliliters of acid could be expelled from dispensers up to ⅜ inch in diameter, after a six hour delay, consideration was given to embodying dispensers in Gravel mines. To keep the mines as small as possible, it would be desirable to store the acid in the stiffener. Two approaches are being evaluated, a channelled dispenser and a diaphragm dispenser.

In the first case, the acid would be stored in channels within the stiffener. A delay device would be connected to the stiffener from the outside of the mine. It would most likely be a simple matter to mold a plastic channelled stiffener. At this laboratory, however, we are not equipped to mold such pieces. . . .

(3) CONCLUSIONS

The self-sterilization of Gravel mines six hours after sowing seems to be feasible. Concentrated hydrochloric acid has been found to completely destroy lead azide in less than two hours at any temperature between 0 and 125 F.

A six hour delay may most effectively be obtained by the attack of 30% hydrochloric acid on cellulose acetate barriers. The required thicknesses to give a six hour delay at any temperature between 0 and 125 F. have been established. It is believed that the barriers may be thickened to give a twenty hour delay. It remains to be seen, however, whether the same technique may be used to give a delay of four to seven days. . . .

(4) RECOMMENDATIONS

A number of problems that have been considered during this contract need further study. To this end it is recommended:

1. While the quantity of concentrated hydrochloric acid

needed to destroy lead azide has been measured, the amount of 30% acid required to sterilize Gravel mines which contain also RDX, ground glass, and a Cab-O-Sil in trichlorethane gel has not been determined. To keep the disarming unit as small as possible it would be desirable to keep the amount of acid to a minimum. The amount of acid required to react with the lead azide in the mines should be measured. It should then be determined whether this quantity is sufficient to sterilize the mines. If it is not, the effect of acid on the other components of the explosive mixture should be studied.

2. The thicknesses of cellulose acetate needed for a given delay at any temperature between 0 and 125 F. may be estimated from the enclosed data. It should be verified that the estimated thicknesses will indeed give the specified 20 hour or 4 to 7 day delays.

3. A search should be made for plastic materials from which the dispenser may be fabricated. . . .

4. Means of embodying the disarming unit in the mines, preferably the stiffener, must be studied. Both the channelled type and diaphragm types have given sufficient promise to warrant further investigation.

5. Finally the disarming units should be incorporated in Gravel mines and a sufficient number should be tested to insure that they meet all requirements.

ACKNOWLEDGMENTS

The author is indebted to Sam K. Crone for drawing the figures shown in this report. The experimental work was performed by Sam K. Crone, Carl Dock and Barry Rothman.

I can shoot off fireworks galore whenever I'm at his country house. No neighbors to complain, no cops waiting to pounce. I can shoot real guns on the shooting range, all the guns I could ever imagine, and more. If I'm lazy and don't want to trudge up to the range, I can plink with a .22 right in the driveway. Just don't assassinate anyone or anything, he'll say.

I am taking a fantastically long, dangerous shot at a sparrow across the road on a power line. It's beyond the bottom of the hill, which must mean it's at least 400 yards away. I take careless, quick aim at that brown speck with an old scopeless, rusty, single-shot .22 rifle—the one we call the Scopeless Hopeless— and what the hell, that speck does fall. It takes me several hours to find the corpse in the underbrush, but when I do, it's warm and red and tiny and I am sick sick sick, and pledge to God never to kill another living thing.

One of the worst moments in my life: I am twelve years old and calling my father from the phone booth around the corner. I am trying not to cry, but it's not working. Somehow I've got to get the words out: Last night I was arrested in a synagogue. The charges: breaking and entering, possession of stolen property, petty larceny, trespassing. Soon I'll have to go to court. If I'm lucky, I'll get probation and mandatory psychiatric counseling (the latter having been demanded by my mother in front of half a dozen police officers. "I don't know what to do with him any-more, I can't reach him, somebody else has to try." I could've shot her). I don't want to think what could happen if I'm not lucky.

I'm expecting a bitter, angry rejection. I'm expecting to be shut out, given up for lost, beyond redemption. It doesn't help that I've also been charged with half a dozen other burglaries and petty thefts—most but not all of which I committed. The most ridiculous charge is trespassing on a construction site. The most serious is breaking into and entering a local country club, vandal-izing the soda machines, stealing all the money in the coin box, and drinking about three cases of orange Nehi, my favorite soda. A couple of my friends were in on most of these gigs, but none of them have been charged as heavily as I. I'm crushed. It's the end.

"I did pretty much the same when I was about your age," he says. No anger, no resentment or rejection. Sounds like he's *proud,* like I've just copped a medal. "Only I wasn't quite so young. Maybe about sixteen. Me and a few friends broke into a tennis club and had a great time causing lots of damage. We weren't as lucky as you are. They didn't have probation then. You either paid back the damage and went to jail or you just paid back the damage. Fortunately I just had to pay the lion's share of the damage. If I'd been a year older I would've gone to the slam."

"How long did it take you to pay the owners back?"

"About two years. I worked at a doughnut factory filling cream doughnuts. Can you imagine the idiocy? I know how you feel. You feel like the dumbest jerk who ever drew a breath. Right?"

I'm choking I'm so amazed. I feel *closer* to him than I've ever felt.

"Right."

"Don't worry about it. It'll pass. Just be glad you got it out of your system now."

Six months later, he and Dawn have come to be with me on my day in court. I meet him at the train station. Again I'm terrified. Could his generosity be real, his *tenderness?*

"What time is the hearing?" he asks while we're walking back to mom's car. He could be asking about the weather.

"One o'clock."

This is the only time I can remember having my mother and father standing behind me, literally standing right behind me, backing me up, giving me strength. I am poised before the juvenile court judge's bench. My two friends and their parents are to my left. I ignore them. It seems as if the judge is ignoring them, too. All the time he is reading the charges, he seems to be reading them to *me,* not *us.* What can this mean? Am I going to reform school? The nuthouse? Prison? What special treatment awaits me because of this judge's special favor?

Now he's looking through my school records. They're not impressive, but they're not pitiful. Maybe a few inches above average in more subjects than not. Especially science and social studies.

He ponders so long that the court falls deadly quiet. Finally, in a deep, frightening, judicial tone:

"Why did you do it?"

"Stupidity, I guess."

I don't think those words, they just fall out of my mouth with half my voice. No one says anything. I am sentenced to a year of probation and a year of psychiatric counseling; one of my friends gets six months' probation; the other gets off without so much as having to spend one minute in a probation office or under the eye of a New Jersey shrink. I'm enraged but say nothing. Walk out with my father and mother behind me. Walk out into the hall where Dawn has been waiting for my father, for us.

Later I ask my father why the judge picked on me.

"He wasn't picking on you. He was respecting you. He was honoring you by asking you why. Those other guys were too dumb to know better. He knew you could do a helluva lot better."

8

Mom

An unusually cold, rainy night in a warm season. A quiet, clean, civilized suburb of a major city in the northeastern United States. A quiet, clean, civilized living room in a modest neighborhood. A son comes home to talk with his mother.

We talk briefly about the length of the cassette tapes. I'll be using thirty-minute cassettes. She's distant for a second, then snaps back and says she was just thinking about them having thirty-minute orgasms. She laughs. "I got my thoughts crossed."

We do the interview in one sitting while the rest of the house is asleep. It's not really an interview; it's more like listening in on her private monologue, a stream of consciousness that has been flowing through her blood for almost three decades. I am surprised to get her to talk so openly for so long—all of two and a half hours. After all the bitter years, I am shocked by how willing she is to talk, how *committed* she is to passing on these fragments of what she calls "our childhood." Not that she makes a great show of her desire to talk; quite the opposite. It's just that, after agreeing to do it, she offers herself honestly and compassionately. I get the feeling it is not unlike the way she must have offered herself to my father when they were both young and foolish.

She is surprisingly unemotional, clinical. She talks with a mature woman's acceptance of the early days of their marriage and why it failed. She leaves out much of herself, but that's all right. I don't push her or even try to lead her where she doesn't choose to go on her own. She has suffered enough, maybe too much. Too many deaths. What she offers will be enough.

There is a feeling coming from her of something opening and closing, very delicate and childlike. My mother is emancipated in the sense that she doesn't care what anyone thinks of her thoughts or hobbies or occupation. She couldn't care less what "the girls" think. She is domesticated in the sense that something very womanly and feminine has been wounded in her by this man's world, or her surrender to it, or both. She once told me what she wanted most out of life: to be alone. Solitude is the one gift she has never received from anyone, never given to herself.

"It was a long time ago. About twenty-eight years ago. Do you think this is going to work? Well, ask me specific questions because I don't know what you want.

"It must have been early 1952 when we met. I had been working since I graduated from high school at the Cancer Research Institute. I had come there hoping to be a biologist. I wanted, more than anything, to be a part of that bright new generation that was going to wipe out cancer in my lifetime.

"Barry came to work there as a bottle washer—the job I held for two years before being promoted to laboratory aide. I was nineteen and a half, which seemed very young, and I had no idea how old he was. He seemed older than that, and he was looking for sex, he was looking, I think, I think really he was looking for love spelled S-E-X. I think he was very much looking for love.

"I don't know how we first noticed each other, but since we worked in such close proximity, it was probably over the sink. Pretty soon he was quoting poetry at me. His favorite poem was about a whore named Senera. What was important to him were these lines: 'Senera, my Senera,/With thy ruby lips and raven hair,/I will be faithful to thee in my fashion!'

"Throughout his life that meant something to him. It was a talisman. I don't really know what the significance of it was for him—possibly it had to do with his mother being a whore. He had found her in bed with another man, other than his father, I think at the age of ten, and that screwed him up for the rest of his life. But aside from the fact that the lady Senera is a whore, the line 'I will be faithful to thee in my fashion' became very significant words to both of us, which lasted, I think, till the end, till his death. I never felt that he thought of me as a whore, but it was the faithfulness in my fashion that was important.

"I'm giving this importance out of all proportion, but I think it was a touchstone. It began and ended our relationship.

"Anyway, he was hot and panting and speaking poetry at me, and I succumbed. I had always told my girlfriends that I would lose my virginity when I was twenty, and also that I would marry a Jew. Well, they both came true. When I was a teen-ager, I had three very close girlfriends. The four of us were very close for several years, a good many years, and it was they whom I shocked tremendously. This was when I was maybe fourteen, fifteen, sixteen years old. I shocked them tremendously because they were good Christian girls. . . ."

I can see my mother now, young and ripe and on the farm. Her friends are shocked, of course, but this is part of the reason they love her. They never know what to expect from her. Here is a good Christian girl, just like themselves, from a first-generation German Lutheran family, a family just as boring as their own, and one day she's telling them she'll go to bed with the first Jew who tries to seduce her, and the next day she tells them she'll marry that Jew.

On other days she'll tell them about the snakes she catches in the cornfield—all the different species, including diamondback rattler. She'll tell them about the tiger salamanders in the stream next to the house, and how beautiful they are. She'll tell them how long it takes to hatch an alligator egg, and that the female alligator is the only reptile that digs a nest, lays its eggs in the nest, and guards the eggs until the baby gators hatch.

She'll tell them that one of these days she's going to hitchhike down to the Florida Everglades and go "collecting" all by herself. Her friends think she's crazy, but they love her in spite of it. Or maybe because of it.

. . .

"He was kind of an insinuator and a wheeler-dealer and a manipulator. He was supposedly sleeping with a girl named Joan Brown, and he used to delight in telling me that he'd been having sex since he was eleven. He said it started with a black girl—which influenced his choice with Dawn; one always goes back to one's beginnings. Anyway, his first was on the school fire escape at the age of eleven. He was thrown out of school for such things repeatedly, and finally expelled.

"He was trying to get me to sleep with him by holding Joan Brown over my head. He was saying that if I did it, he would give her up. Well, I was very innocent . . . before we started sleeping together, he gave me this clock radio, for which he paid twenty dollars. It was the only twenty dollars he had seen in six months. He had been saving it for a special occasion. I was special.

"He gave it to me at work, but that night, on my way home, I dropped it while going through the subway turnstile. That was a very bad beginning. I felt terrible, absolutely terrible. I'm not sure he ever forgave me. That was the day he wanted me to have lunch with him, because he had something to tell me. When somebody says they have something to tell you, and they're very, very serious about it, it sometimes scares you. So what I really thought, since I thought he was a lot older than he seemed, was that he had an illegitimate child somewhere, 'cause I always thought the worst. He was that kind of person. You immediately thought the worst, and usually it was true. But this time it wasn't. He was really upset, and he was afraid to tell me what it was.

" 'Barry,' I said, 'you know you're really scaring me. You mean to tell me you have an illegitimate child somewhere?'

" 'No!' he said.

" 'No?'

" 'No!' he said. 'I'm seventeen!'

"It was quite a shock, 'cause I thought he was older than me. Although he was very mature, he was an old young man. Anyway, we got over that. I started laughing, and forgave him for being two and a half years younger than me. That really wasn't so bad. I was very relieved, because I really believed he had a child somewhere.

"I never knew whether this Joan Brown was a figment or not.

But we did sleep together in his father's metal shop—in the attic, in the dark—and it was *sooooo* filthy. Oh, my. We couldn't put a light on 'cause somebody might see us. What children won't do.

"After that, he assured me he had completely given up Joan Brown. It's true—I mean, I never doubted it. I still don't doubt it. That was just not part of our relationship. She never came into the conversation again."

I can see my father now, the wheeler-dealer, the manipulator— a sallow, pimply kid with an oily aura and the tact of a sex maniac. He is washing bottles and she is studying the mating habits of fruit flies under a microscope. There are other workers in the lab, but Barry ignores them. It's sex he's after. Pure and simple.

"If you go to bed with me," he says between suds, so all can hear, "I'll give up Joan Brown. I've been fucking her for two years now, but I'll give her up for you. I'll be faithful to thee in my fashion. . . ."

He is relentless. She pretends she's not listening, but she is. With both ears. In fact, she can no longer keep track of who is fucking whom under her watchful eye.

"I started when I was eleven. I've had a lot more practice than any of the other guys around here."

A few stares. A few grumbles. A few giggles.

"I started with a little black thing named Belinda. She lived upstairs from me, and we used to do it on the fire escape at her school. I'm sure glad I didn't have to lay on the bottom."

The lab is silent now. Everybody is listening to the bottle washer.

"What's the difference between a black pussy and a bowling ball? If you had to, you could eat a bowling ball."

"So then we had a really, really hot relationship, and I really thought we were children. We were very happy, and, repeatedly, you know, we had to be scolded for kissing and necking and petting and other things in the lab, where we could be seen. We were very indiscreet. We were crazy. We had a great time. We both nearly got fired—we got reprimanded severely—and eventually he did get fired because of it."

My mother doesn't remember details, so I am forced to imagine what my father must have thought and felt when he discovered my mother also loved snakes. He could tell her how long he's wanted a corn snake for a pet. He wouldn't have to explain why, because she would already know it was because they are such a beautiful reddish orange, that they eat well in captivity, and that they're very good-tempered. They rarely bite and almost never get sick. Even if they've grown up in the wild and have eaten live mice and birds all their lives, they can be trained to eat mice and rats that have been defrosted from the freezer. This is good, because the Cancer Research Institute throws out hundreds of dead mice each week that they've used for experiments. Part of my mother's job is to kill them by breaking their necks. No one will complain if she takes a few home and tucks them in the freezer next to the chicken breasts and green beans.

"Of course my parents hated Barry. They were very strict, and they absolutely disliked him. I can see why now. He came across as a real sex maniac, and he had that oily quality and a hostility aimed at everyone and everything.

"But this didn't stop me from telling my parents that I wanted to go to college and live in a dorm and get a degree in biology. I would have needed their permission and their help, because I wasn't making enough money on my own.

" 'Oh, really?' they said. 'So you can have Barry every night?'

"Which was true, of course, but that didn't slow me down either. I went for the obvious: I wanted permission to marry Barry on Thanksgiving of 1953.

" 'Over our dead bodies,' they said.

"Since I was still under twenty-one, the only solution was to elope, which Barry pushed for very, very hard. But I had a little more sense—at least that's what I think stopped us from eloping

—I'm not sure. I think I would have been a little more sensible than Barry. After all, he didn't have a job and I wasn't making much.

"I had some friends at the lab who went away on weekends, so I got one of my good Christian girlfriends to cover for me, but she didn't lie very well and my parents got very suspicious. But we managed to get away with it and sleep together on weekends.

"But it didn't last long. I acted so miserable around the house that they finally gave in, thinking I'd probably run away and do it anyway.

"We got married in April of 1954 at my house, and it was very nice. Well, it was a miserable wedding because my parents were so brokenhearted. They had it against him that he was a Jew. I don't even remember that his parents were invited, or if they were invited, that they didn't come because I wasn't Jewish. I remember how forlorn the atmosphere was. Marty was as much against the wedding as my parents, and there were a good many reasons. Barry was a kid without a job and not a likable person. Barry told me that his father's housekeeper straightened his collar and kissed him goodbye, and he walked out of his father's house alone. His father wouldn't even say goodbye.

"The justice of the peace was a real deaf old man. We had to keep reminding him of the words. Strange, I remember a lot of daffodils. I picked them that morning. I was very happy. We were just determined to be happy.

"We must have started out living with my parents. We had a room there on a separate floor. On our wedding night we went to see a movie called *Captain's Paradise* with Sir Alec Guinness. Guinness leads a double life in the movie. We had a good time. We were like two kids. Barry gave me a black nightgown, a very sexy nightgown. I was supposed to call my father the next day and tell him I was all right, so I did. We stopped at a phone booth in the morning. We had been out walking all night—I think we just walked all night. We were very happy and I think by that time he was working at the Lincoln Institute, so he had a job. I was making more than he was, but at least he had one and we did all right.

"I got pregnant by accident, naturally, and he wanted me to have an abortion. But abortions were not simple in the 1950s, and we didn't have the money and we didn't really have the guts. It would have been an illegal abortion. So fortunately I didn't do it and I had you.

"I intended to have you by natural childbirth. My doctor spoke out of one side of his mouth, literally and figuratively. He said he was all for natural childbirth, but he really wasn't. He knocked me out and I was furious, but I was mostly awake. I told Barry he jolly well better be there, but he was late, which was very sad because he could have been with me at the time you were born. It would have been very exciting.

"I had to hold the nurse's hand rather than Barry's because he wasn't there. I suppose he just couldn't make himself be there. Again, it was a case of not being able to get ahold of him. I don't know where he was, but he just wasn't where he was supposed to be.

"He had been neurotic, but gradually became more and more divorced from reality. He'd always carry guns as a symbol of his masculinity. He never felt like a man without it. He slept with it in the headboard of our bed and tried to give me one. I refused, and it bothered me a great deal to sleep with it in the bed because he was very unstable. I don't know what you could call them, maybe flights from reality, but gradually they became weekly. The crises became weekly.

"I remember sitting at the lunch counter at the zoo with a mutual friend. We were talking about Barry. This friend started a sentence and I finished it. It went like this: 'Half of his experiences are imagination . . . and the rest are fantasy.' We sort of laughed a gallows laugh, because things were, you know—it was a very serious situation. Barry's state of mind, I mean. This friend said it must have been a great relief for me at that moment to know that someone else knew this. He was right. Both of us were shielding Barry from the outside world, although neither one of us had ever indicated to the other that we knew the experiences that Barry went through were not real. Or at least you never knew which were real and which were not. Because *he* believed them. If you faced him with any doubts as to whether something that he claimed had happened had actually happened, he would be exceedingly hurt and that was as far as you got. Most of Barry's friends took it in as, 'Wow, you know something's happening with Barry all the time. He really has these wild experiences.' But none of them may have been true. Nobody will ever know.

"He was losing more and more and more contact with reality. Finally he became incapable of sex. He really became completely impotent. This was part of it. He left me for many months. He had something like a nervous breakdown. He said he had to live by himself. I think he did. He would call me every once in a while to tell me these crazy stories about things that had happened to him. He was always the center of the stage. They got more and more bizarre, but after a while his sex drive came back, but never again with me. He didn't hurt me by telling me —he wasn't trying to hurt me—but he said that it was coming back slowly. He was able to feel it again. He got more and more destructively oriented and he was working for the Lincoln Institute, trying to design devilish devices.

"There again, nobody ever knew if he really did the things he said he did, but he had this real consuming drive for destruction. I was a biologist, I was still working in cancer research, so this major schism developed between us.

"He taught me to shoot, and I probably am still a very good shot. When we were married, we used to spend weekends dynamiting boulders for extra money. We'd always come home with a nitroglycerin headache. That wasn't very good for either of us, but we had good times. He had lead poisoning a couple times. This was real. He was in the hospital and he had to be chelated to get the lead out. Lead can affect your mind, and his mind was just going. His sanity was going. Partly it was guilt because he was designing these killing or crippling devices for the Lincoln Institute. He loved it, it was his passion in life. And here I was working in cancer research. He was faced every day with a life-and-death schism, so it was as much a philosophy division between us that broke us up as it was the general disintegration of the relationship.

"We were separated for many months before our divorce, close to a year, and he talked about killing himself. I don't know whether he was manipulating me or what. You just never knew what to believe anymore. He was quite capable of doing that for sympathy. It was a very strung-out time, the late months of 1959 and the early months of 1960 and into 1961.

"He came back, but he had turned away from me. He didn't want me anymore, so I asked him to leave, and he did. I think it was the day after his twenty-sixth birthday in 1961. I started divorce proceedings in April and it was final in August.

"Then he gradually got better, got himself together. He was sleeping with a lot of women. I knew because he kept telling me every chance he got. I was utterly miserable. I never got any support from him. Oh, well, it was a real mess for years. There was one year when I was raising you kids when I did get support from him. It wasn't even a full year. The rest of the time I never got any. Just a mess. I've heard it said that death is often better than divorce because it's final. The bitterness doesn't drag on for years, grievances don't keep adding up."

Times were pretty lean then, she has told me over the years. For the first two or three years after the divorce, my mother ate six eggs a day so she could afford to buy me hot dogs and frozen vegetables—so we would have something close to a balanced diet. She worked all the time, six and seven days a week, fourteen hours a day. Her full-time job was at the Cancer Research Institute. Her part-time job, which she did in the evenings during the week and on weekends for extra money, was in the herpetology department of the zoo. My mother counted scales on preserved snakes in order to keep enough grub on the dining-room table.

"I was glad for him when he met Dawn. He introduced me to her at some party. He'd just been going with her for a couple weeks. He was trying to start his own business, and she was supposedly a technician in it. I liked her from the beginning. I thought she was good for him.

"The psychotic episodes kept occurring at weekly intervals. He would call me up and tell me about them as if they were absolute fact. You never knew what was true and what was fantasy. It became a way of life. I don't know if any of them were true, but there was a crisis once a week. He had to be the center of the action.

"He got Dawn this gun—this was significant—he got Dawn to carry a gun in her handbag. He could never get me to do that. This gun bit. He never felt secure without it. He used every ruse he could think of to carry one. He lied to get permits if he couldn't get them legally. If he couldn't get a permit at all, he'd carry it anyway. Kept wanting to give me one. I never—I could never accept it because I didn't share his obsession. Dawn understood this in him and agreed to carry one. Maybe she lasted longer with him for that reason. I don't know. But he was not faithful to her either.

"Dawn and I never felt—we both had enough sense—we'd talk to each other once in a while. We never felt that one of us was better than the other or more able to hold him. He had so many destructive drives. And what seemed to be better in one relationship eventually turned into the same after a few years in another relationship. Both ended in similar ways.

"He had only contempt for women. He hated himself with a vengeance. Dawn and I understood each other pretty well. We could have been friends, as a matter of fact, by the time you got into trouble with the law. The two of them came up to visit and spend the day in our apartment. The three of us were very close because of our mutual concern for you. There were no constraints among us. We regretted the geographic distance, because we could have been very close friends."

I must be twelve or thirteen. My mother has driven me all the way to Hill House, a five-hour drive. I can't travel by train because I have a broken leg from playing football. It's summer, my favorite time of year to visit him: I can play in his woods with all his guns and ammo.

But the vibrations coming from my mother make the trip unbearable. After an hour of awkward silence, I'd rather turn around and go back. Anything but be bombarded by the relentless heat of her bitterness, or whatever it is. I'm too young to know or care. I just want to get out, away from her, out to his

*woods where I can be free to do all the things she forbids me to
do, all the things that explode in a young boy's heart in the
fiercest heat of his teen-age summer lust. There is no girl to give
it to, so I put it into fire, and smoke, and ash, and sweat, and
explosions that shout my name back and forth in holy echoes
across and around and through the ridge upon which Hill House
is built. I want to make an explosion that will rock everything to
its foundations, that will stop everyone and everything in their
tracks long enough to listen to their own heartbeats, to the silence
that follows an awesome sound. I want to shatter every molecule
of stone in the bedrock upon which I stand. I want to lose myself
completely and forever in that moment when everything is torn
asunder. I'm just a boy, but I know what the soldier and the
bombardier and the general and the submariner know: Lose it,
lose it, lose it all. Tear away the armor and the plastic. Break
your very own ribs just to feel the heat of creation and
destruction.*

*We pull into the driveway and my father and his harmless
Doberman, Attila the Hungry, greet us. I struggle out of the car
the moment it comes to a full stop, and drag my suitcase up to
the house. I don't want to be around while they talk. Never know
what she'll say. Don't want to know what she'll say. Later he'll
tell me that she wouldn't even get out of the car to have a cup
of coffee and yak for a few minutes. "She's put on a lot of weight
since I saw her last," he'll say. "Maybe she's afraid to show me."*

"During the psychotic episodes he would say he witnessed a
murder or had to go away to Maryland because a fireworks
factory blew up. Now this could have been true, but when they
happen once a week with great regularity, you don't know what
to believe. They were always very bizarre stories. One of his
friends was killed, but I never knew the person. After a while,
they'd just go in one ear and out the other. You couldn't let
yourself get emotionally tied up. Other people finally began to
realize this, but just as many were taken in for many years.

"He died the night before his forty-first birthday, and I'm
quite sure he programmed himself to die at the age of forty,
because by the time he was nineteen or twenty, he used to say

he'd be burned out by the time he was thirty and dead at forty. He believed it and he was.

"There were some good years, too. I know that we had some good years. I remember telling him in one of our phone conversations that after so many years I was finally beginning to see our time together as a mosaic of pain and pleasure, and not just pain. I was beginning to remember the good times, too. Dawn and I both felt the same way about him. We both felt we could never stop loving him and we both felt that he was probably the most unforgettable person we had ever known.

"He spent a lot of time talking about how he designed this new device called the Gravel mine. He was very much involved with it mentally for a long time. I don't know whether he was really doing it or not. He was a technician, but I don't know how much responsibility he had or whether this, too, was his imagination, whether he was designing these weapons for himself in his own mind or if he really was doing them for the Institute. Nobody ever knew. Maybe not even the people at the Institute. This was during the early years of the Vietnam War. It was a mine the size of a pack of cigarettes. It could be broadcast in great numbers from planes and it would break the bones in a person's foot. That's the only device I remember specifically. Completely crippling.

"This was before what I consider to be his breakdown. The responsibility preyed on his mind and yet he loved passionately, he loved the idea of designing a destructive weapon. But he wasn't completely amoral, so the consequence of his country using the mine in great numbers also weighed on him. I don't remember how he would talk about it, but he was very articulate. I do remember that most of it had to do with guilt.

"He had a habit of going to sleep as an escape. Sometimes he would go to sleep in the middle of a conversation. He was tormented by guilt about his work. What drove him out of the Lincoln Institute . . . his mental health was virtually going downhill. That was the turning point. That's when he tried to start his own tear-gas business.

"In the early years of our marriage, we made tear-gas bullets at home. It was awful. He also designed a tear-gas pengun, and he felt really good about that because he could enjoy the creativeness of designing it, knowing that it wasn't going to kill anybody. I hated it because we both suffered terribly. You know, it's miserable stuff, and it was extremely tiring. He was trying to make money with it, so he was taking orders for it. It was a very exhausting and miserable business. But I didn't mind that so much. It was in the early years of our marriage.

"He was always trying to corner markets. He did fireworks shows, too, occasionally. Mostly tear gas was the big thing. It's a wonder you weren't born defective. Seriously! From all the tear gas we breathed in, all the tear gas I breathed in while I was pregnant.

"After twenty-five years, memories fade. You'll have to hypnotize me to get me to remember details. He probably said things about the CIA, but I don't remember. If he did, it would have been that they were after him. He was pretty paranoid.

"Do I remember much about his childhood? I was practically *there*. He was seventeen, for Pete's sake, when I met him. I lived part of his childhood.

"His sex life started at eleven, and that was the main thing with him throughout his life. When he was a kid, the problem was getting girls, because girls at that age wouldn't. He got thrown out of school for fucking, and after we were married he finished high school through a high-school-equivalency course. Other than sex, his main childhood interest was rocketry. He'd spend his weekends shooting off rockets. That was another thing we did together.

"I suppose his contempt for women came from his relationship with his mother, whom he had nothing but contempt for. He despised his mother.

"I think his relationship with his father was good, although it was pretty uncommunicative. He and Marty just never did understand each other. But there was no hatred there. He respected Marty. They were even fond of each other. Barry was essentially a poet, and Marty was essentially a steelworker. They just didn't speak each other's language. But I think there was real affection between them.

"At one time or another, we kept most of the world's reptiles.

Practically anything you could mention. We had a very good collection of rattlesnakes. We kept mostly lizards and snakes. We worked very hard together on that collection.

"I would guess our animals were his favorite possessions. I don't really know. Maybe the movies he made of animals. He spent a lot of time making movies. He did a lot of photography of snake eggs hatching.

"He kept trying to get people interested in making pornographic films, but somebody always backed out at the last moment. They wouldn't go through with it. Never did get very far. We could never get the act together. He would have loved to have made pornographic films 'cause he was a voyeur at heart. He never got it together with me, but maybe he did in the second half of his life. He just couldn't get the people together in the first half. Nobody was ever quite as dedicated as he was.

"I don't know if he was a lot more uninhibited for his time than the rest of us. You try and get a bunch of your friends together to make a porno film. Everybody becomes self-conscious. One person after another backs out. They might think, Gee, this would be great fun, but they always back out.

"He was also always trying to get an orgy together. I don't know if he ever succeeded in that endeavor either. He may have. I suspect he did.

"Yeah, I guess among our group of friends he was probably considered the most uninhibited. This was a matter of pride to him. In some ways he was telling the world he wasn't afraid of all those dangers that most mortals are afraid of, like working with explosives. He liked to court danger. But that was actually a charming part of him, although he antagonized a lot of people with his uninhibited speech, saying what he felt like saying. It was his hostility that antagonized people more than his lack of inhibitions, because he was a very hostile person. Very biting sarcasm. He'd hurt people if he felt like it. But in other ways his lack of inhibition was part of his charm, when he wasn't hurting people with it.

"We were very much involved with herpetology. Heavily involved with herpetologists. Almost all of our friends were herpetologists . . . or stock-car drivers or librarians. And see, even the stock-car drivers and librarians were sympathetic. They weren't afraid of snakes.

"He essentially had two things going. One was herpetology. The other was trying to make money. Free-lancing with tear gas and fireworks. He went about free-lancing the way you go about free-lancing. Exactly the same. Trying to get orders and having them canceled after you've already made them, or not getting paid because the powder got wet or because the smokes didn't go off, so you don't get paid for that either. The tear-gas bullets don't fire, so you don't get the order renewed. Or getting an order for twenty-five hundred tear-gas bullets in twenty-four hours, so you stay up for twenty-four hours making tear-gas bullets. God, what a horrible job!"

On January 13, 1981, my mother wrote:

Dear Dave,
I am thinking of you on this 5th anniversary of your father's death. And tomorrow would be his birthday. I don't know which was more traumatic for his world. Certainly he was the "most unforgettable character" I've ever met. Had a great impact on my life as well as yours, for good & for bad. I lost my parents within 9 months of each other when I was 30. I didn't remember the dates of their death very long but I still miss them and still "see" them the way I remember they looked in middle age, not when they were 60, and about to die. I still remember that their birth dates were Jan. 5 & 10 and since I've been a child I could never remember which was which, and now I do not try.

I do not come from a long-lived family. No one before my generation has lived past 65. I used to think that was my limit. But as I get closer to it I don't believe I have a limit. Of course I realize this may be wishful thinking, but I now intend to live to be 80, and pretty healthy. And I intend to *live* till I die. I intend to beat the system. So there.

Here is a poem I thought you might like to have. I wrote it the day after your father died. It's a haiku, and attempts to say how I felt about his death:

Barry

No place, nowhere to
*   mourn first love's extinguishment.*
No time for dying.

Another snapshot of my mother:

I'm sitting in the dining room talking with my sixteen-year-old brother about drivers' licenses. "When you work on a farm," he says with great enthusiasm, waving his hands to make sure he has my full attention, "you learn to drive very young, sometimes thirteen or fourteen, even younger."

Our mother, from the kitchen, adds her two cents: "I learned how to drive a tractor when I was ten."

"You never told me that," I say around the wall that divides these rooms.

"There's a lot I never told you. There's a lot you don't know about me. Maybe if you took the time, you'd get to know me."

"I try to. Every time I see you, I learn a little more. I try to. At least I think I do."

No word of reassurance. Silence from around the bend. My brother and I go on to bigger and better things: girls and bikes, snakes and turtles, bikes and girls. When we're done, I walk to the kitchen to try to walk through the door she just opened.

"Well, why don't you take the time and tell me about yourself sometime?"

"There's nothing to tell."

She gets up from the chair and makes her way past my brother and me.

"I'd like to watch some quiet TV," she says.

PLAYBOY INTERVIEW

PLAYBOY: Were you ever asked to work with drugs?

MR. DEATH: Only twice that I remember. My contact brought me half a gram of LSD sealed in twenty-seven different bottles inside of each other, delivered in the lunchroom of the institute.

Normally, his manner was laconic, straightforward. In this case, he was edgy. This was in the Fifties and I had no idea what LSD was. I had to pump him for information. Finally, he started giving me a skeleton outline. That specific job gave me the very distinct, creepy feeling that it was under the counter even for them. I didn't know what the hell he was handing me. If it's botulismus toxin or something, screw you, Jack, I don't even want to get near the container. But, at any rate, he finally handed it to me. Well, I loaded LSD onto cough drops and resealed the packages. I put it into cough syrup. I had a whole box of Neo-Synephrine spray bottles that I loaded. Mostly cold remedies.

PLAYBOY: What dosage were you using?

MR. DEATH: Enormous dosage. Probably wipe you out forever.

PLAYBOY: You mentioned two instances. What was the other drug you worked with?

MR. DEATH: The other was called BZ, and I wouldn't ever want to get dosed with that. It was something like LSD, but the dosage was much lower and you had to work with it in a glove box, because it was administered by breathing. I saw some very frightening films of soldiers who had been given BZ. The guys were reduced to catatonics. They would just sit there, drooling, with no control over bodily functions. Unless they were given commands, like "Get up" or "Put your helmet on," at which point they would go berserk and attempt to kill the guy who had given the order. This effect, I understand, lasted weeks.

PLAYBOY: What was the purpose of working with BZ?

MR. DEATH: Area denial, I would imagine. Chemical warfare, that sort of thing.

PLAYBOY: Did you design anything for domestic use?

MR. DEATH: I think just about everything I had worked with up until the LSD and maybe those snake pens was not for use in the U.S. But I think that the pens were used here. Don't ask me why, but I got the feeling that it was a local gig. The LSD really impressed me as being something that even they were nervous about. And you're not going to find your basic Muscovite taking Neo-Synephrine or Vicks cough drops.

PLAYBOY: When did you work with the BZ?

MR. DEATH: Near the end of the Fifties, I think. Sometime near the end of my stint with the [delete] Institute.

PLAYBOY: What made you leave the institute?

MR. DEATH: I began getting disgusted around 1960. It had nothing to do with CIA types or anybody else around. I was getting very unhappy. First of all, by that time, my psyche was really fucked up. My marriage fell apart. And I had been eating what is now known as speed.

PLAYBOY: Where did you get speed?

MR. DEATH: From the CIA. It was an auxiliary service. Meprobamates—Miltown, downers—and speed. I initially got some from a doctor, but even in those days there were only so many times you could refill a prescription. And one day I casually asked my contact if he could help me with that. Well, he brought bottles that were like industrial mayonnaise jars. And very deadpan, he said, "Is this enough?" I was on speed for about two and a half years. I'd wake up in the morning and have three cups of coffee and a palmful of Dexedrine. I must have been taking sublethal doses. I think the turning point came when I met a very sharp girl. She made me realize a lot of things. I started to reappreciate the fact that I was really a lecherous character at heart and that I had been taking all that energy and sublimating it elsewhere. I had forgotten how good fucking could be. That kind of woke me up. Then she gently pointed out to me that I was killing myself with speed. Finally, one week I took off and locked myself in my apartment and kicked it—absolute cold turkey.

PLAYBOY: How bad was the withdrawal?

MR. DEATH: The word "agony" is not good enough. Most of what I remember was uncontrollable muscle spasms. That was most distressing. Nausea. Oh, nausea. And my head—thoughts racing, just trying to keep control of myself. I was very sick, but I was also very determined. Because I knew if I was going to continue with speed, it would kill me and I'd just as soon put a gun to my head and get it over with. When I came out of it a week later, I was pretty wretched, but I was out. And that's when my creative urge came back and I designed a little device that fires a small powder charge and blows out a chemical irritant. At that point in time—where did I hear that phrase before?—there was a wave of rapes; I almost said a rape of waves. That's kind of poetic. Anyway, it started me thinking. There must be a way for a woman to defend herself. And this gadget came into my head. I got someone to promote it and a company called [deleted] was formed.

PLAYBOY: Meanwhile, were you still in contact with the man from the agency?

MR. DEATH: No; once I left the institute, they called him off. I never saw him again. They were probably just waiting to see what happened. So I guess it was a year later, when this little company was doing well, and then I was contacted by a different guy, who came out to visit me at work.

PLAYBOY: When someone contacted you, how did you know he was from the CIA?

MR. DEATH: In this case, the guy showed me CIA credentials. An I.D. card. Also, you kind of got to know what they looked like. When this guy came, he looked so weird that my secretary came in and said, "There's a guy out there who must be a cop." And he certainly did look like a cop—square jaw, flinty eyes.

PLAYBOY: You could spot those guys just by their looks?

MR. DEATH: Well, there were other telltale signs. When he showed up, he was accompanied by a very bad guy who bore a vague resemblance to King Kong. When he sat down, he clanked and I made some comment like, "Whatever it is you've got in that shoulder holster must be something to see." He just kind of smiled and opened his coat and in there was a .44 Magnum. I have never seen a man before or since who was large enough to conceal that handgun in a shoulder holster. Anyway, I asked to see it; he unloaded it and handed it to me and there was no serial number on it. It hadn't been removed. There just wasn't any. So he was either president of a firearms company or a CIA operative.

PLAYBOY: Did you ask him about that?

MR. DEATH: No. He wasn't the type you'd ask that sort of thing. He wasn't exactly talkative. If I remember correctly, he spoke in guttural monosyllables. I don't know what he said, but it didn't matter. When he talked, you listened.

PLAYBOY: What did your new contact want from you?

MR. DEATH: Well, he looked at our little company and said, "This is an ideal setup. It's private, it's quiet. You can do a lot of useful things here." I gave him a few gadgets to look at. Later, he came back and said, "There are a lot of things that we want loaded into special shells. Can you do it?" I made shells loaded with poisoned fléchettes, little ballistic darts, phonograph-needle-size. I made them loaded with poisoned shot, with incendiaries.

PLAYBOY: What types of poisons were you using?

MR. DEATH: Most of what I worked with in those cartridges was sodium cyanide and an anticoagulant. I remember I dipped the fléchettes and dried them. There were a couple of exotic cartridges that converted [deleted] into a hand grenade. Some were loaded with HE [high explosives] and shot to get a frag effect. I developed a small land mine—I guess you'd have to call it that—that you could slip under a rug.

PLAYBOY: What could something like that be used for?

MR. DEATH: Who knows? Liven up going-away parties. As I said, I really have no direct knowledge of what happened with any of those devices.

PLAYBOY: What other projects were you working on at [deleted]?

MR. DEATH: Sometime in 1962, I invented the miniature distress signal. I had also screwed around with soft plastic-cased grenades. [Deleted] was doing a lot of riot-control work. I started screwing around with those to see what I could come up with for the CIA. And I loaded some special ones. They were mostly concussion grenades, designed to produce horrendous blast effects. It was like a giant firecracker initiated by a regular grenade fuse. I did this type of work until I was able to form my own company to do industrial research. That company staggered along and I had no CIA contact whatsoever. I was going broke. And I finally got a lovely order for some pyrotechnic devices from the [deleted] government that we couldn't fill. I had invented the device, I knew how to set up production, but I didn't have enough money to start. So I picked up the phone one day and called a large firearms manufacturer and they bought us out and hired me. I got my very own laboratory and a nice comfortable salary. I was running the whole show, basically. What I really wanted was to get into the commercial end of this business. The military-ordnance business was going to hell rapidly. Vietnam was going to end and there we would be, selling military equipment. Unfortunately, I was very quickly pressured into getting into military research and development.

PLAYBOY: What form did this pressure take?

MR. DEATH: Oh, it was very indirect. Like "Get us into military R and D or hit the street." I was told that by the officials of the company. They were manufacturing [deleted] for the army with a great deal of success and wanted more contracts. So I obliged them and started work on an improvised munitions program, which was funded by the [deleted] Arsenal. I wrote a couple of proposals. Again, one of those hypothetical situations: The Special Forces are dropped behind enemy lines with access to virtually nothing in the way of sophisticated materials. And I sold a program of improvising things, literally out of nothing. For example, you can make white phosphorus from sulfuric acid, bones, and charcoal. It's a pain in the ass, but you can get a nasty incendiary weapon out of it. Thermite presents two problems, getting granulated black-iron oxide and getting granulated aluminum. The iron oxide is easy to make by burning steel wool. You can make 40-to-100 mesh consistent granular aluminum by melting scrap aluminum in a shallow iron pan and stirring it as it cools. Without going into any of the exotic demolition stuff, those were the types of problems I was solving.

PLAYBOY: Now, meanwhile, what was going on with the agency?

MR. DEATH: Nothing. I had no contact. This work was for the military, the official, aboveboard work of the firearms manufacturer. So we generated our first report on improvising munitions and, I must openly say, it was a damn good piece of work. Because, literally, we showed a guy with an I.Q. on the order of a twelve-year-old's how to make black powder, nitric acid, sulfuric acid, nitroglycerin, detonators by starting with nothing and winding up with some pretty sophisticated sabotage and demolition stuff.

PLAYBOY: But at the time you moved to the firearms company, you said there was no CIA contact.

MR. DEATH: Not at first. But apparently that report got some wide circulation, because the next thing I knew, I got a call from someone at work who said, "There will be another agency contact." And a group of five guys came down and we talked. They did not identify themselves, but I knew from what was said that they were CIA men. At any rate, they were mostly touching base. "What are you doing?" "Where are you?" An es-

tablishment of a new kind of link. More official, really. Somewhere in there, a general manager was brought in over me at my
request. I couldn't handle the whole operation. I just wanted to
do the research. They brought in [deleted] who became my
liaison to the Central Intelligence Agency. I was clearly instructed
that absolutely no one else was to be aware of this sort of work.
The very first CIA task was a rather sizable one. And that was
the development of a handbook, which I dubbed *The Devil's
Diary*. It was an offshoot of the improvised-weapons thing, but
instead of being oriented toward explosives and munitions syn-
theses, it was specifically aimed at chemical and biological weapons and systems. It was to be written for anyone with no more
than a high-school chemistry background. I will tell you right
now that I was not very much in favor of that whole idea. I
began to realize that that was really dangerous information to
assemble all in one place. That is something that, if it ever got
out anywhere, would give somebody the ability to take over or
even destroy large cities with very little investment in time or
money. But I got the word. "Write it. One copy. No carbons."
So what I did was survey the plant poisons. There are so many
plant poisons that it bends your mind. Common things you can
walk out and find right now in your backyard can, if treated
properly, yield very deadly poisons that are not easily detectable.
I think I included about forty plants and instructions on how to
use them. The agency was very pleased with it. I went on from
there to biological systems. I came up with a number of agents
that could be made without too much grief. There are a fair
number of those. You do need certain safety precautions or
you're going to wipe yourself out. It's pretty dangerous.

PLAYBOY: Are you referring to things such as anthrax, botulism?

MR. DEATH: One of the most toxic materials known to man is
botulismus toxin. The lethal dose is on the order of a twenty-fifth
of a microgram. There is a very slim chance of recovery. The so-
called R strain developed by the agency is even more potent than
the garden variety. So, in *The Devil's Diary*, I told a guy how
to breed botulin, identify it, keep it under vacuum. You could
literally set that up in your own kitchen and then extract the
lethal agent in a form you could disperse. You need a little more
sophisticated equipment for things like botulin, but there is easy

access to [deleted]. You can find [deleted] in the soil. Or pneumonic plague, the airborne form of bubonic plague. As history has shown, it can get out of control very quickly. At any rate, I wrote all this up and sent it in and apparently they were happy, and then they said, "Now you can do the chemical section and systems." And that's when I did some work using extremely simple materials to deliver those agents. You know, sprinkle this on a car engine block, throw that in ventilating ducts. One system I gave them is so simple, using a material you can get in any hardware store, that you can't even print it, because you'd have kooks tossing it all over the place every time they got pissed at someone. Spritz it around and no one can enter the area. Put some of that mixed with [deleted] extract, for example, in jars and drop them off tall buildings or out of a plane and you could deny admittance to the island of Manhattan in a matter of hours. That stuff is unbelievable. Just unbelievable. A canister of it chucked into the subway system and you've messed up tens—perhaps hundreds—of thousands of people. Incidentally, in the *Diary* is an extremely simple method of synthesizing a rather potent nerve gas from a material that is easily available on your grocer's shelf right now. It requires no time or effort, really.

PLAYBOY: Do you want to go into that?

MR. DEATH: No, I don't even want to mention it. I don't even want *you* to know what it is. Right now, you can walk in and buy enough of it to do all kinds of ferocious damage. It's not as toxic as VX or some of those things, but damn close to it.

PLAYBOY: What's VX?

MR. DEATH: The most potent nerve gas they had at the time I was working for the CIA.

PLAYBOY: How long would it take to synthesize your grocery-store nerve gas?

MR. DEATH: Two hours for enough to do a large building, like a high-rise. Low dosage, inhalation or skin contact, either one. So that also was a very pleasing thing for them. There is also a form of heavy metal—I'd rather not say which one—that's readily available. It has a natural tissue-penetrating property. Put a drop in someone's shoe and he'll absorb it in time. Then he has heavy-metal poisoning, which is frequently fatal. Where did he get it? They'd never know. Similar in potential were some very peculiar plant poisons that are little known, although the literature's there. These are all things that are buried in the avalanche of scientific paper. For example, there is a substance that can be extracted from a plant that grows in the Southwest. It's a neurotoxin, orally administered, but it has this remarkable six-month delay before any symptoms show up at all. By that time, it's irreversible. You deteriorate steadily. Like muscular dystrophy. A tribe of Indians used it long ago.

PLAYBOY: Would they ever be able to figure out what had killed the person?

MR. DEATH: It's very unlikely.

PLAYBOY: Do you have any idea what they wanted that document for?

MR. DEATH: Well, there was one peculiar thing about *The Devil's Diary* and that was that I was specifically instructed to orient it toward domestically available materials and plants. Plants that grow in the U.S. and materials that are sold in the U.S. What that means, I don't know, but it makes you wonder.

PLAYBOY: And how much did you get for *The Devil's Diary*?

MR. DEATH: I was not paid directly by the CIA at that time. The firearms manufacturer was being paid. I would cost out the project, report the price to my supervisor, and he would take care of any administrative details. I have no idea where the money went, who knew about it, or what they did with it. I believe I told [deleted] the CIA should pay about twenty thousand for *The Devil's Diary*.

PLAYBOY: It was just understood that you would work for the CIA as part of your job?

MR. DEATH: Right. I had a pretty decent salary. I was happy with it. I had a lot of fringe benefits. Like a big car with a telephone and a modified, built-in console that concealed a revolver. Very nice car. Also, a sawed-off shotgun, a Mafia special, overall length eighteen inches, clipped under the dash.

9

IMP

From Science to Alchemy

Thrust into underdeveloped areas for lengthy periods, how do Special Forces synthesize and compound explosives and propellants from primitive raw materials? This, in essence, was the problem.

With more or less sophisticated components and materials like blasting caps, Primacord and military explosives, it is relatively easy to construct a host of ingenious and effective weapons (for example, guns, grenades, demolition and incendiary items). But what if ready made components and even basic raw materials are not available? In such a situation little if any guidance was to be found in existing field manuals.

Thus, the development and dissemination of practical methods for field manufacture of explosives from commonly available materials would substantially increase the independence, mobility and effectiveness of Special Forces in remote areas while further reducing the requirements for logistical support.

Initial work on this improvised munitions program was approached from the view of the man in the field. Our effort was aimed at uncomplicated techniques that were reasonably safe and which would require neither sophisticated materials nor equipment. The first phase of the work involved field synthesis of the prime ingredient for black powder: potassium nitrate. A literature search turned up some intriguing possible approaches for field manufacture. One of these systems, used by the French in the 16th and 17th centuries, involved boiling down fermented urine and subsequent water extraction of the nitrates. Although we had no difficulty in procuring large quantities of the raw material there were considerable problems in its refinement. Mainly, it was necessary to crush a rebellion of the technicians involved.

It was also quite obvious from the initial tests that the odor created by boiling several gallons of fermented urine was readily detectable for quite a distance downwind. This feature would certainly compromise any secret powder processing factory. Most important, yields from this process were too low to make it practical.

Another approach involved hot water extraction of potassium nitrate from the earth. This rather simple process requires only a large container, like a 55 gallon drum, hot water and some pans. In brief the water is poured through a bed of dirt and filtered through sand and/or charcoal. The extracted liquid is then boiled or dried in the sun. The crude nitrate from this process is then purified by simple recrystallization. Surprisingly large yields can be attained by this process, in some cases up to 1% by weight of the raw material. Organically fertilized earth is, of course, the most profitable source for nitrates. This includes the soil under old farm buildings, compost heaps and graveyards.

Potassium nitrate synthesized by the method described yielded surprisingly good and quite serviceable improvised black powder. When combined with agricultural sulfur and improvised charcoal, and mixed in a water slurry, the improvised material gave gun performance about 85% as good as factory grade material. Apropos, we found no feasible way to extract or synthesize sulfur from any commonly available materials. Excellent charcoal was readily manufactured by means of a simple kiln.

Flushed with the success of improvising black powder from compost we investigated the improvisation of high explosives. Since many worthwhile high energy explosives require the use of nitric acid we approached this aspect of the problem by field manufacture of same. By concentrating automobile battery acid via simple boiling, and mixing it with field grade potassium nitrate, the combination could then be heated and the resulting nitric acid vapor collected in a simple two bottle condenser.

Despite the horrendous impurity of the raw materials one could with relative ease brew up useable quantities of red fuming nitric acid on short order.

The next step, which we approached with some trepidation, was nitration of anything that would yield a worthwhile high explosive. Although glycerin was a logical choice, the material is not readily synthesized in the field, and impure glycerin can lead to rapid disaster in field synthesis. However, drug store grades can be and were readily nitrated with improvised acid in a simple field system that required three jars and some cooling water.

Nitration of improvised or commercial grade methyl alcohol and antifreeze grades of ethylene glycol proved to be easier and safer.

Very serviceable improvised dynamites were formulated by simply mixing the explosive liquid with suitable adsorbents such as sawdust and paper pulp.

Field manufacture of nitrocellulose from improvised ingredients would not yield reliable results. However, a rather unique pipe bomb was constructed from paper towels saturated with field grade fuming nitric acid. The towels were placed in a 2 inch diameter cast iron pipe coated with wax and a premeasured quantity of acid poured in. The device could be detonated with either improvised or commercial blasting caps.

Field grade nitric acid could be used to formulate "Sprengel" type explosives based on mononitrobenzene.

Urea nitrate at this point also appeared to be a good candidate for field synthesis. While relatively easy to prepare—from nitric acid and urine—it suffers from several disadvantages. Namely, improvised urea nitrate requires heavy confinement and very strong initiation to achieve high order detonation and even when successfully detonated it is not a particularly brisant explosive.

RDX also appeared to be a worthwhile addition to the family of field improvised explosives. The base material for synthesizing RDX, hexamethylenetetramine, a relatively common drug store chemical, is also available as a field ration heat source. RDX can be synthesized with field grade nitric acid. However, the yields with improvised ingredients and equipment are about 20% lower than laboratory preparations. Thus, as with urea nitrate, the tradeoff of time and material is poor and effort is better directed to higher yield explosives such as the nitric esters.

Improvised Primary Explosive

Considerable time was devoted to evolving a family of primary explosives for use in improvised detonators. The fulminates of mercury and silver are readily synthesized but both have drawbacks: Mercury metal may not be readily available in many areas and silver fulminate is extremely sensitive and difficult to handle safely. Since silver is commonly available (at least in the form of coins) some effort was devoted to reducing the impact sensitivity of the fulminate. This was accomplished with partial success by adding easily available desensitizers such as corn starch or flour.

Ethyl alcohol is also essential to the production of fulminates and the synthesis of this material was rapidly accomplished by our skilled technicians. Ethyl alcohol of excellent quality was readily prepared from corn mash in the field. This material has other uses besides the preparation of fulminates: For example, it is an excellent disinfectant and solvent. For these reasons large quantities were prepared for investigation.

On the more sober side, mercury fulminate was manufactured with improvised ingredients and apparatus in relatively large quantities. Generally, it proved to be a most reliable initiator in blasting caps improvised from metal tubes and small arms cartridges.

While not generally well known, and not used commercially, the double salt of silver acetylide and silver nitrate proved to be a suitable material for improvised initiators. This double salt can be readily synthesized in the field from silver coins, field grade nitric acid and acetylene generated from calcium carbide.

Hexamethylenetriperoxidediamine is perhaps the only organic peroxide that has been seriously considered for commercial initiators. This primary explosive is probably the easiest and safest to manufacture in the field. The requisite materials for production of HMTD are hexamine, hydrogen peroxide and citric acid, obtainable in drug stores and food stores under the name "sour salt." We found that the common 6% hydrogen peroxide solution used as a hair bleach was satisfactory in this synthesis. HMTD can be prepared at room temperature in a single jar with remarkable ease and safety.

The optimum initiator case material appears to be small diameter metal tubing and, specifically, roughly quarter inch diameter soft copper tubing such as that used in plumbing and vehicles. Initial tests were conducted with ¼" diameter copper tube caps containing straight, unconfined charges of improvised mercury fulminate. These caps were fired into 50 gram target charges of prilled TNT (DuPont "Pelletol") confined in paper cups. Results were erratic. Radically improved reliability was observed when the mercury fulminate was hand-pressed in the tubes. As expected, compression also increased the initiating efficiency of other improved primary explosives.

Compound caps, that is, caps containing a base charge of high explosive, are generally the most efficient and reliable. When suitable solid high explosives are available they can be used to extend the supply of improvised primaries and provide more powerful initiators.

Both compound and straight improvised blasting caps were tested with a wide variety of military and improvised high explosives. In summary it appeared that improvised mercury fulminate caps were the most reliable. However, improvised and commercial dynamites can be readily, reliably initiated with any of the improvised primary explosive systems.

Incendiary Pyrotechnics

In a second phase of the improvised munitions program the study of the feasibility of producing white phosphorous from commercially available ingredients was undertaken. In brief, we succeeded in obtaining yields of from 4% to 8% by weight of feedstock materials. The process consists of baking a mixture of concentrated sulfuric acid derived from vehicle batteries, bone meal and powdered charcoal. The crude phosphoric acid obtained from the bone meal is heated in an improvised reaction chamber and white phosphorous is collected in a crude but efficient clay distillation retort. The process required for field manufacture of WP is somewhat laborious but the material can be put to good use in delay incendiary and anti-personnel devices.

Greater success was achieved in the improvisation of thermite. The major problem here was the method of producing granulated aluminum. (Black iron oxide was easily synthesized by burning steel wool.) Melting scrap aluminum in a shallow iron pan over a hot coal fire and constantly stirring the molten material as it cooled produced remarkably consistent granular aluminum ranging from 40 to 100 mesh. The coarse material was ideal for thermite mixtures and the fines found use in improvised pyrotechnics. To determine the efficiency of improvised thermite an arbitrary steel plate penetration test was set up using a metal funnel, ¼" thick steel plate and some cement to hold the assembly in place. In a series of tests using this apparatus, one pound charges of improvised thermite were compared with equal charges of commercial material. The plate was penetrated in all tests and there was no visual difference between improvised and commercially manufactured thermite.

Pyrotechnic flares have probably been used as tactical signals since the invention of black powder. Thus, the ability to improvise such signals from commonly available materials is logistically valuable. Our approach to the improvisation of flare mixtures and signals was based on the assumption that only one prime oxidizer would be commonly available, i.e., potassium nitrate. Evolution of a white flare mix based on potassium nitrate and bronzing grade of improvised aluminum powder was rapid and quite successful. This relatively simple flare mixture may be bound with shellac solution and readily fabricated into ground or aerial flare munitions.

Attempts to improvise color flare mixtures were not as successful due to the unavailability of suitable flame coloring materials. Applicable barium or strontium salts are not commonly available and, for that reason, green and red flares cannot be readily improvised in the field. A satisfactory yellow flare was evolved using sodium bicarbonate.

Construction of improvised pyrotechnic and incendiary devices is wholly contingent upon available materials and application. With such gross variables, it is impractical to describe devices in other than generic terms. Improvised thermite has essentially the same performance as commercial and some military grades. Grenades can be readily improvised from tin cans, pipe, flower pots and the like. Improvised thermite must be heavily tamped to insure complete combustion and heavy walled containers are preferable to insure a directional flow for maximum metal penetration. If magnesium or aluminum tubing is available, added incendiary effect can be achieved. Anti-personnel or scattered incendiary effects can be built into thermite bombs by imbedding an initiator and explosive (improvised or otherwise) in the base of the charges.

Small chunks of oil- or grease-coated white phosphorous proved to be useful and uncomplicated booby traps. Strategically planted so as to be ignited by mechanical crushing and exposure or human action, is probably the most useful employment of improvised WP. Similarly, oil-coated WP pellets can be loaded into improvised shotgun shells that are quite annoying at ranges up to 30 yards.

Finally, it can safely be said that, in this project, shovelling the manure and mixing the vinegar and urine was worthy of our time, patience, and money. The study of cemetery soil was also a worthwhile if grave undertaking.

10

Death Clone

He looked so much like my father, they were often mistaken for brothers. He spoke as well and as quietly, emanating a slow gentleness even when discussing technical problems *they* were having with some of the most destructive weapons ever invented by the human race. Even their initials were the same: BR.

Bob Rightman. I must have met Bob more than half a dozen times before I was sixteen. My memory is usually photographic *and* phonographic, but I can't recall a single detail about any of those meetings. I do remember that he moved slowly, as if nothing in this world could make him jump or run for cover or raise his voice above its basic nasal monotone. I remember he was thin, of average height, and probably in his late twenties when we first met.

Those meetings probably took place before, during, and after some of my father's most violent, beautiful, ambitious fireworks displays. Most of them were on the Fourths of July from the mid-Sixties and into the early Seventies, when my father was director of research for Western Weapons. My father and his team of fireworkers were allowed to use "scraps" from the explosives labs, plus odds and ends that might be lying around in unused storage bunkers. Their credo: *Anything Worth Doing Is Worth Overdoing.*

Bob was part of those displays. He worked in the lab, so it was natural for him to be part of the crew that spent most of the week before the Fourth pasting bombs together and tying fireworks to boards and fusing everything to everything else. It was a family occasion, and it never failed to bring out the best in my father. His charm was on full-blast, his warmth red-hot, his humor in fifth gear. Some fathers get drunk from watching a football game. My father tripped out on bombs and flashes.

I was always proud to be near my father while he was going through his paces as The Fireworker. I was *Barry Rothman's son*, I was another fireworker. I got special introductions to all the girls. I was noticed. I wasn't afraid of fire and explosions and bombs bursting in air. I loved the smell and heat and fury of a hundred different fireworks going off at once, each of us lighting our designated fuses, each appointed to our special tasks.

I was usually a runner. I would carry huge shells—the kind that produce magnificent designs across the sky—to the men hunched over the mortar tubes. They would light each shell as I dropped it into its steel tube, which was buried in several feet of sand and earth so it wouldn't explode and take us with it.

Bob was one of those men who lit the shells the old-fashioned way, with a pyrotechnic torch, similar to a highway flare, instead of firing them with electrical charges from a much-too-safe distance. I was one of the handful of special teen-agers whose task it was to deliver the shells to the men at the front lines, who would fire them as fast as they could set the shell in the mortar and touch the fuse with their fire stick.

It was glorious! All the excitement of war without the mess. When it was over, even a virgin teen-age boy knew he had just made love to the sky.

I never saw Bob run from a shell that misfired. I don't know what he did when it happened—and it always did—because I was too busy running for cover. But I know he didn't run. If a tree caught fire overhead, threatening to detonate our fireworks prematurely, he wouldn't even raise his voice. Did he *walk* away?

I call Bob at work to request an interview.

"Sure," he says. "I'll talk." He doesn't ask for details now. He makes small talk: how long it's been; gee you were just a kid when I saw you last; how long ago was it really?, etc., etc., etc.

His house is nondescript. In fact, I walk up and down his

block several times before I knock on a door. It blends into the woodwork so well I can't remember a single distinctive feature.

His appearance is also nondescript. Skinny, average height, hunched shoulders, whole body hunched forward. He wears big sneakers and T-shirts and corduroy pants even in summer. He looks like Woody Allen, only with a Fu Manchu moustache.

He's very polite and considerate. We're interrupted several times during our first conversation, and each time he apologizes, explains that it was unavoidable. I share a steak with him, and half an hour later he remembers that he didn't offer me dental floss.

When I arrive to do our second interview, he says we should talk up in his bedroom because "there's an air conditioner up there. That is," he adds, "unless you have any objections to entering a strange man's bedroom." It so happens I have just such an aversion. I have a vague apprehension that he's going to come on to me (what the hell would I do?), but I stifle this fear and proceed like a true professional. I sit on one side of the bed and he slouches on the other, my microphone between us.

So much he doesn't remember: his own childhood, details about Barry's early personality, escapades from youth that didn't involve guns, the movies they made . . . What *does* he remember? What *does* he hold on to?

He was working for this company that made rocket propellant, but he got disgusted one day and quit. Worked for a company that was doing simulated chemical warfare . . . kind of a fun job for a while . . . had been reading a lot about rockets and playing with some neat explosives . . . but quit one day because he had nothing better to do. Went to work with Barry at Western Weapons and they went out of business. Did some consulting for a few months. Sold some machine guns to the wrong guy and got in trouble with the government. "And that's where I am now."

Now he's working for BOMCOM, Inc., a munitions company that bought the Western Weapons spread.

"It's basically the same thing, only BOMCOM does more of it and they do it better."

This is the same "plant" I used to visit in my teens, the same place we used to shoot those fabulous fireworks shows. After our interviews, Bob promises to give me a tour.

Flash. He's telling me the technical details about the construction of a napalm bomb. I wonder what he would feel if someone dropped one on his house and that cloud of flaming gel burned into his wife's and his cat's and his own nostrils and throat and lungs. If his esophagus choked on a product distilled by OPEC and good old Yankee know-how.

I note how skinny his arms are. About as skinny as the average Asian peasant's, but probably not half as strong. What would he do if he had to walk across this continent? Would he survive? Hardly. Not even with his "devices."

He speaks in flat, even tones. When he's telling something funny, there's a very short laugh, and then the smile disappears from his face and he looks blank again.

Blending into the woodwork.

In the car:
"Have you ever worked for the CIA?"
"No."
"Are you working for them now?"
"No."
"Have you ever *tried* to work for them?"
"I sent them my résumé once, but they never answered."
"Would you give me a different answer if I turned off this tape recorder?"
Turning to me, not smiling. "No."

Things get weird. Nothing surprises you. You get jaded easy in this biz. Come up to my bedroom and let's talk. Death toys and dollars-for-death and dialing-for-death and push-button death and powdered death and aerosol death and dispersion-system death and poison-tipped-umbrella death and blasting-goats-to-death death and death-in-life death. Improvised-munitions death from commonly available materials, with which a twelve-year-old can deal death.

Have I gotten it all? Have I dug deep enough? Have I asked the right questions? Have I been quick enough, slick enough?

Have I beat them at their own game? Am I being followed? Is there (deleted) in this orange juice? Is the ticket seller at the train station recording my vital statistics? Are there any cameras in this station? Is that trainman one of The Group? Is that cabbie a hired gun? If I buy a candy bar, will it be coated with (deleted)? Is that pretty girl a double agent? Is it worth my life to make a pass? Will I be shot if I speak out of turn?

In some men you can see the little boy very easily. He's right there under the surface, sometimes smiling, sometimes just standing quietly in a corner. Sometimes he's waving and screaming and shouting and beating his fists against windows.

I can see the little boy in Bob, the boy who knows he's smarter than the rest but never gets any credit. Always gets pushed around. He's another Mr. Death but without the glitter and flash and fiction and intrigue. Instead, he's got a whole lot of technical expertise. He knows his formulas the way a grand chef knows his recipes. By heart. Backward and forward. In his sleep. Half drunk. He'll get it right every time. And he cringes every time someone else gets it wrong.

"Oh, hell, I don't know how old I was when I met him. I was playing in the playground behind my school . . . must've been fourth or fifth grade. Barry came walking through the alley holding a box. He got to talking. The box was full of a high explosive he'd gotten somebody to make for him, because it wasn't a commercial item. If you want to keep your records accurate, it's nitrobenzene and potassium chlorate and it was all partridged up in a box. I seem to recall it was a Railway Express shipment. At that time you could ship small bombs via Railway Express.

"He was about seven years older than me. We walked over to your grandfather's company and he put the stuff down in the basement. We talked a little bit. He took a little bit out and hit it with a hammer and it went bang and I was very impressed.

"I was about thirteen when Barry and your mother got married. He was working for the Lincoln Institute and was making .38 tear-gas cartridges on the side. He had or feigned a great sensitivity to the stuff, so he used to pay me to load them down in the basement.

"I went over to his house once and your mother started talking and it was obviously a little personal. I wondered if I should leave and she said no 'cause she knew I had known him for a long time. I don't remember exactly what was going on but I think it had something to do with his drinking. Soon after that they split up, and he left the Institute and went into the tear-gas business.

"Barry was putting on fireworks shows, too, and I helped him with some of them. He had a partner in the tear-gas business, who I'd rather not name, and they had a disagreement, too. I don't know the details 'cause I heard very biased opinions. It may have been money, or Barry may have been playing with the guy's wife, but I think it was mostly money, 'cause I knew the wife and I don't think they were anything more than friendly with each other. But there was rumor to that effect, so I mention it.

"I went to work for a place in the city doing rocket propellant and chemical warfare, that sort of thing. One day I got disgusted because they weren't giving me enough work, I was hardly ever busy, just counting time on the clock. I drove out to see Barry at the farmhouse he was renting after leaving the Institute. I can still see the sign for the exit when you turn off the highway. There was a dump right there and I guess they didn't have much work either, so we sat there shooting rats all afternoon. Not too many showed up.

"But pretty soon he got some orders for a device he called Teleshot, a small explosive charge that's fired from a shotgun to scare birds off runways. That was one of your father's more ingenious inventions. We did some development work on it, and very quickly realized we had more work ahead of us than we could handle. So he got in touch with Western Weapons and asked them if they wanted to buy him out in order to give him more space and resources. They went for it. I moved into a trailer behind the plant. Did a couple jobs there. The Teleshot was the major product in the beginning, and there were also a couple research jobs for a couple arsenals. Hired two more people, Betty and Dawn. It's the same plant I work at now, even though a different company runs it now.

"To backtrack: Barry was manager and I forget what other titles he held. We started to get more jobs. The place grew. We got into more explosives. They hired another manager, and Barry became technical director or something like that. Around that time he took a trip to the Smithsonian and discovered geodes, which are spherical rock formations that are ugly on the outside but contain beautiful crystals on the inside. Some are hollow, some solid. He thought they were neat and he'd be able to sell 'em as a mass-market item. So he got into the rock and crystal business on the side. Eventually he and Dawn had a roarin' mail-order business. But that's later on.

"The place started to build up. This was the mid-Sixties. Business was going along pretty good.

"I don't have any real strong memories of personality going back to very young. I remember doing some things with him and I remember having conversations, but I really couldn't tell ya. He was somebody who I was reasonably friendly with. He was fairly funny. He used to tell good stories. My later impressions of him are that his life did not turn out as it should have and it was due—this is a personal opinion—due to a wrong image that he had of himself.

"Technically, he was not what he thought he was. He was very good at language. Had he gone into marketing or sales or writing, I think he would have been a much bigger success, wouldn't have had so many problems. Because what would generally happen is he would sell somebody on an idea. He was pretty good at initial concept, but once things got past that initial point he didn't have the background to be able to really pursue things and get them going. He was very, very good at getting things moving, but then it would stop and he would not be able to contribute much more and he would find something else to do.

"Generally he was a very, very funny person. I liked to talk to him when he was in a good mood. He would periodically get into not-so-good moods. After he died, I talked to Dawn and it was interesting. There were some things that I thought he did that were entirely fiction. A lot of it was fiction.

"For example, I always thought he was dealing fairly heavily in pornography, and it turned out that his dealings were very, very minor. He was a major collector. He used to buy the stuff for himself. When we were still kids, he used to buy porn from some guy down in Providence. This was just after he got his

license—maybe '63 or '64. The guy was a vaguely shady sort of
guy, and sometimes Barry didn't want to drive down and get it.
He'd pay me and I'd take a ride down. I'd meet the guy on the
Massachusetts Turnpike. There's a Harvest House right in the
middle and you can drive in from both sides and turn around
and leave. That was my early sexual education, as it were.

"When I was younger, he was a lot more direct and I thought
he had more technical expertise than he did. A lot of the stories
he used to tell me I took for fact and later found out they were
fiction. I don't know how much truth was in them, or if there was
any at all.

"Some very big stories, for example, are the ones in the *Playboy*
interview. When I read it, I said this is a load of nonsense. I sat
down and wrote—and I hardly ever write anything; I'm not
much of a correspondent—I wrote an eight-page letter that I
was gonna send to *Playboy*. I wrote it in longhand, and nobody
can read my handwriting. Before I mailed it, I talked to somebody else I'd rather not name. I'd had my problems with the
government and he was contemplating having problems with the
government . . . and he said just cool it. Don't stir the pot. So I
didn't. But it's ninety percent fabrication. There are broad, sweeping things that are true, but in detail they're not, 'cause I was
right there at the time and did some of the stuff for which he
took credit. And I wasn't looking for any recognition, but what
I don't know is if *Playboy* knew this.

"Some specific things.

"One: The exploding .22 was not his idea and it wasn't mine,
so I'm not taking credit for it.

"Two: I know all the silencers he was involved with, and there
were only two. I used to have a picture of it in my wallet, but I
cleaned out my wallet and threw it away about four years ago.
Had a picture of it for years, carried it right there next to my
heart.

"Three: Barry gave a mutual friend of ours a .22 rifle on his
eleventh or twelfth birthday. Eventually this friend got a little
older and I made a silencer for it. We cut the barrel off so it was
shorter and cut the stock off. A few years later, Barry paid the
guy to have it back. So if you ever see the silencer, it's about
this long [spreads fingers several inches]. It's a big aluminum

thing and looks like it obviously fits a single-shot .22 rifle with the stock and barrel cut off.

"When we were developing the exploding .22 at Western, somebody got the bright idea of trying to sell it to the Mafia or the CIA. Same dif, really. I don't recall who suggested that, gee, they'd work okay in a pistol; wonder if we oughtta show it to 'em as a possible assassination weapon; be pretty nifty with a silencer. This was actually why Western never did market it. It really was pretty good for that. The things'd go in, you know, and blow up. Not a whole lot of damage, but a lot more than your basic .22.

"One story in the *Playboy* interview involved getting on a plane and going to South America. At the point he places that, I know for a fact he had never been on an airplane. The first time he was on a plane was about '67 or '68 for some boring business trip. Had to fly to Kentucky or something. He never did like planes. Later on he got accustomed to 'em, but he would talk about 'em as being very unsafe.

"If I went through it sentence by sentence, I could pick out all sorts of stuff like that. There were some things that involved me that I could feel personal animosity about, but it was all really far in the past. Most of what involved me was at least six or seven years old and really didn't have much to do with anything—it was more a matter of this is not true. If you're gonna tell a story, it's okay if you let people know at some point that this is a story. You don't tell stories that are self-aggrandizing at the expense of somebody else, even though nobody will ever know who the other people are. You're kind of stealing credit from people a little bit.

"We had a contract with a big arsenal to design improvised munitions from commonly available materials. That was the only one I really got irritated about, because I did seventy percent of the technical work and Dawn did maybe twenty percent of it and we got the last sentence in the report that said, "With thanks to. . . ." His name got on the cover—which didn't bother me 'cause I figured, well, he's the author, he wrote the thing. But that was pretty much all he did with it. He sold it all. The work was done for him and he wrote up the results.

"What really bothered me was the next phase of the same contract, which I didn't work on. Dawn worked almost exclusively on that. It was on incendiaries and some other stuff that was not overly successful . . . I'm not putting that blame on her, it's just that it was a technical problem. But at that point he was becoming involved with Dawn and as a result her name got on the cover of the second report and that's what irritated me. He didn't like boys, he liked girls. That's what he was saying.

"I was ready to quit and in fact I did. I got a job with the police department's ballistics lab. I gave him notice and then there was this big meeting. I was taking a cut in pay to go work for the police, just because I didn't want to be part of that anymore. Then they gave me a raise that would have meant a fortypercent cut in pay to work for the city, so I stayed.

"The improvised-munitions program was a full, multifaceted thing. Got to look at the problem, go out and do research in the library, talk to people, go back and refine it a little bit. The customer didn't really have anything specific in mind. The idea was to present him with a number of things that would all suit his purpose. Explosives that you could improvise anywhere. How to make the stuff. That was the first time I successfully made nitroglycerin.

"We wanted to make urea nitrate. Instead of going out and buying urea, which is kind of cheating, we put containers in the bathroom. Everybody got to urinate into it. By the time we collected enough to try it, it was pretty ripe. Then we had to boil it down. Didn't smell too good. That was in the 'interesting' category.

"Making fulminates of mercury and silver is interesting to watch because it just sits there and looks like nothing's happening for a couple minutes. Then it begins to bubble and boil and all these fumes come out of it. Then it all subsides and the fumes go down and the stuff's still in the container. It's neat because it's just sitting there doing its thing. It looks like something Boris Karloff might make in a movie. Makes a pretty good grenade.

"There was only one other time when he did something in a personal sense to me. When I was fifteen or sixteen, I was working for Marty, and Barry knew somebody who was selling carbines. I gave Barry the money to buy one for me and the only thing I ever got was a story about how the guy left with the money. It wasn't that much money and it didn't really hurt me at the time, it was only thirty-five or forty dollars. That's more than it is now, but it's really no great amount of money and periodically I made money from him. But here he was acting as the agent . . . he had a much better job than I did. I was working part-time for something under minimum wage and he should have done something about it. At least given me half of it back.

"I know he told at least one true story. I never got all the details straight, but there was a girl at the time that he knew. She was probably a graduate student. By the time I met her, she had gotten her doctorate. I remember going over to his house a few days after it happened and he said, 'You won't believe this story.'

"Somebody set him up with this girl, and they went out to dinner and wound up back at her place. In like fifteen minutes they were in bed, and she was a virgin. That was the end of that story. He embellished it a little bit, but that was the essence. He said he always thought he was pretty good but not *that* fast, especially considering the fact that we're talking about the early Sixties.

"A few years later, I dated her for a few months, so I know the story's true. She'd decided it was about time and she'd asked all the girls she knew for a referral . . . 'cause everybody was apparently involved with everybody else. She asked for someone who was reasonably experienced and could bring the matter off without too much trauma. His name was brought up and that's how it happened. So that's a real story.

"By the time I was in my mid-twenties and working at Western, I'd heard so many stories from him that I knew weren't true that I didn't believe it when he said he had a heart attack. Must've been around '68. I don't think many other people knew him well enough to doubt he'd had a myocardial infarction. I didn't believe it because there were some problems at work right at that time and I figured he thought he'd be better off at the hospital than at work. I wasn't even sure when he said he had the second one a year later. . . .

"He would really get involved, and then it would become just like any other business, relatively mundane: You're making a product and you're trying to sell it, and to do that did not fit his image of himself—you know, big things. It's one thing to sell somebody on the idea of setting up a big fireworks plant, but then it's another to keep it running without blowing everything to smithereens. I'm of the opinion that temperament is all it takes to be a manager. You may not have to know all that much, but he knew more than enough. He would sell his basic idea and, once it was sold, he'd lose interest. That was the only reason all his businesses died.

"There was something in the *Playboy* interview about snake venom. He was living in Millville at that time and he bought a couple spitting cobras. He had 'em for a while, but once he was cleaning out the cage and, even though he wore protective clothing, he got very sick because he inhaled dried venom that was stuck on the walls inside the cage. He didn't keep 'em much longer after that.

"He always used to have a couple poisonous snakes lying around the house. I think mostly to show off to somebody coming to his house for the first time. It's one thing to have plain old ordinary snakes, it's another thing to have spitting cobras.

"I remember he got a package once at Western while I was living in back of the plant in that trailer. I knew it was a snake and I was curious, so I opened it. I'd handled snakes, but, not knowing what it was, I very cautiously got the thing into a bottle. Nasty-lookin' critter. I don't know if you remember the Gaboon viper he used to keep in the basement, but that was it. If I had known what it was, I wouldn't have handled it. I think they're only one of the most dangerous snakes in the world, isn't that right?

"I remember he had a black American scorpion and an African scorpion on his desk in little aquariums. Probably more stuff like that, but that's what I remember."

I am thirteen. He sends me a tiny black American scorpion and a huge African scorpion—both dead—mounted in the same glass case.

"In the beginning, in the mid-Sixties, there were only a few people working at Western. I considered myself part of manage-

ment 'cause I functioned as part of management. It took a while
before I was officially made part of management, which I guess
was another thing which caused some resentment, because technically I did a lot of the work. It wasn't until much later that I
got credit for it. The unofficial view was that I had the authority
to do almost anything in the place. I could tell anybody to do
anything. I could control projects with approximately equal
authority. I couldn't sign a final purchase order, but I could say,
'Here, buy this, you need it.' I could direct the people in the plant
to do whatever I wanted, but there was no official recognition
for me. There's a little bit of resentment.

"I'm a less than hard worker. I'll put in bursts and then slow
down, but I'm reasonably conscientious in that I come to work
on time. Starting about late '67 or early '68, Barry started to
slough off and had very little to do with the operations at the
plant. He would come in and raise a fuss for a while and then
you wouldn't see him for a day or two or three.

"We had a couple mass-production jobs loading fuses, and
there was the likelihood of some big loading jobs coming in.
The war was really building up at that point and they sent down
some new management. That was about the time they hired an
auditor. I know Barry had the company buy stuff for him personally. I don't know if the auditor ever caught that . . . but
anyway, the new manager was down for a long time. I don't know
what discussions they had, but Barry went away very abruptly.
No warnings. They paid him off and eventually he went into the
fireworks business.

"He could sing fairly well. Had a good voice. Occasionally I
would hear him sing 'Lord Randall.' It's a child ballad. I still
remember the words. I remember him singing it when he was
feeling whatever.

"He was very active toward the women in the place. Compulsively so. There was a girl named Jane who I was kind of interested in but never pursued properly. He pursued her and was
too blunt or something, but, anyway, she quit or he fired her.

"I had this trailer out in back of the plant. He used to ask me
if he could have the key, if he could use it for an afternoon. He'd
always give some long story about why he needed it. I wondered
why he didn't use his own apartment over in Millville, but I

never asked him about it. If he wants to use it, let'm use it. It wasn't until much later that I found out he was sleeping with Dawn in my trailer. This must have been only two, three, four months after he hired her.

"A great number of women complained about him after he left, but who do you complain to when he was essentially running the place? There was an undercurrent of animosity between some of the women and him. Some really unlikely people made comments about him. He was not one to always pick the most visually or mentally desirable.

"He was not a machinist. Occasionally we hired a machinist or two for a special project, but I did most of the machining, so I should know what went on in the machine shop. I would say I had a ninety-nine-percent awareness of everything else that was happening in the plant, and there was no cloak-and-dagger stuff. No connection with CIA. No times when somebody came in and said, 'I want a few hundred of this special bullet—we don't want to do it, so we'd like to ask you to do it.'

"I would have known about it, 'cause I always knew who the customer was, where and when the item was being shipped. We just didn't make sophisticated stuff. It was all pretty straightforward. We didn't have any great expertise in any area that would have been useful to them. We had all run-of-the-mill parts and machines and explosive components. And to just give them a box of this—well, they could get it easier in a thousand other places; why come to us for it? And as for putting anything sophisticated together, we never did any sophisticated work like that. I would have known about anything that needed machine work. To be really honest, Barry might have loaded *one* item, *possibly*. But if the order were for two or more, he would have somebody else do it. In which case I would have known about it, because he probably would have asked me to do it.

"I've only had limited contact with government agents, and that was only when I sold some machine guns to a federal agent, which is the wrong guy to sell machine guns to. I don't feel super-bad about it 'cause there was somebody paid in between. But you know I did it. It was only the selling of 'em that was a problem. They couldn't have done anything to me if I hadn't actually sold 'em, 'cause I acquired 'em in a legitimate fashion, sufficiently legitimate. They could have confiscated them, but the only people they could have prosecuted would have been Western Weapons, because they shouldn't have let me keep them when they sold out to BOMCOM.

"What I'm saying about your father might sound a little bit negative and I hope it's not causing any . . . I see it as the story of a man who lived the way he thought he lived or the way he told people that he lived. . . . Deep down inside, I don't know how honest he was with himself. From about the time the fireworks plant blew up, he was just down. Dawn told me he used the shopping-bag technique for paying bills. He would get all his bills together in a pile, put 'em in a bag, and when the bag was filled he'd throw 'em out.

"I talked to her after he died. I can't remember if you were at the house then or not. I remember you stayed at the house for a while. But when somebody close dies, most of us grieve for the personal loss. I got the impression that she was grieving over what he left her with, which was a helluva lot of debt.

"He described himself as a man of intrigue, mystery, a dweller in dark places. He thought of his presence as a wisp of smoke. He was, in his own mind, a Director of Doom—which, in a lot of ways, he was capable of. He had some technical knowledge. He was obviously a lot more expert than the man in the street, or even perhaps a little bit above that. And I would say that he knew where to go for information if he needed it.

"But he never acted much of that out in a real sense. He didn't tote heavy books around on these subjects. It was mostly verbal and in mood and character. He had a period where he wore all black. He shaved his head for six or seven months in the late Sixties and wore nothing but black.

"He was aware of his powers of persuasion. He had a great deal of success with women for various reasons. He once told me a story about a guy who used to go to the beach and just ask every girl if she wanted to fuck. Supposedly this guy never had to walk more than two or three blocks down the beach.

"As you get older, you realize how true this is. You think back on all the times you might have scored if you had just asked. So I think the shotgun approach was part of his technique. And it didn't have to be somebody he was working with. If you met him for the first time, you realized right away he was an excellent speaker, a superb talker. I would imagine he told great stories with the right hints of whatever. I don't know what his percentage rates were for success, but in absolute numbers they were quite high.

"The only physical thing that I can think of that would possibly have thrown women off was his breath. He had really bad breath. But my wife's brother has unbelievable B.O. and he got married, so that's kind of the family joke. So these things are not necessarily impediments, and maybe when I was around him he just hadn't bothered to brush his teeth.

"He had various inclinations toward women. Marsha was short and round. Dawn is tall and thin. The girl that had a committee select him was big and heavy. Most of them were relatively bright. He was a bright guy, and most bright men, unless they're chauvinistic and don't ever want to have a conversation, will gravitate toward people who are relatively bright.

"I don't know if it was his suggestion, but whenever we got a new person in charge, we'd put a whistling bomb in their car on the first day. There was one guy in particular who didn't think it was very funny, but I doubt that had anything to do with Barry's problems with the administration.

"Barry used to smoke those thin cigars once in a while, and I got him once with silver fulminate. I kind of actually almost caused a real problem, 'cause he was drivin' through D.C. on a business trip with this thing in his mouth when it blew up. It threw tobacco all over the inside of his car and he almost had an accident. I went over and really apologized to him, 'cause he was really mad. But after a few days he saw the humor in it. There was some guy comin' from the other direction that Barry almost ran off the road, and he said he'd always remember the guy's eyes.

"There was the great Fourth of July picnic, which hadda be '68 or '69. We used to buy commercial fireworks to celebrate the Fourth and supplement them with leftovers from the plant. We'd work all week before the Fourth, just getting everything together. We had a lot of aerial shells and Roman candles and that thunderstorm at the end of the show. It went from real little firecrackers to the medium-size ones to bigger ones, and there was

all this stuff goin' off at once and then the big boom that was
really a bucket of flare mix.

"The flare mix was supposed to go up in a big red flash, but
instead of just stickin' a fuse into it, we put a cherry bomb halfway down into the bucket. It acted as a detonator. We put a hole
in the side of the bucket so it wouldn't light the flare mix before
lighting the cherry bomb. So the cherry bomb went off and blew
all the powder in the air, and then it all caught fire, and because
it all happened so fast, it caused an explosion. There was a crater
there the next day. It blew out I don't know how many windows
in the farmhouses in the area and the light reflected off the clouds
and turned off all the streetlights. People dove under their cars,
laughed and cried at the same time. It was funny as hell.

"He and my cousin and a couple other guys from the neighborhood used to make movies when they were in their early
teens. Melodrama of the worst type. You know, heroine tied to
the tracks and curly moustaches and all that crap. I don't know
who has them. Barry used to have them, about eight or ten reels.
I haven't seem 'em for fifteen years.

"The most interesting project I worked on while at Western
Weapons was probably the improvised-munitions program, which
was the earliest thing I worked on there. Another interesting
project was one I did right at the end, literally as the place was
closing. It was classified, but it involved reentry of missiles. Warheads and a way to hide them. They were probably the two
most interesting in a personal sense. They also had the largest
dollar volume. They never really had any big contracts at Western, but they had a couple interesting ones.

"He was there when we were loading the FMU fuse. We had
the complete contract for the FMU-7. It's the fuse that goes into
the napalm bomb, which is interesting because you don't need a
fuse for a napalm bomb. But the military mind being whatever
it is, they figure if you don't have a fuse on it, then it must be
armed all the time. So this way you can take the fuse out and
it's safe. To my knowledge that's the only reason they use the
FMU-7 fuse in the napalm bomb.

"Napalm bombs are just these big light sheet-metal containers
full of napalm. One fuse sat in the nose and one sat in the tail.

They were electronically armed and fired a burster tube that was in the middle of the bomb. Supposedly the idea was that the bomb would hit the ground and the fuse would go off and the burster tube would rupture it and blow the napalm all over the place.

"On the other hand, if you think about it, if you have this little sheet-metal container full of this explosive jelly and it hits the ground at three or four hundred miles an hour, you don't need a fuse to light it. The friction is almost always enough to light the stuff. It's possible that if you landed it in water or on really soft sand, it might not explode; but by and large, on normal, average terrain, it always lights.

"We had a guy working on our crew who had been in the air over there and he said they tried the experiment once. They just left the fuses off and told the guys, 'Drop these somewhere and see what they do.' Their reply: 'Eh, they work fine.' That's neither here nor there, but I mention it for history's sake.

"We made maybe fifty or a hundred thousand of 'em. A very, very old fuse, very antiquated. They kept saying they weren't going to buy any more, but we'd almost be done with an order when they'd say, 'How 'bout makin' another ten thousand?'

"I think we must've made a quarter of a million of the 344s.

"In the *Playboy* interview, he claimed he got out of military work for moral reasons. Since he did not do any weapons work after leaving Western, at least none that I know of, it's possible that he had an abrupt about-face. On the other hand, he took several guns with him, including at least one silencer. He also owned some number of weapons at that time and during all the time I knew him. So offhand I don't think very much of that statement.

"Up until very close to the end, we were playing around with stuff that involved high lethality, and he didn't seem to be any less interested in the destructive aspects of the work. He may have been bored or pissed off that he was about to be fired, so I can understand him saying that because it's a good rationale for not being involved with military work. It's quite possible that he was fed up with military work. I wouldn't doubt that 'cause everybody's fed up with military work. A lot of aggravation. But if you make things that go bang, that's usually who you sell them to. His about-face would have had to take place in less than a year.

"When he joined Western his income improved a helluva lot. He was able to indulge himself more. His life-style improved considerably. That was the period I had the heaviest contact with him.

"What does this say? He got a phone put in his car for absolutely unknown reasons. He wasn't dead serious about it, but he let it be known. He didn't jump into the office and say, 'Wow! I just got a phone put in my car!' I think he was sitting in the office one day, and calmly said, 'I think I'm gonna get a phone put in my car.'

"Everybody sat around and said, 'What for? You're either here and nobody calls or you're home and never answer the phone.' A little umbrage was taken, and the subject was dropped. But he had it put in anyway. He complained because they hadda have his car for two days to install it. It was really ridiculous because he never did any traveling for the company during the day when they would have to get in touch with him. He went on maybe one or two short business trips by car. It was really a personal thing. Billed to the company, of course. He was still there when they stopped paying for it.

"I remember a story he told me about George. He used to say that George had the whole trunk of his car outfitted with handguns and machine guns and grenades and all sorts of goodies. Well, I got to know George pretty well and I guess he's just not as mysterious and exciting as he used to be, because his trunk was and still is as normal as yours and mine.

"I don't think I tell stories as well as he does. Even when everybody knows there's a story being told, I'm not the raconteur. I'm a little more solid. I pay my bills. I think he was a better administrator than I am. I think I'm technically more competent than he was. I'd say we're both dissatisfied with how we lived. He may have had a queerer idea of what he really wanted to do, and maybe he didn't. It's hard to tell. We both liked sex. I think he had a little more experience than I did. I started going with a girl and then I lived with her for eleven or twelve years. Then we broke up and I had a little bit more excitement. Then I got married. None of the above implies absolute fidelity anywhere. It's all relative.

"I think he felt he was born ten or fifteen years too soon. I'm not sure if I was born too soon or too late. I was either born ten or twenty years too soon or I was born seventy-five years too late. I haven't decided which. Things are always loosening up sexually, so he would have been happier now than he was twenty years ago. He had an obsession for sex. I prefer to think of mine as a great interest. I would like to be able to enjoy more, feel a little younger now, to enjoy what's going to come about in the near future with technology.

"Or maybe I was born too late, because the great period of free enterprise is over. I would have enjoyed being around then, because if you came up with any idea at all, nobody regulated it or told you it was morally bad or socially repelling or ecologically damaging. Too much of that stuff now . . . you could play with guns a little more then. The great period of gun development was about 1900 to 1910. They were doin' a lot with explosives then, too. The laws on fraud weren't so tough. I'm interested in certain types of fraud which didn't used to be considered fraud. I'm involved in some mail-order stuff and I've always told people exactly what they were getting. But you used to be able to be a little less precise. Even now, it's amazing what you can tell people that they're getting and they'll still buy it from you. 'Buy This Worthless Trinket.' People will send you money for a Genuine Worthless Trinket.

"People flew airplanes with much less regulation then. Course they weren't as reliable, but they were a lot more fun.

"I'm certain that Barry had nothing whatsoever to do with the Bay of Pigs. He would have told stories about it. That would have been too choice. He may have supplied something to somebody, but if he did, I'll bet it was peripheral.

"Let's go into an old allegation he made that I suspect is also highly unlikely.

"When I was nineteen or twenty—this would have been the early Sixties—your father showed great interest in that silencer I told you about earlier. More importantly, he said the CIA showed great interest in it. He told me that he called this guy at the CIA and described it, and that he was very, very interested;

they sent some guy up and they had a long talk about making poisoned bullets or whatever.

"Nobody ever got to meet this guy, which of course was reasonable. I never thought much about it, except one day I realized no orders ever came. Soon after that, I became interested specifically in weapons. I did a lot of research, and suddenly it dawned on me: Why the hell would they get in touch with him for something so crude? Why would they be interested? They don't need anybody to make 'em half a dozen poisoned bullets. Particularly if they're .22 shorts drilled out with a little cyanide in 'em. That's completely ridiculous.

"I can't say, no, it never happened. But considering the general level of expertise that they have right on their own premises, and the way these things are usually done, I would have to say it's very, very, very, very unlikely. Unlikely to the point of being impossible.

"It's like this: If you're gonna load poison bullets for somebody, you don't load 'em with cyanide or even snake venom. There are much better toxins than snake venom. Snake venom is poisonous, but it's not a really toxic material. There are much more common things that are much more toxic.

"There was a Bulgarian dissident living in England. He was assassinated recently in such a bizarre fashion that it raised all sorts of big questions, because somebody went to a lot of trouble to make it known that some very sophisticated organization went to a lot of trouble to do him in. He was a defector and they just shot him with a very tiny pellet that had cross-drilled holes in it. It was probably shot out of an air gun. The pellet was made of platinum and was only one or two millimeters in diameter. The cross-drilled holes were a few thousandths of an inch in diameter, and somebody filled them with ricin, an organic toxin distilled from a plant I would prefer not to mention by name.

"You can get your own ricin in this country. You can buy it in this state at any agricultural-supply store—by the *pound*. What was sophisticated about that assassination was the little platinum sphere. They used that because it has a high density and will go farther with more force if it's only being shot out of an air gun. An air gun has so many obvious advantages in terms of noise, bulk, and how easily it could be recognized as a weapon. Fact is, it couldn't have been. You could cross any border with a weapon like that and do anybody in and nobody would ever find the murder weapon.

"If you want something nifty and mean, you don't use cyanide or snake venom. If you don't want something nifty or mean, you don't have to go to somebody else to do it. These people know how to do this stuff. No big trade secrets in this business. No new technology. You can paint all sorts of nifty nerve gases on toilet seats or doorknobs or spray 'em in somebody's shoes. Absolutely nothing new under the sun.

"I don't know how much you know about physics, but all the air around you could pull away from you so you couldn't breathe. I'd go on breathing and you'd be left in a vacuum. You might explode or maybe you'd just suffocate. There is no reason for that not to happen. It's just statistically unlikely. All that stuff is moving randomly, but no one can promise you it will never decide to avoid your lungs. It's just not too damn likely. I would put most of your father's stories in the same category."

11

Walking Wounded

Today I am cruising across this New England landscape with an
ease that is utterly astounding, stationed at the helm of a snow-
white Cutlass Supreme. Last night I borrowed this luxury automobile from a friend who's visiting from the Midwest. He's a
young doctor, and his chariot wears Illinois plates. The perfect
vehicle with which to crash a bomb factory.

I hold an image in my mind of a huge green pie that has been
sliced and apportioned and sliced and apportioned again and
again, gouged and plowed and planted and fertilized. That pie
is the American dreamscape that flows past me, glides by in a
hundred thousand shades of green. There are silos full of grain,
and cows munching and making milk, and streams gurgling, and
crows crowing. High above, one hawk holds us all in his merciless
grip.

Imagine a dozen and more roads and side roads leading closer
and closer to boyhood memories, to a "plant" where the death
clones do their thing in peace and tranquillity. Bob gave me
directions that one might take to a county fair to enter a contest
for the best baked goods in this part of the state, or to an estate
auction where one might hope to purchase first editions of
Emerson and Thoreau, or to go see grandma on the occasion of
her seventy-fifth birthday, or to fish a trout stream that no one but
you has ever heard of, or to dig for Indian relics in a quarry.

At the bottom of a hill on my left, there is a huge wooden sign
planted high on the embankment. In big black letters on a white

background, it says, simply, BOMCOM, INC., hard and black, with very sharp edges. There is an eight-foot fence topped with barbed wire. This fence is obviously manicured regularly, because there are no rusted links or twisted strands of wire or wild grapes or poison ivy growing on it. The grounds are well groomed, the grass is very green and very short. There are warning signs everywhere: signs with black dogs baring huge teeth, signs in yellow and red, signs in green and white—signs, signs, signs. All with one warning: GROUNDS PATROLLED BY ARMED GUARDS. TRESPASSERS WILL BE PROSECUTED AND/OR SHOT. As I turn into the driveway, I wonder who thought of this last bit of humor, but already I have decided not to try to find that person.

Three plastic cones, the kind the state police use to direct traffic around an auto wreck, stand in the middle of the driveway by the security gate. The gatehouse is a plywood shed with no windows, paneled with what appears to be quarter-inch-thick linoleum. The only guard in sight is a sturdily built blond woman armed with a white pearl-handled, long-barreled .38 revolver. Her blue uniform fits her well, almost too well. Her hips and bust are well defined, almost too well defined. I wonder: Would my father have tried to make her, or would she have been too much even for him? I am tempted to ask her name and how she got into this kind of work, if she's overworked and underpaid like everyone else except the president and his band of merry stockholders, but I change my mind as I drive closer. She's tough. Too tough for me. At least that's my first impression as I pull up to the cones and roll down my window.

I speak before she has a chance to.

"My name is David Rothman and I'm here to see Bob Rightman." I say this firmly, with conviction and ease, as if I am now in exactly the right place at exactly the right time. I *belong* here.

"Does he work in the lab or the office?" replies my blond.

"I'm not sure. Probably the office." I look her straight in the eye, sublimating that quiver in my stomach.

"You're probably right," she says, amazingly. "Sign here. Display this badge at all times while on the premises. The office is straight ahead on the right. You'll see it. Can't miss it."

I sign in, purposely leaving the "occupation" and "purpose of visit" boxes blank. I pin the plastic I.D. badge onto my shirt, just left of my heart. She removes the obstacles from my path, and I roll into the boom-boom womb.

If she had asked for some identification, I would have been stuck like a pig on a spit. I don't even have a driver's license because I've failed the tests so many times I've taken it as an omen. Conceal everything, a tiny voice says deep inside. Invisible is not secret enough.

Imagine a pre–Civil War farmhouse with walls two feet thick, surrounded by half a dozen sheds and barns. There is no apparent order to the ground plans. A barn was built here and a shed constructed there, as if according to someone's unpredictable whim.

I walk into a small, bunkerlike building made of old fieldstones. An attractive, middle-aged, motherly-type woman looks up from her cluttered desk and smiles. I could be in a doctor's office. I state my business and turn to sit down, expecting to see some office chairs, but there aren't any. There is a row of armchairs, the kind they use in high school, with the little rack underneath the seat for your lunchbox and extra books. Maybe these are for working out problems on the spot, when the inspiration strikes. What would you prefer if you were an engineer waiting to see the boss about a problem that had been rattling around in your head for months, and suddenly, minutes before you were to see him for the nth time this month, a light bulb lit over your head and the answer came all in a flash? Great for working out little bomb problems, ironing out the kinks.

"How are you," Bob Rightman says. It's a statement, not a question. He's under fire for some project snag or other, and my hunch is this is not going to be a leisurely stroll through the guts of BOMCOM.

"I'm sorry," he says to fill the vacuum, "but we're gonna have to make this kinda short. We're having some problems over in the lab and the boss is givin' me heck."

I say that's okay, something is better than nothing, and we walk out into the bright late-afternoon sun.

As we walk across the gravel driveway toward a narrow asphalt footpath that connects all these buildings, I think: The last time I was here I was twelve years old. Half my life ago. It was the Fourth of July, and it was the greatest. I was Barry Rothman's son, I was the son of the fireworker—I played with danger, too.

If he was *the man who could cheat death*, I was *the son who played the same game—and won*. People looked at me differently, I thought, when I was around him. They—especially the women —looked at him differently, more romantically, than at other men. People watched in awe as we ran from firework to firework, lighting fuses with matches and cigarettes and even Roman candles. Lighting fuses with anything that would burn. That was *it*, that was what life was all about: setting fires whenever, wherever you could get away with it.

People noticed me more when I was around him. I liked that. Loved him for it. The Fourth was the best day in my year. I savored the taste and smell of burning charcoal and sulfur and saltpeter—the basic recipe for black powder—for days and weeks after it was over. I brought those tastes and smells back home with me. They would keep me alive—burning inside—for the months when I wouldn't see him, for the months when I would starve. Nourishment for a growing boy. . . .

But now my guide is pointing out the different kinds of buildings and their purposes. On our left are two new gray steel "barns"—not like any barns I've ever seen. Were they here when I was here last? No. They went up soon after BOMCOM bought out Western Weapons. What're they for? I ask as innocently as possible. "Oh," says the right man for the job, "they're for storing stuff that's about to be shipped."

His tone of voice doesn't leave much room for a question-and-answer period, like: What sort of stuff? Shipped where? By what vehicle—Atlas moving van or parcel post? No more Railway Express? Who is eating shrimp and lobster bought with war profits in peace time? Whose hands signed the papers, or was none of it committed to paper because of its sensitive nature? Does it matter that I have a sensitive nature and don't like being so close to so much death and destruction, even if it's asleep in a barn? Does anybody around here care about Deeper Psychological Paradoxes: that maybe I like being near so much death and destruction almost as much as I hate it; that maybe we all like it and always have and always will, because why else would we tolerate it, let alone thrive on it? Maybe I like to measure myself against *it*. Maybe I like to imagine who is stronger: those devices or the muscle in my arm and the brain in my skull and the pen

in my hand. *The pen may be mightier than the sword,* a ghost
whispers in my ear, one of the many who hover above this barn,
but a bomb will blow your shit awayyyyyyyyy.

Each building, no matter how small, is wired for electricity. But
why are the poles that carry the wires double-masted, like the
masts of old sailing ships ready for the worst possible storms?
How much juice are they using here? My mind briefly contem-
plates megawatts, electric chairs, nukes going bang in the night,
the smell of Frankenstein's singed hair.

Eight eighteen-wheel semi's are lined up in a makeshift parking
lot, all without cabs, as if their carcasses are all that's needed.
Storage? Lab projects that can be broken down quickly and
moved to an even more remote location? An image: eight huge
hogs dining at a communal slop-trough.

There are signs everywhere that say:

SMOKING

CARRYING MATCHES

OPEN LIGHTS

ABSOLUTELY PROHIBITED

Yet everybody I see is sucking a cigarette or cigar or pipe, or at
least has a pack of matches tucked away on his person. If I set off
a belt of firecrackers, would anybody get uptight?

An old-fashioned fire truck is parked in a shed, and it's even
painted red. The company logo is painted white on the doors,
plain and simple: BOMCOM, INC.

The Clone is walking fast now, guiding me on the narrow
asphalt footpath, up a slight incline, to a reinforced concrete
bunkerlike building. It has a number on the outside—they all do
—but I forget which one it is as soon as I try to remember it. As
we approach the heavy steel door, a calm young female voice
announces over an unseen P.A.: "Bob Rightman, please call
sixty-six. Bob Rightman, please call sixty-six." Flushed with the
importance of his position (though feigning the proper amount
of disgust at the aggravation, obviously loving every second of it),
my guide apologizes and lurches for a phone that is hidden from
my view behind what appears to be a closet door to the bunker.

My disorientation and confusion quickly engulf all of my senses. Hungry to scribble every shred of revealing tour-guide talk, aching to remember every relevant and irrelevant detail, I am suddenly afraid that too much will escape me, that I am not good enough for the job. Not that someone else could do it better, but that no one could do it the way it should be done, the way it *must* be done. There is too much to tell here, the story is too big, the implications too awesome—the connections to all of history, to what has come before us and what is with us now and what we will leave behind, what will perish and what will endure—it is all too vast for a fumbling, confused, angry young man to grasp. A platoon of scholars couldn't do better; they'd only add to the confusion. There's too much. It's too big. I can only hope to bring back a few shards worth remembering. I cling to this resolution, hoping none of my doubts are revealed in my voice or face or body language.

I look off into the distance, knowing that it really doesn't matter what I write down, it doesn't matter what I see and hear, it doesn't matter how much realistic detail I capture in twenty minutes, it doesn't matter how much I miss, how much I forget. What's important is that I am here, now, standing where my father once stood, where we never had a chance to stand together, admiring a view he must have admired. Imagining the beautiful sunset that will spread tonight across the western horizon. Both of us loving colors in the sky.

My guide returns from his closet with more apologies and more aggravation. He knocks twice on the heavy steel door, but opens it before anyone could possibly have proper warning. Two young white women, smiling like cheerleaders or small-town college students, appear in front of us. He ignores them, stepping forcefully into a small, half-lit room full of more machinery that I couldn't understand if I studied it for ten years. He mumbles something that I also can't understand, something about operations going on in here. I know he isn't referring to surgery, but my mind can't help but flash on legs and arms popping on and off, heads being disconnected temporarily, basic dismembering.

I don't get to know much more about the rooms we just passed through until I'm outside. I squint in the sudden sunlight. I turn for one last glimpse while my guide is already trotting off to another building. I see a sign above the back door, the door that I just opened and closed: CAUTION! EXPLOSIVES BEING MIXED!

He's walking about ten paces ahead of me. I figure this is just one small tactic to avoid my questions, so I try extra hard to think of one that he'll have to answer.

"What's that big thing over there?" I point to something that looks like a giant guillotine about 300 yards away.

"A drop tower," he says, and nothing more. He's still ten paces ahead of me. I don't try to catch up with him. I'm still trying to slow him down. I wait a few seconds for some more, but that's it. He's making me work for every scrap.

"What's that?" I say it with the proper amount of hesitation in my voice, trying to make it irresistible to take the time to answer. Who knows where this line of questioning could lead? If he's got the answer and I don't, I know it's gotta be causing him extreme discomfort not to dish it out. This is one of my few tools—or weapons. "Could you tell me a little—"

"We put a bomb up on top," he says abruptly, over his shoulder, still walking. "Then we drop it. When we send 'em out, they don't have to work. They just shouldn't go off if something happens to 'em that shouldn't."

"Like getting shot at or falling off a plane?"

"Yeah."

We approach one of the largest buildings on "the premises," as Bob calls this place. It looks like a small airplane hangar. He opens the heavy steel door and holds it open for me. When I step over the threshold, I am bombarded by the roar of heavy machinery. Two or three young white men (I haven't seen anyone darker than albino yet) peer up from their work and look at me through welder's goggles. Sparks fly and wheels grind. I smile and nod hello. They look me straight in the eye and don't smile, as if to say, What's there to smile about? You got a problem, take it somewhere else. I look away and follow Bob, who is opening another door to another quieter, hopefully safer room.

He points to a "tablet machine." Here is where they pack HMX—a high explosive—into tablets, which eventually fit into bombs. Which eventually kill strangers across the seas. Which eventually explode in kindergarten classrooms. Which eventually make mincemeat of goats and sheep. Which eventually turn the soil over, but make it unfarmable for years—possibly forever—because of the trash they leave behind.

As he walks away, I ask to see one, touch it, feel it. Contemplate it.

"You mean one of the items?"

"Yes."

He doubles back, exuding knowledge and expertise in the way he knows exactly where to look; but not because he spends eight hours a day packing them—because he spends eight hours a day telling other people how and where and when to pack them. There is a row of carriers lined up against the wall, the kind hospitals use to dispense little cups full of pain-killers. These trays are full of tablets, but they're not pain-killers. They're pain-producers. Pain-promoters. Pain-inducers. Pain-growers.

"Here's one of the items we're making for————" and he names a fairly well-known European client. A country. A major industrial nation that is a member of the Common Market. This particular country, to my particular knowledge, has not been at war since 1945, has not even paid attention to the Cold War.

"Can I hold it?"

"Sure." He hands me a silver aspirin-size cylinder that has a hole in one end. He explains the reason for that hole and what happens when a firing pin punches into it and what happens after that. There are at least 200 trays within sight and at least 100 tablets on each tray. I try to count the deaths but lose it real fast. Should've brought my calculator.

I must be hiding my feelings very very well, because the Death Clone answers my next question with alarming ease.

"What does one of these tablets fit into? I mean precisely. . . ?"

"Oh, a five-hundred-pound bomb. Your basic general-purpose device."

The facts drift into and out of my cracked consciousness.

1. There are ten HMX machines in this hangar.

2. All of the tablet-packers are women. All young. All white. All quite innocent.

3. All of these machines are older than I. All were built in the early Forties—with the exception of a few new ones in the new wing. (This last fact courtesy of my guide. I didn't even have to ask.)

4. How to describe these machines? Take an old-fashioned electric mixer, magnify it 100 times, and you've got the powder-mixing part. Take an old-fashioned cookie cutter and dough mold, magnify it 100 times, and you've got the tablet-packing part.

We're out of the cool and dark and into the hot and bright, only now my guide isn't walking quite so far ahead of me; he's only about a pace or two in front of me, and he even slows down to let me catch up. I'm gaining ground. I'm guiding him, but he doesn't know it and probably/hopefully/definitely never will.

We approach another small, bunkerlike building. Its individuality is amazing considering the sterile, conformist architecture and atmosphere in which it lives. This fact is obvious to me from 200 feet away, even though it looks just like all the other buildings.

A radio is playing quite loud and spilling out from under the reinforced steel door and through the concrete walls. The first song I hear goes like this:

> Summmmm . . .er
> Is my time of year

The next, which picks up where the other leaves off:

> We will,
> We will
> *Rock you!*

We step over one more threshold (for some reason I think of mistletoe and Christmas). The air-conditioned air feels good on my sweaty skin.

The radio goes down immediately. Two young women are washing up after a hard day at the lab.

"This is where the young ladies mix wet explosives all day,"

Bob says, leering toward the taller, blonder, more attractive of the two. "Miss White, say hello to the writer Mr. Rothman. I brought him over just for you."

A blond, big-busted T-shirted woman in her late twenties turns and smiles sweet as pie. I'd like to fuck her, right here on the wet-explosives packing table. With this awful smell sticking its finger into our nostrils.

"Oh, shit," says Miss White, "if I had known he was coming, I wouldn't have worn my bra. Woulda dressed down."

I can't think of anything to say except "*Wanna fuck?*" so I just smile awkwardly and mumble something about how it's still nice to meet you even if I can't see your nipples. Besides, everything I might have wanted to ask has already been answered: How do you feel about your work? *Do* you feel about it? What's it like playing with wet explosives all day—sort of remind you of mud pies you made when you were a kid? Isn't this a man's job? Do you have to deal with male-chauvinist bullshit on the premises? If so, how do you deal with it? Do you think of yourself as a "survivor," which seems to be a very popular phrase among women these days? Does that smell ever leave you alone? Are you ever able to wash it out of your hair? Has your boyfriend ever complained? How often do you wash your hands? What's a nice girl—er, woman—like you doing in a nasty place like this?

The most chilling vibes to have so far penetrated my skin are being emitted from a very small bunkerlike building that, according to Bob, is used for "hand operations." Again, I'm pretty sure he's not talking surgery. Or handjobs.

There is an even larger version of the old-fashioned electric flour mixer—more than 1,000 times the size of the kitchen model that was so popular in America during the decade in which I was born. This mixer is silent now.

There is an "ultralow refrigerator." I look closely—the dial says it can go down to forty degrees below zero. This ultra-icebox is humming furiously.

There is a wooden contraption, painted red and obviously handmade, that has screens and windows and miniature doors and levers. It is oddly out of place with all this heavy metal. I ask my guide what it is.

"Just a box," he says. And smiles.

In one stockroom, he points out the fact that the M-57 detonator is mounted with the 505 fuse and fits into a 20mm shell.

In another stockroom, he points out that a certain bomb, when fitted with all the necessary apparel, weighs 136 kilograms.

In yet another stockroom, I ask him what those little silver things are and what they fit into. "Oh, I dunno," he says. "Must be some sort of fuse for some sort of assembly."

There are trucks everywhere and bulldozers and parked cars and young men without shirts and with muscles and great tans riding around looking very productive.

My tour comes to an abrupt halt. I hadn't noticed that this footpath, which winds up to and around more than a dozen buildings and other "facilities" (i.e., the drop tower), eventually leads back to the front door of the main office. There is some symbolism here, but I'll never grasp it. (Rats in a maze? In our beginning is our end? Can't tell the dancer from the dance?)

"Well, I hope that was of some help," Bob says. "I'm sorry I didn't have more time."

I say that's quite all right, I appreciate everything you've done for me, I've really learned a lot just by being around you and your facilities.

I sit in the parking lot scribbling notes and generally trying to get some attention, to work up some suspicion, but nothing happens. Messages fly back and forth over the P.A., as usual. Workers wander to and fro, on their way to appointments with destiny or their boyfriends and girlfriends and wives and hubbies. The generators hum and the pellet-packers pack. Men crawl out of reinforced-concrete bunkers looking like they're returning from a place called Hell. Cars start as other workers decide it's time to give up and go home. I'm tempted to push my luck even further —to start walking without an escort and poke around some more, maybe strike up a conversation with Miss White about the hassles and hazards of packing wet explosives—but I don't have that much *chutzpah*, my balls aren't that big. A tiny voice inside tells me I could be shot.

I scribbled in my notebook very openly while the Clone and I were walking and talking, while he was introducing me to machinists and ladies behind steel counters—and now, in the parking lot, alone, after my guide has gone home, I continue to scribble very openly, and no one notices, no one stops to ask who I am or what I'm doing here or what I'm scribbling or whom I work for. I'm a paranoid spy, all right, a spy in the heart of the heartland, but I've got nothing to worry about.

I pause from this introspection to examine a piece of evidence that has been so close to my heart it has gone unnoticed: my I.D. badge. On the front, at the top, in fine print, it says: "Display this badge at all times while you're on the premises." Okay, I've done that. I've been a good boy.

> BOMCOM, INC.
> Best-Of
> Manufacturing,
> Inc.

```
V
 I
  S           NO
   I          ESCORT
    T         REQUIRED
   O
   R
```

There's even a little I.D. number at the bottom. It comes as no surprise to see ".006" in little black numbers.

On the back, it says:

This badge must be visibly displayed at all times while on company premises.
This badge is company property and must be surrendered to the Personnel Office upon termination of employment.
Should this badge be lost or mutilated, a replacement fee of $3.00 will be charged.
I hereby acknowledge and agree to abide by the above.

———————————

(Signature)

If found, please drop in any U.S. mailbox. Return postage guaranteed.

Everything is quieter now—most of the bosses and workers have gone home—but the generators, the holy and eternal generators, still hum.

I try one last time to look suspicious, but nothing happens. Then I try to look like I work here, and again nothing happens. Finally, after I've scribbled all my notes for this time around, I start my car and go back through the gates of wrath. I surrender my badge (but nothing else) to my blond, and head back the way I came.

I take one last look through the rearview mirror, and I see the gates are still open behind me. Ms. Tracy has not bothered to put back the cones. Why should she? It's Friday afternoon, right?

There is an Atlas moving van parked in the shade by the side of the road, just outside the perimeter. Waiting.

12

*Take This Job
and Shove It*

WESTERN WEAPONS FIREARMS DIVISION

INTERORIFICE

To: Dawn   Customer or Subject: IMP
Date: March 8, 1968

Per discussion with Bob Rightman today, the following items were resolved to determine the remaining work on the IMP contract:

1. Attempt to evolve a colored smoke (red-orange) formulation based on iron oxide derived from burned steel wool and a solid chlorine donor. Suggested start would involve use of paradichlorobenzene "mothproofing" crystals.
2. If a suitable solid chlorine donor can be found, formulate a screening smoke based on it and improvised aluminum powder.
3. Evaluate incendiary agents based on red lead (oxide) containing paint and powdered aluminum and/or improvised iron oxide.
4. Evolve a white phosphorous-loaded shot shell (.12 gauge). (See me before attempting this.)
5. Evolve a yellow flare based on KNO_3, aluminum, shellac and table salt or Na bicarbonate.
6. Check out sulfuric acid initiated incendiary systems.

Rightman was completely satisfied with our improvised thermite.

PS: Keep it wet. The powders I mean.

Barry Rothman

cc: S.D. Stodler

WESTERN WEAPONS FIREARMS DIVISION
INTEROFFICE

LONG RANGE R&D EFFORTS FOR
THE FIREARMS DIVISION

The need for area denial weapons has grown sharply since the inception of the war in Southeast Asia. A classic example of such weapons is the gravel mine, a simple tea-bag like affair that is armed by solvent evaporation and disarmed by chemical action. Millions of gravel mines have and are being used in Viet Nam. The use of gravel mines in Viet Nam has tipped our hand and a need exists for the development of a generation of new area denial weapons. Following are some ideas on the subject:

MINIATURE INCENDIARY MINE (MIMI):

It is presently conceived that MIMI would function in the following manner:

MIMI is a non-adherent plastic envelope about the size of a pack of book matches. The package is tough and capable of surviving an air drop. After release from the main munition housing, MIMI arms by dissolution of the outer envelope. This dissolution is accomplished by exposure to the atmosphere and/or chemical triggering by solvent evaporation. Ideally, the outer envelope decays to leave only a thin and very sticky film to cover the main filling of the mine. The main filling consists of white phosphorous dissolved in carbon disulfide. The latter liquid ignites on contact with the air and causes deep and painful burns. The sticky surface of the armed mine would enhance its generally disagreeable performance. It is also feasible that a micro MIMI could be built consisting of a small gelatin capsule size version. Either version could be made extremely inexpensively. A built-in disarming feature could be incorporated by secondary decay of the inner envelope.

CS ANTI-INTRUSION MINE:

A gravel-like mine with a CS-gas output could have considerable tactical application as an anti-intrusion warning device. A tea bag size mine that produced a visible cloud of CS gas would not only disrupt infiltration operations but could also provide a visible warning.

THIRD GENERATION GRAVEL MINE:

One of the major disadvantages of the current gravel mine is that it frequently contrasts with its environment and is easily detected. There is no universal camouflage that will mask the mine in such varied terrain as grassland, sand, rain forests, and mud. An intriguing way to overcome this problem would be to make a transparent gravel mine that automatically matched all environments. One possible way in which this might be achieved is by use of methyl nitrate, a water-clear and very powerful high explosive with a sensitivity equal to that of nitroglycerin. Jelled methyl nitrate could be used in place of the opaque-white RDX/lead azide combination currently used in gravel mines.

We have a number of ideas for other pyrotechnic and explosive munition systems that I believe may have major interest to the military. These are as follows:

1. NEW METHODS OF GENERATING COLORED SMOKE:

Colored smokes are the only effective daylight pyrotechnic signals. Colored smoke is generated by the pyrochemical heating of a volatile organic dyestuff. In this process the dye is melted, vaporized, and expelled into the atmosphere and recondensed in the form of a brilliantly colored particulate cloud. This system is remarkably inefficient, cumbersome and expensive. More than half the dye is lost in the combustion process, and colored smoke mixtures are notoriously difficult to blend and load. Much effort has been expended to improve the performance of colored smoke mixtures. Even a 15% increase in overall efficiency would be considered a major breakthrough. Feasibility studies can be made in several areas: These include pyrocatalysis of dyes and dye intermediates, inorganic smoke mixtures, and colored particle clouds generated by use of freon and/or other such materials.

2. SEA MINES:

To avoid slighting the Navy, we have some ideas for a new generation of sea mines. Our new mines could best be described by a code name like "Jelly Fish." This proposed family of devices is unique in many respects. For example: The mines are almost entirely transparent, are armed by an unconventional osmotic system, and are fuzed with all plastic hydrostatic liquid sensors.

3. LIQUID PYROTECHNICS:

Liquid pyrotechnic systems, usually based on low viscosity fluorocarbon and magnesium, already exist and are being explored for use in illuminating systems. Possibility of miniaturized long-duration liquid flares should be explored. Long-duration battlefield illuminating flares based on liquid systems could and would have considerable military interest.

4. PSYCHOACTIVE FLARES:

Bright lights flickering within a given range of frequencies will induce narcosis, epileptic seizures and, at the least, headaches and a rapid optical fatigue in human beings. It is conceivable that such effects can be achieved under battle conditions with blinking flares. Indeed, it may be possible to build flares with an order of brilliance that will penetrate even closed eyelids. Flares of this sort could be of considerable tactical benefit. Oscillation could be achieved by a multi-layer tabletting technique in the loading procedure.

WESTERN WEAPONS FIREARMS DIVISION
INTEROFFICE

To: Management   Customer or Subject:
Date: April 13, 1968   RESEARCH and DEVELOPMENT

It is necessary to sharpen the focus of both short and long range R&D goals.

For the past four years, we have labored under a crippling burden of unrealistic R&D sales requirements and, in many instances, misplaced emphasis. For almost three years our "laboratory" consisted of a 10x15 converted milk shed that lacked even the most rudimentary equipment. . . . It took this length of time to commit Management to the urgent need for at least basic facilities. Despite this sad picture, we managed to acquire and successfully perform four military and industrially sponsored research efforts, in addition to constant load of production engineering tasks.

I firmly believe that the future of this operation and, perhaps, that of the entire Firearms Division may rest on our efforts here. I also believe that research efforts should be devoted exclusively to the development of an advanced line of consumer orientated products. Although I cannot argue that considerable money is available for military R&D, and that we could (with major investment) build a profitable military-orientated facility, I feel that such attempts would be ultimately foolish. At best, the return on such investment in personnel, facilities, and sales effort would result in a constant "feast or famine" picture. The tides of gun sales are ebbing, both in the military and civilian markets; without diversification, Firearms Division faces a lean future.

It is time that management faces this problem directly and with decision. Specifically, I believe that we can concentrate R&D on commercial devices that will give us and the

Division the broad base of "razor blade" type consumer sales that will fill the projected loss in gun income. Several major changes, mostly in basic policy, are required to accomplish this:

1. Management must commit funds and thinking to a straightforward self-proposed concept. This is without the idea that we can have our cake and eat it too by paying for everything with outside funded work.

2. Management must face the fact that most, if not all, of the products developed here cannot be sold through Western's existing sales and distribution network. New systems must be devised. (The tie-in with Union Carbide on the organic insecticide device was a major step in the right direction.) A new sales force, whose umbilical cord is attached here, is imperative.

These are the two most urgent and difficult changes to be made. With such policies in effect I am certain that we can (1) generate a new product every year for (2) a modest research budget on the order of $50,000 to $75,000 per year. We will also need a few more people; a research assistant type and two additional technicians. With the exception of an office or two, I believe we can operate effectively in the lab space we currently have.

There is, I think, no point in reiterating the sundry commercial products that I have proposed in the past two memos or those already in the early stages of development.

A detailed milestone program awaits clarification of the above points. In the meantime, I shall pursue the organic insecticide development without derailment.

                                                    Barry Rothman

13

Black Widow

I have returned to get her side of their story.

We meet on a sunny afternoon on the same Main Street I haunted four years ago. We don't kiss, but we're not awkward either. We're cool, close, distant, and warm. Is there true affection in the way she says it's good to see me? I think so. I have been afraid that she would refuse to talk with me, but I should have known better. There is nobility in Dawn, too, even though an eavesdropper may never have guessed from the way she is trying to distill divine destiny down to a business transaction.

"Are you here on a mission or just for the day?"

"I'm definitely here on a mission. I'll be around for at least a few weeks."

It's obvious she's hoping I'm just passing through. Nothing personal, you understand. I get the feeling she has made an entirely new life for herself, a life I can know nothing about. She has worked very hard at burying the past, which she seems to have done admirably.

Most of our first conversation is informational: What do you know about his childhood? What books did he like to read? It's only when I ask about their courtship or his sexuality that a sense of innocence comes over her. There are moments when we both double over with laughter—full, easy laughter from the bottoms of our souls—and I think if he were here, he'd make some terrible comment about how you'd be able to see her blush if she didn't have such a nice tan. Sitting at this picnic table in the sun, our talk turns from light to dark with no warning.

"I'm learning to be cautious in my old age," she says, laughing, and a new kind of sorrow echoes behind that laugh. Dawn never used to be so cautious. What happened? Why start now? I realize this is going to be a tough one, possibly the toughest. How do I approach her? How do I ask her what he was like in bed? I have to lead her, take her by the hand. And she goes along, but stubbornly, kicking up dust every step of the way. It's a challenge, but, hell, I like challenges. Do you hear that, dad? I'm gonna get your story out of her if I have to pay for each raw gem with sweat and blood.

Only later, while driving home, do I realize she could very easily have changed her mind in the middle of the interview, could have closed the door.

I take the curves slowly, with caution. Scenes are reenacted. Their lives unfold before me like a very intimate home movie, a movie that is played out in every room of Hill House.

"I don't remember an awful lot of detail about his childhood, except that it was unhappy and underprivileged. Extremely lonely. He didn't have many friends, no one who was much like himself. They were all out there tryin' to make ends meet, survival type of thing. His mother left and he was literally tryin' to take care of his sisters by himself. It was a pretty run-down neighborhood.

"I think he got discovered taking care of the house by himself when he was caught stealing food. He knew where his father was, but he was bound and determined not to contact him for help. I don't remember him sayin' much about that. Only that he was really resentful that his father left, he was very bitter about that. He felt his mother *had* to leave, but I don't know why. I'm sure he knew the reason prior to her leaving. When she finally left, he was just determined not to have to say to his father, 'Hey, you know, I need you,' or, 'We're in bad shape.'

"The resentment carried over when Martin discovered their living situation. Martin took the daughters, but Barry wanted to be on his own, so he didn't go live with his father. I think he had a bed there and tried it, but he was mostly back into the street. Workin' odd jobs, hangin' out at different places, helpin' out. They really never could get together. His father still thought of him as a kid, and Barry thought of himself as a more than capable adult. Martin wanted to restrain him and pass judgment on how Barry thought and did things. I can remember him sayin' he built some rockets and stuff in his father's house, but it didn't last long.

"Madeline was his first sexual experience. Housekeeper, black housekeeper, I do believe. That was when he was living with Martin. Martin was working and hadn't remarried yet, so he hired Madeline to keep house. I suppose she kept house pretty well, because Martin discovered Barry and Madeline in bed. That put an end to Madeline.

"Prior to that, he had not had much luck at love, so to speak. That was his eye-opener. It was pretty thorough from what I can tell. If you gotta go the first time, why not go all the way? Ah, him and Madeline. According to him, everybody should have a Madeline at least once in his life. For the first time anyhow. Oh, I think anytime.

"There were bathroom scenes, you name it. She literally seduced him. He said it started with little subtle things like her touching him, helpin' him on with his clothes and he was already an old kid, remember. Walking into the bathroom without knocking, stuff like that. It really didn't dawn on him right away. She literally had to lay hands on him before it hit him. I think he was in shock before he realized what was goin' on. I think she really flat-out seduced him. And that was the end of that. His innocence, I mean.

"I don't think he was ever stymied after that. He just figures she's just a lustful, dirty old woman. It's all right with him. That's all. And I wouldn't think anything more of it either. Why would any grown woman wanna seduce a scrawny kid like that? Circumstances. He was there and she was . . . probably . . . a plain dirty old woman! Period!

"When his father found out, they had pretty harsh words. Everything just came to a head. All the stuff that was touch-and-go came crashing down on both of them, and that's when he left. Martin really raised holy hell.

"When Martin remarried, his second wife tried to bring them

back together, but it never worked. That's when the household became more of a family, probably more than it had for a long time, and Barry felt excluded from that atmosphere. Which is reasonable. His sisters were much younger. They were thought of as victims, and even though Barry took care of them, he wasn't as victimized as much as they. At least his father didn't think so. His sisters had to be protected. He wasn't so young. Especially after Madeline. I'm sure Martin laid some of his own guilt on Barry just to keep him at a distance.

"The fireworks was always there. Always building bombs. Always. He was doin' it when he was very little and playin' in the back alley. Somebody'd find some caps or take some fireworks apart. I suspect it progressed to guns when he went to work for the Institute, because then he was workin' with bigger things than caps and little firecrackers. There were a lot of explosives and devices. So whatever interest he had in fireworks matured after he graduated to the Institute.

"When he left his father's, he had to find a real job, so to speak, and that's when he went to the Institute. If he didn't go there right away, it was pretty soon after, because he was still very young when he started there. His youth had a lot to do with getting caught up with the romance of making devices. . . . I know he felt very romantic about all that. He felt a lot of things later, but initially it was very romantic for him.

"I don't know anything about possible CIA connections. To this day I don't know how much of that was real. *I do not know.* I'm not absolutely certain that any of it was real. When kids are in high school, they're often approached by the CIA, but whether he accepted that challenge, I don't know.

"If Barry was ever involved with the CIA, I suspect it was between the ages of fifteen and eighteen. I'm not certain about any later contacts either. Later in our marriage he talked about CIA involvement, but I'm not certain he wasn't pulling on a memory of having been approached by them as a kid. Later on in years he really went back to that same romantic flavor of things. And whether the CIA was used to enhance that romance, I don't know.

"I'm sure he met some characters at the Institute who had lots of involvement, 'cause they worked on some real heavy-duty stuff.

That could have supplied fuel for his stories that came out later on, because I'm certain he worked with people that were in the CIA, or at least did things for them. I better not say that, you're tapin' this damn thing, I keep forgettin'. I don't care. I've learned to be very cautious in my old age.

"I don't know much about his life during the early Sixties. That was before I met him at Western Weapons. I know he and Baskum Slokum got together on the tear-gas pengun. One would think they were a partnership, but they were not. Barry worked for Baskum. I know this for a fact, because I've had contact with Baskum's company for other reasons. Barry worked for Baskum on the pengun in the lab. He was more or less instrumental in its development. Baskum was the businessman, the moneyman, and Barry was the lab tech.

"When Barry broke from that company, he felt bitter about having been taken advantage of. And he may have been used, but no more used than any other employee with that kind of talent. I don't know if he got paid correctly for what he did. But that's all he was. A lab tech. Barry felt he was getting screwed when Baskum got a patent on it and his company was growing because of it. Baskum didn't want to give him a share of the company, because he didn't feel he had to. So Barry decided to go some-place else. That's when he sold himself and a few new ideas to Western Weapons.

"Baskum's company is still marketing the tear-gas pengun. Indeed. Oh, extremely well. They're a multimillion-dollar com-pany. They not only make tear-gas guns, but they make a number of items. Baskum is no longer the full owner, but he's the president of the board of directors. He has a major controlling interest in the company, a very successful company. Big line, big factory. It's a small business, but it's a very successful small business. They just built a new facility—big, beautiful facility. They're making archery equipment and a gun kit for collectors to put together themselves. Centennial models, flintlock replicas, head-gear for hunters, a whole complete hunting line, gun-cleaning kits, rifle-cleaning kits, rifles, targets—you name anything that has to do with the gun industry and they're selling it.

"You see, they were substantial even before Barry worked for them. So because he boosted one product doesn't mean he should

have become a partner. He didn't put any money into the business. He put some talent into it, but that was only one of several
products they were developing at the time.

"I think it was a time when he was addicted to drugs. A very
heavy user, very heavy drinker. That was of course prior to my
knowing him. In fact, he could have exaggerated that whole era
just to dramatize the trauma he had gone through, because when
I first met him there were syringes all over his apartment. I knew
they hadn't been used for a long time, but it was a curious thing.
I didn't think drugs at all and he told me he was a diabetic. Don't
look at me like that! That's what he told me. He might have kept
the accouterments just to pretend he was a drug addict, as weird
as he was.

"But that period really is vague to me. He told me he had
experimented with LSD and still had flashbacks. That was a
couple years after we met. He'd do one of these numbers and
say that's still a leftover from his drug period. Big D for Drug. I
really can't confirm anything. There was no solid indication to
me that he'd been heavily involved in drugs. He may have gone
through a stretch where he was very unhappy, like when he and
your mother broke up, and he could've been drinkin' with the
gang who went out for lunch and had their martinis. He coulda
tried an upper or a downer and considered himself a drug addict
just to accentuate that period, The Traumatic Period in Barry's
Life.

"It was such a horrendous thing. He never did anything normal.
A lot of people go through divorces, a lot of people go through
unhappy times in their jobs, a lot of people are depressed, but
Barry could never be just that. It hadda be something horrendous,
no matter what it was. Earth-shattering. It hadda be more than
just your average everyday human type of thing. Hadda be
superhuman. God only knows.

"When we met, I was very innocent. I was applying for a job
at Western Weapons and he had all the aura about him that
anybody who meets Barry Rothman sees. He was gonna conquer
the world and do all these fantastic things, in spite of the
horrendous odds he had overcome. Only his brilliance was gonna
save the day—and anybody who came along with him. Such an
intricate, involved, intelligent person—curious, creative, inven-

tive, all those things. You can extrapolate from anybody who ever met and talked to Barry and put 'em all together. . . . I was no different, I saw all those things, too. That's the image he created for himself right after the Institute period. It was almost like a creation. Of his own.

"Western Weapons was his first taste of what could have been a success. He'd never been in touch with that. He really did believe a lot of good things were gonna happen. That was a turning point in his life. I can remember hilarious letters he was writing to his creditors: 'I only have one crocodile left, so if you want to come and get it . . .' It was only a matter of time before his ship was coming in, and he was gonna bring all his little brothers and sisters along.

"He had his first private secretary. It took me a long time to realize that he hadn't had anything like that before. So he was really takin' a chance and was really gonna jump into it, and he did.

"Western is a big red-tape, gray-flannel-suit company, so naturally they'd have zillions of meetings. They weren't about to come down here, so naturally they'd fly him up to their meetings. It was really a big deal for him to have to hop on a plane to Canada and New York City and Providence. That was really a charge for him. But, see, like everythin' else he did, he let that whole thing get carried away into a fantasy. He romanticized it so much that he lost track of the reality. It took several years, but that's what happened. He started neglecting what he should have been doing and playing a damn role, and that was his downfall.

"Who tries to sell a new product the way he did? You try to get it *on* the assembly line, not *off* it. He didn't even do the feasibility studies. He didn't push enough out the door to see if Western was totally sold on a new idea before he embarked on a new project. All that Western had to know was that an idea could work and that this little branch of the company, directed by Barry Rothman, could be manned by this local group and it could make some money for them. He didn't give it enough of a chance because it didn't get that far. He was so busy buying new Pontiacs and having them fitted with radio telephones and shit like that . . . sunglasses and shaving his head bald . . . I'm tellin' you, he played it to the hilt!

"He had his secretary come to his house for this or that, cartin' her around takin' notes on nothin'. He was playin' a game. I'm not kiddin'. Anything he did had to be dramatic.

"Bob Rightman was doin' a lot of the work. Workin' his butt off while Barry played the game. That's when the Bob and Barry team started disintegrating, because Bob was always the little brother. Bob did a lot of the engineering, paid attention to the details. He did the personnel work, tried to set up the factory while Barry was experimenting, tryin' to make his product better and tryin' to duplicate reports and doin' what a lab tech should do. Barry was playin' more like, 'I'm the owner, I'm the president of this world and I wear the dark glasses and shave my head bald and have the car with the . . .' All that shit.

"Bob did his part, too. He bought his first fast car while he was at Western. No wonder. They had their first taste of money. I don't blame 'em for buying all the things they bought and playin' all those games. But they didn't protect their interests. Certainly Barry didn't protect his, although Bob did quite a bit more. He was smarter. He was much smarter.

"Bob became resentful 'cause Barry would sit in his office and get nothing done and neither would his staff, while Bob was workin' his butt off. . . . Barry started taking off from work. He wouldn't come in for three or four days and couldn't care less about it. Took off for trips without any notice. Spent money like crazy.

"And then, to reinforce that, he had his first heart attack. Boy, that just told him he had to be more reckless, there's only so much time left. He felt his mortality, probably for the first time. He just knew he was gonna die. He was scared shitless. Just plain scared. I've never seen a person so afraid and preoccupied with death as that day he had the first heart attack. *Scared to death!* 'Sixty-three? No, you're right, it was '68 when he had that heart attack. We were goin' together. That's when he wanted to get married *right away.* He wanted to get married *in the hospital.* I'm not kiddin'! Stop makin' me laugh!

"We waited till he'd been out of the hospital two weeks. I found Hill House when he was in the hospital, because he didn't want to go back to the house he'd been living in. That was a complicated situation, too. Well, not that complicated, but it was definitely a messy situation. . . .

"The local police chief was his friend and helped him find the house he lived in while he worked at Western. The chief had a girlfriend who lived with her family, and she wanted them to live upstairs. So they both moved in. Two weeks later, Barry's screwin' the whole family. She was gettin' more demanding, and her kids . . . the whole works was getting sticky. So he didn't want to return to that after having a heart attack at thirty-three. Which I did not know about at the time, incidentally. I think the chief knew. That's what was worryin' Barry.

"I never did understand. I just figured he wanted to have some place of his own and be settled and all that bullshit. All I knew was that he didn't want to go back there, so he had me and a couple real-estate agents looking for a place while he was in the hospital. He was adamant about it.

"So I found a place for him. And mind you, on no money. He always did miraculously incredible things. One of them was to procure money whenever he needed it. Of course I didn't realize what his financial situation was. I didn't know if he had money or what. I just figured he had enough to do whatever he wanted to do, and if he didn't have any money and wanted the house, that was okay, too. Because he had the wherewithal to do something about it.

"But I found a house for no money. It was a lease-purchase. The minimal amount of money down. I had a couple hundred bucks and he had three or four hundred. That's what we gave 'em for a down payment and that's where Hill House came from. X number of years we'd have to make settlement, but his ship was coming in. So within the next few years, when the ship arrived, there'd be plenty to make settlement, so it wasn't a concern.

"Between the two of us, we were making a damn good salary. After we got married, we figured we'd have plenty, so I wasn't bothered about the financial obligations of getting married and buying a house at the same time. But it didn't quite turn out that way. Not long after that, we both left Western. He hadn't saved any money, so there wasn't anything to fall back on. But he kept gettin' things for nothin'. He just kept getting things anyhow. He had credit, and people would let him get away with spending money without having any . . . it was just horrendous. I never understood how people let him do that. But he was a good sales-man and he was believable. That *image*. He still had that aura about him. And then the rest is history. You know about the rest. That sort of fills in the gaps, doesn't it?"

She tries to get up and force an end to the interview, but I persist with more questions. Fortunately, she relents.

"Our courtship was extremely whirlwind-romantic. He played the sugar daddy to the hilt. He told me stories of far off which I had no reason to disbelieve, and with the guy's surroundings one would tend to believe him. He had all kinds of weird things and knew all kinds of weird people who did things that were alien and interesting to me, and that's basically what it was. He'd tell me about some of the sad times in his life and make me feel like I was the best thing that ever happened to him. So I felt I had a part of his life and was needed and I fulfilled something for him as well as his being able to fulfill something for me. It was a mutually satisfying relationship when it started. I don't think he was ever able *not* to be that sugar daddy. Not only to me, but to anybody.

"Initially I thought we had both created a situation that became difficult for him, but then I realized he wanted to be the sugar daddy and he wanted me to be the dependent woman. He wanted to be the smartest one, he wanted to be the one to provide, to make the decisions, and he just wanted an attractive, quiet, unassuming woman for a wife, to look up to him for all the answers. He didn't want the woman to say, 'Hey, hell, we're in debt, let's go out and work and make some money and let's save and let's . . .' None of that. Not even with his closest friends. If I wanted to have a small gathering with intimate friends, he wanted to have a bash, and we'd have a bash. It's the same way with his life all the way down the line.

"His clothing was part of the game-playing. I call it his costume. He'd dress up in a black suit, gangsterlike. The white tie and dark suit. He got away from that later on. Started being jazzy.

Remember that stage? Started being a little less dramatic. But always the black boots, black belt, black pants. He had a ton of black pants. That was the Gable look. Mysterious! Dark glasses, the flip-up shades. The mysterious look, with the black car with the black interior with the black shotgun that he had a little post built for in the center of the car . . . the black radio.

"That was another weird thing. I shoulda gotten the hint right there. But you see, he always used to tell me he was goin' somewhere, always on a mission, his whole life was a mission. It's hard to find somebody runnin' around with a shotgun mounted in the center of their car. Guys in the KKK aren't that obvious. With all that regalia on. When you think of it, it *is* pretty tough! You could go out on Highway Eleven with a roadblock and you'd be hard pressed to flag a car down and find someone inside like that.

"See, I had to be nuts to believe all that shit, too. God. Pit vipers in your kitchen. Course that's not as totally weird as the rest, but it fit, it just fit. The whole damn thing fit. The vipers added to all the mystique about him that everybody loved. Everybody loved Barry. Of course you could get away with that more in the Sixties than you could in the Seventies. He was really running out of ammunition. It started getting hard for him to beat everybody else gettin' so weird.

"The mission was whatever was going on in his head. I think he was doin' a lot of stuff which I knew nothing about. He deliberately did not tell me and I never really questioned it. Never questioned it. At all. But I had no idea what that was. Coulda been sellin' guns. Coulda been . . . coulda been makin' devices. I don't know.

"An FBI agent came to the house one day. Barry was as surprised as I was. He had some guns in the trunk of his car and wanted to know if Barry wanted to buy them. They were illegal guns. I think it was a setup. It's the only time I can remember his having any contact with the FBI. The guy literally identified himself. Isn't that weird?"

She's getting into her car, and suddenly she calls me back and says there is one more thing she remembers that might be of use to me. It's the first time she has offered a piece of the puzzle without my having to ask, and I assume it will be the last. It's a short story about one of his last con jobs, when he deceived a local town council into fronting him the money for a Bicentennial fireworks display six months before the Bicentennial—just a week or two before he died. I had already heard of one scam that cost a modest burg several thousand dollars and the fireworks display of a lifetime. I didn't know there was *another* Bicentennial pyroscam.

"Yeah," she says, chuckling into her knuckles. "I found out about it the other day. Overheard it somewhere, or somebody called and told me. There's only one person on this planet coulda pulled *two* jobs like that. Your father. I'll tell ya, the eternal fireworks display."

Since she appears to be in such a generous mood, I ask if she still has a copy of *The Devil's Diary*, and if so, could I borrow it for research purposes? I ask for the hell of it, just to see if she kept it as a souvenir, because I recall seeing it on a bookshelf in their bedroom several years back.

"I looked for it before I came down here today, but I couldn't find it. Whether it got lost or thrown out, I don't know. But I feel kinda bad about it, 'cause I'd like to have it around for my own sake, too."

"Yeah, right. Never know when you might need it."

"Well, these things have a way of coming back to haunt me."

PLAYBOY INTERVIEW

PLAYBOY: That must be taking us close to the end of that type of work for you.

MR. DEATH: Yes. There was one last major job that was a very rush program for a barometrically operated bomb that released cyanide gas, rather than exploding. It was to be very small, "as small as practical to wipe out a commercial-size airliner"—that's a quote from my contact. The emphasis was that it be something they wouldn't discover after the plane crashed. So I built one into a domestically available aerosol deodorant can, with a barometric switch, two batteries, a miniature blasting cap that

shattered an ampule of [deleted] in a casing of [deleted]. I delivered two of those and they had asked specifically that the
deodorant cans be from domestic sources. They were set to go
off at five thousand feet and I have no idea what they did with
them.

PLAYBOY: You say that was your last job. What made you decide
to stop working for the agency?

MR. DEATH: I have not touched on the fact that things were
changing with me psychologically. The real change was initiated
when I started with the firearms company. First of all, I had met
and fallen in love with [deleted], my lab assistant, and we got
married. And I really didn't want to make any more weapons.
Although I was originally enchanted by the James Bond *macho*
trip, it had worn out and I was much more interested in living
than I was in building things to kill people, including myself.
I don't believe I mentioned, either, that I have very nearly
blown myself away a few times.

PLAYBOY: Did you ever find yourself getting paranoid, thinking
that maybe it wasn't an accident?

MR. DEATH: Of course, but you have to watch yourself or you'll
go crazy. The one time I was really suspicious was when I developed a miniature white-phosphorus grenade. It was loaded
with powdered aluminum to give the fireball a better spread.
Nifty little thing. Anyway, I ordered some six-second grenade
fuses. A case came over labeled as if it contained six-second
fuses. I screwed one in, pulled the pin, and—whomp!—it was a
one-quarter-second fuse and it blew me away. I was in the hospital for a very long time. The thing that saved my life was the
fact that, because it was experimental, I had put too much aluminum in the mixture, which made the white phosphorus disappear and not stick to me.

PLAYBOY: Then you think someone was trying to tell you something?

MR. DEATH: No, not really. But it has made me wonder. Anyway, I had begun to resist fiercely any of the military R and D
the firearms people wanted. But I couldn't talk that kind of sense
to them.

PLAYBOY: What was their response?

MR. DEATH: There was all kinds of chickenshit pressure.

PLAYBOY: Was that pressure from the firearms company or the CIA?

MR. DEATH: The CIA had said nothing at that point. But in the firearms company, some of the key people from the main office were absolute wretches. Anyway, I had been worn down physically and emotionally to the point where something had to give, and that's when I had a heart attack. Then they tooled me off to the hospital and plugged me into the EKG and a few other things and said, "Man, it is an acute myocardial infarction." I was not very old, and there I was, wondering when the next blip was going to come. The chest pain was terrible, like somebody stabbing me with an icepick. It's steady, relentless.

PLAYBOY: When you recovered, did you return to work?

MR. DEATH: Correct. I hung around, but a year later, almost to the day, I had a second heart attack. I had started an exercise program and used to jog every morning, which, quite frankly, was overkill. One morning, it was just too much, and zap. Three months later, I went back to work, but with the express purpose of quitting. I had been out of work for so long they were just glad to see me leave. I think it was no more than a few days after I had officially separated that there was a phone call at home and I met one of the CIA contacts. And he was just supposedly inquiring about my health. But he was also obviously inquiring about my social life. You know, very oblique, casual references, but it was unusual. "How are things going at home?" I mean, that question was never asked. There was some vague probe: Had I made new friends? Meaning new radical friends. I'm pretty sure that I made some kind of sarcastic remark, "Yes, and they're all Weathermen." It was obvious to me that he was concerned. So I said, "Look, I've had two heart attacks. That's enough, and I'm kind of revising my whole life-style." I just didn't want to do any more weapons work. From the change of expression, it was apparent that he wasn't very happy with that statement. That's when questions started to come up about political feelings, which they would never have discussed before. They were paranoid: If you ain't with us, you're against us. And he did ask me if I had kept a copy of the *Diary*, which was reasonably indicative of what he was thinking. I told him, "No, and I'm not involved with anybody and don't intend to be." My wife and I managed to coast for a while and I got involved in all kinds of endeavors, consulting work, and so on. We made ends meet.

PLAYBOY: Did they leave you alone then?

MR. DEATH: Not by any means. I know that I was followed. There was always a pickup car as I turned out of our street, no matter what time of day I left. There was one guy I began to recognize, who looked like Slim Pickens. The phones were also tapped. I would call somebody: "Fred, I'll be leaving at such and such a time," and, sure enough, there would be a pickup car out on my route. I started addressing friends as "Comrades" and other sophomoric things, just to relieve the tension. Well, then I started bumping into CIA guys in very peculiar places, like little restaurants that nobody ever went to. It was deliberate, to let me know they were watching. They were so obvious. Clever little oblique questions like, "Hey, did you ever walk off with any machine guns before you quit?" I think that I probably aggravated the situation by responding with what I considered to be humor. Statements like, "No, I'm too busy preparing botulismus R strain for radicals," or some other nasty thing.

PLAYBOY: What was the last meeting?

MR. DEATH: The last confrontation that I had was when my wife noticed she was being followed. That was the first time she realized that somebody was behind her all the time and it frightened her. That did it. I made a phone call and set up a meeting with two CIA types at the [deleted], a pleasant, quiet restaurant. I walked in and sat down. They ordered drinks and asked if I wanted one. I said, "No, thank you, I just came here to make a statement, which is this: Very briefly—if you continue to fuck with my life, if you continue to keep me under surveillance and act as if I'm involved in some kind of political bullshit, particularly now that you've involved my family in it, I'm telling you right here and now that I will detonate a canister of VX in the central-air-conditioning system in Langley," I said. "If anything unusual happens to me or my family, I have arranged to do this and it will be done." And I got up and walked out.

PLAYBOY: Were you bluffing?

MR. DEATH: No, I was not. I worked with biochemical warfare

long enough to be able to make that threat very real. They were well aware of what I had done *for* them, so they knew damn well what I could do *to* them. So at this point, it's kind of a Mexican standoff, if you will.

PLAYBOY: Are they still after you in some way?

MR. DEATH: My impression is that they've dropped it, at least from within the CIA. I don't think they've completely given it up in other ways.

PLAYBOY: What are your plans, now that you're out of weapons design?

MR. DEATH: I've started working on designing toys. I have patents and some backers and hope to be bringing out some toys soon, with any luck.

PLAYBOY: Doesn't that strike you as odd, working for so long designing assassination devices and then switching to making toys?

MR. DEATH: All my life, I've liked to fool with things. I'm just doing it now in a way that will entertain people instead of kill them.

14

Freedom of Misinformation

Dear Mr. Rothman: 24 Apr 1980

This is in response to your request for information which may be held by this Agency concerning your father, the late Barry Rothman. We regret our delay in responding, but we still have a very large backlog and have only just reached your request in the queue.

Our file search has produced the documents listed below. They have been reviewed and are released to you in sanitized form, with the exception of the last two items, which have been found not releasable. All deletions have been made in accordance with exemption (B) (3) of the Freedom of Information Act. Please see the accompanying sheet for an explanation of this exemption.

The documents are:

1. Form 644, 3 February 1964.
2. Form 864, 5 April 1965.
3. Form 1024a, 3 May 1965.
4. Form 237, 14 May 1965.
5. Form 1024a, 5 May 1965.
6. Form 1230, 10 May 1965.
7. Memorandum for the Record, 5 April 1965.

The following are not releasable:

8. Form 1841, 27 January 1964.
9. Form 1841, 5 April 1965.

Please be assured that the only substantive information concerning your father in documents 8 and 9 is his name, address, and date and place of birth.

In addition to the foregoing Agency material, we have found reference to other material in which your father's name appears which originated with the Federal Bureau of Investigation. This has been drawn to the attention of the Bureau for review and direct response to you.

The deciding officers in this case were Mr. Warren Priestley, Chief of the Information Review Group, Office of Security (documents 1–7), and Mr. Dan King, Executive Officer, Office of Logistics (documents 8–9). Under the provisions of the Act, I am advising you of your right to appeal their decisions, through me, to the CIA Information Review Committee.

Sincerely,

Charles E. Savige
Acting Information and
Privacy Coordinator

Enclosures

Everything has been ickied out with black Magic Marker.

Dear Mr. Rothman: May 12, 1980

This is in response to your letter of September 19, 1979, to the CIA requesting records concerning Barry Rothman. The CIA on April 15, 1980, forwarded a copy of your letter and three FBI-originated documents.

We have reviewed these documents and determined that deletions be made pursuant to Title 5, United States Code, Section 552:

(b) (7) investigatory records compiled for law enforcement purposes, the disclosure of which would:

    (c) constitute an unwarranted invasion of the personal privacy of another person

    (d) reveal the identity of an individual who has furnished information to the FBI under confidential circumstances or reveal information furnished only by such a person and not apparently known to the public or otherwise accessible to the FBI by overt means

The CIA has requested that certain information be excised from document ten pursuant to Title 5, United States Code, Section 552:

(b) (3) information specifically exempted from disclosure by statute (National Security Act of 1947 and the CIA Act of 1949)

If you so desire, you may appeal to the Associate Attorney General from any denial contained herein. Appeals should be directed in writing to the Associate Attorney General (Attention: Office of Privacy Information Appeals), United States Department of Justice, Washington, D.C. 20530, within thirty days from receipt of this letter. The envelope and the appeal should be clearly marked "Freedom of Information Appeal" or "Information Appeal." Please cite the FOIA number assigned to your request so that it may be easily identified.

                Sincerely Yours,

                David G. Flanders, Chief
                Freedom of Information-
                    Privacy Acts Branch
                Records Management Division

Enclosures

UNITED STATES DEPARTMENT OF JUSTICE
FEDERAL BUREAU OF INVESTIGATION
BOSTON, MASSACHUSETTS
MARCH 2, 1967

BARRY ROTHMAN, also known as
Martin Rothman

(DELETED), employed by Western Weapons, Inc., of (DELETED), Mass., as an (DELETED) has provided information to the Boston Office of the FBI to the effect that Rothman, manager and Director of Operations and Research, Western Weapons, Inc., (DELETED), Mass., deliberately ordered quantities of explosives from Aberdeen Proving Ground, Md., in excess of that required for certain tests conducted by Western Weapons, Inc. He stated that on December 1, 1966, he was instructed by Rothman to place 36 demolition blocks, M5–A1, in Rothman's car, that he did so, and that Rothman intended to trade the explosives for a Russian DP38 7.62 mm machine gun. (DELETED) advised that Rothman has a carbine in his car and is armed with a revolver.

(DELETED) further advised that in November 1966, he assisted (DELETED) in the loading of 90 pounds of composition C–4, U.S. Government property which was being used in a U.S. Government project, into Rothman's personal automobile. (DELETED) mentioned to (DELETED) several days later that he had reported Rothman's taking of the explosive to the FBI. (DELETED) stated that about two weeks later the explosive was returned by Rothman, apparently the same material in the same quantity, and was unloaded by (DELETED) and (DELETED). (DELETED) knew of no U.S. Government property missing or stolen from Western Weapons, (DELETED), Mass. He volunteered that (DELETED) has insinuated several times he has worked with the CIA but has never been shown any CIA identification by (DELETED). (DELETED) has mentioned he worked

with the CIA at the time of the Bay of Pigs incident in
Cuba. When (DELETED) asked for details (DELETED)
refused to elaborate. He further stated (DELETED) for
a period of time, was also driving his automobile around
with the letters "CIA" on the trunk.

On February 23, 1967, (DELETED) again contacted this
office and stated that a man, driving a 1967 Buick Riviera,
Massachusetts License AK–47, stole an undetermined
amount of C–4 and headed in the direction of
(DELETED), Mass. (DELETED) became incoherent
upon being asked for details and subsequently stated he
was being intimidated and that his life had been threatened. Massachusetts License AK–47 is listed to Barry
Rothman for a 1967 Buick Riviera.

Information has previously been furnished to the Boston
Office of the FBI to the effect that (DELETED).

This document contains neither recommendations nor
conclusions of the FBI. It is the property of the FBI and
is loaned to your agency; it and its contents are not to be
distributed outside your agency.

15

Soul Brothers

How can I do Ian O'Hennessey an injustice? He's short and
dumpy. He's quick with his hands, eyes, feet, and tongue—not
in that order—even though he's pushing sixty. It's easy to see
how he has made a career of entertaining roomfuls of deadheads.
For the past few decades he's been teaching English Lit. at a
small liberal-arts college in a suburb of Boston. He has made
excellent use of such close proximity to our greatest natural re-
source: He was my father's pimp, or "bird dog," for the last ten
years of my father's life. He was recently chosen to teach a
black-literature course. The black students actually chose him
over a black professor that the administration offered. His explanation: "I talk nigger better than anybody in this town,
including the blacks."

We met when I was ten or twelve. It must have been one of
those Fourths of July, the holiest of my childhood holy days. It
was probably on a slow July afternoon when all sorts of people
were wandering in and out of Hill House. People bringing fireworks, buying fireworks, stealing fireworks, putting fireworks
together, trading fireworks, sneaking out to the woods with fireworks and a few of my father's Marlboros to light them and
smoke on the way. People, young and old, like me, trying to
get into the action, trying to belong to the First Family of
Fireworks.

I was serious the way only young people can be serious. I
would not hesitate to discourse at length about the end of the

world, overpopulation and how to stop it, the staggering crime rate, how many assassinations were yet to come. I spoke on these subjects with a passion that only young people and the truly mad will dare. I made no connection between what part or parts my own father may have played in these apocalyptic arenas. If I had made the connection, my father would have loved it. He would have been proud.

Who knows how many of my father's "devices" fulfilled their destinies? Is there any way of counting? Who knows how many of his minimines screamed beneath bare Asian and South American feet? Who knows how large a piece of the pie belonged to my very own father?

I liked O'Hennessey and he liked me. We've kept in touch over the years. When I published my first article in *Oui* on the possibility of nuclear terrorism, he wrote: "It has the same crack-of-doom feeling as your father's articles might have had . . . if he had ever gotten around to reading and writing articles instead of just looking at the hot pix."

When I was living at Hill House after my father's death, we fell right in together. I didn't know it then, but he was working very hard to hold on to any shred of the ghost that left us behind, and of course I was the best manifestation of that ghost. I didn't know then what he was after, because I was after the same thing. The only difference would have been that I could not have admitted it as easily as he did.

Half my life ago, when I was already very concerned about the end of civilization as we know it, Ian was funny in a way that alarmed me. It was easy for him to crack jokes in front of strangers, a talent I admire and have had to work to cultivate. He told me later it's his way of seeing if this new person is alive.

I was alive but withdrawn—pathologically shy would be more like it—so I rarely responded to his barbs. But Ian had faith in me because I was Barry's son—not because of any apparent gifts of my own, but simply because I sprang from those same genes. That was years ago, when I was a kid, but Ian is still back there, locked in that time, clutching whatever passion is left, seeing me as my father's son and little else.

When I called to ask if he'd like to invite me over to do some interviews, he asked if I had any preference.

"What kind of preference?"

"Blond, brown, or red. Your father always liked browns and blondes, in that order. Almost never a red, except maybe one . . ."

"No, thanks," I said as politely as possible. "That's not exactly what I had in mind."

"I figured if the son of Barry was coming to town, I might as well make sure he came."

Welllllll, on second thought . . . but as soon as I seriously considered his offer, he was off and running about how easy it would be to set up a threesome. That was a bit too much. I wasn't willing to go *that* far into my research. He backed out by saying he understood that was a very personal decision, but I got the feeling he had very little understanding of how personal it really was.

He quickly changed the subject.

"You're probably armed with the same equipment, huh? Well, are you?"

We can't talk on Saturday or Sunday nights because those are family nights. Kids need things fixed, dinner is often late (when is it ever on time?), never know if something good'll be on TV. Basically, those are nights when everybody has a piece of his time, so we should aim for weeknights, after the kids are asleep and the house has settled down.

"Single guys just don't understand it," he says. I agree. "I love kids—don't get me wrong—but sometimes I'd just like some time to do things for myself. Or do nothing at all. Or stare at a wall."

His frustration must have turned to rage a long time ago, and it comes out and out during our interviews and I get it all on tape.

He says more than once that he's a fish, he'll believe anything as long as it sounds good. He also says, more than once, that my father was a snake.

The metaphor is apt. Fish are born and grow up and reproduce and die in schools. Most fish live in shallow waters. Some seas are miles deep, so most of the earth's fishes are found in surface waters. They only go for certain kinds of bait, but when they do, they often take it hook, line, and sinker. Often the only way to save a hooked fish is to rip out its guts and hope for the best. At least you get the hook back.

After our last interview, he drives me home. Before getting out of his car, I say, "Nobody knows where I live, right?"

"Have I heard those words before? Where have I heard those exact words before? *Nobody knows where I live, right?*"

I try to explain that this time it's for real, the generation gap is closing fast, but it's hopeless. Absolutely hopeless. I am my father's son, a trap I can't escape, at least in his eyes.

"Now I'm beginning to sound like him," he says, sighing. "I'm exhausted. Only I did physical labor today. That sucker never lifted a finger. Except to move that incredible equipment."

His Games
(WITH MONEY)

"Like so many intellectuals, when he would get immersed in a project, mundane things like money would not matter. He didn't care how he got it. Barry was like a compulsive gambler. Money doesn't mean anything to a gambler. It's the action that matters. He would have sold his mother to get five hundred dollars on the roll of the dice and lose it. It didn't matter where the money came from, as long as it came in large bundles.

"And the timelessness, the fact that there was a great deal of haste. He didn't do long-term things. He was leasing his house, for God's sakes. Barry had no concept of building equity for a long-term project. That's why money would come and go and he'd spend it suddenly on a toy, on something that fascinated him like a kid. He had no concept of investing, of building something —like investing in a good car and keeping it clean because the resale value . . . no, the car was a useful tool at the moment. Even though, by abusing it, it was gonna cost him money. But that was later. Always later.

"When I met him, he told me his income was forty-five

thousand. When he moved out here and set up his rock shop, the Crystal Balls, that's when he lost his job at Western Weapons, because he was out there three or four days a week when he should have been working for the spooks. That's when Dawn quit working at Western and started working in the rock shop. Their ideal situation was Dawn would run the rock shop and Barry would work with Western and they'd bring in tons of money, 'cause they were still working on their mail-order business, too, which was really hummin'.

"But their lives were chaotic . . . Barry's 'office' was filled with debris and rubble, but somehow he knew where everything was and he'd package up a rock and mail it out, always attaching some handwrit, witty note. That impressed his clients. He had very faithful clients and he was supplied by some shady character I never met who had a bizarre name, a strange name, who would smuggle the stuff in and carry heavy stones. He eventually got killed. We're pretty sure he got wiped out, somebody knocked him over. He drove an old car and was very inconspicuous, but apparently somebody found out he was carrying heavy stuff.

"Barry always had money, he could peel off a twenty . . . he loved to whip out a roll of bills. I was never quite sure where they came from. But he loved to have 'em.

"See, money was the problem. He should have had lots of money. However, he might not have lasted as long as he did if he had had bundles of money, 'cause then he could have given full reign to his fantasies. He'd have bought an orphanage. All those cats—directors of orphanages—they're all phony ministers. Molester-type, you know.

"He was very convinced that barter was the thing. He wanted to return to the barter system 'cause he could trade fireworks for anything. He always had things that people wanted, he had a sense of what people needed. He could size up somebody and figure out their weaknesses right away. Especially if they were the same as him.

"Only thing that interested him more than sex was makin' a lotta money—quick. None of the plans panned out, but he was always struggling at it. I am absolutely convinced that if he had been celibate, he could have been emperor of the world. He could have been a very huge success, *if* he coulda kept it in his knickers. If he could have concentrated on using his inventiveness, his creativity, his knowledge about things technical . . . but *it* got in his way all the time. Soon as he got a smell of it, nothin' else mattered.

"Before he died, he knew he had burned all his bridges. He owed *everybody*. It was getting worse, and there was gonna be a helluva comeuppance. He *had* to know that. Even when he scammed me, he had to be desperate, 'cause I was living in a rented house with no money to buy a house, no down payment, two kids, paying support . . . and he knew my situation better than anybody. And that year, he took me for two grand! *Convincingly*, though! He knew he could always appeal to people's greed and avarice. Of course I trusted his mind, because I knew one of these days he was gonna do it. But to take me for two grand and spend it on a chick—buying her little-girl dresses and whatever paraphernalia was involved . . . the factory was beggin' him for the materials that they paid him for and he never bought . . . it hadda all come crashing down.

"Did he know he was checkin' out soon, and might as well get one last one for the road? Was some clock inside him ticking? Or maybe he just knew he was so deep in debt that he knew he couldn't face it. . . . Can't picture him getting that upset about the money, though, because he was such a slickee, such a con man, that he might have even been able to talk himself out of those money problems."

His Games
(WITH TRUTH)

"Truth was what he thought it was at the moment, whatever was most exciting. Barry had one enormous fear and it really hadn't to do with death or dying or pain—it had to do with *boredom*. He was like a Greek in that respect. His one great fear was being dull, so he would choose to be bizarre.

"He had a showman's sense of audience. All you hadda do

was introduce him to three or more people and he went into his number. He was a *great* guest to have at your house. Whenever we had a party, Barry and Dawn were absolutely required, *de rigueur*. Barry would look over a group of people, especially new fish who didn't know his number. I would lead him a couple questions just to get him rolling, and then he'd take over. Dazzle 'em.

"One of his pet numbers was the Armageddon bit. You have it, too. The sense of doom, that it's all gonna fall apart any minute now. He'd scare the shit out of people. Barry could getcha *trembling!* When he got finished with all the chemical weapons that are corroding in their canisters in Nevada and the ketones that are in the water and we're gonna become mutants because of hot dogs . . . do you realize that if you eat a little too much spinach your urine will turn green and it'll corrode your kidneys because of this chemical reaction? Christ, before he was finished, you were desperate. All this time, of course, he's smoking four packs of cigarettes a day and drinking booze and eating chocolate eclairs and every possible thing that was bad for him.

"I subsequently found on many occasions that he was involved in many projects he had taken credit for, but maybe only peripherally. He didn't do that particular thing, but he was around when it was going on. When he told a story, it was willing suspension of disbelief. It didn't really matter what the truth was. I did and do the same thing. If I'm regaling several people with a story and the facts don't quite add up, *change the facts!* It's not the facts that matter, it's the effect that matters! I think he operated on that level and that's why we enjoyed each other's company."

His Games
(WITH HIS CONS)

"Barry would give you anything, especially if he just borrowed it from ya. Without a question asked. He didn't care about those kinds of things. I guess it comes with great minds, and maybe also that sense of the shortness of it all. You better burn like a comet 'cause it's not a long-term arrangement.

"He could con you into or out of just about anything. To get you to give him money—or anything else—he would approach you with a distracted look, or at least a pretended distraction. He would dazzle you and then say, 'Well, I'm workin' real hard these days on thus-and-such,' and he'd be on the phone at the same time to twelve people in twelve countries. While he's dialing and manipulating, he'd make it known he needed *you*. 'Now, uh, I just need two thousand in order to . . . if I can get this thing off the ground . . . clearly it'll triple your money by tomorrow morning." Then he would go back to his job and you'd think: He didn't really try to con me. It's such an over*whelm*ing con that it's gotta be legitimate. Why else would I have given him money I didn't have?

"People gave him large sums of money for all kinds of projects, although nobody ever looked at his track record . . . when he was on a straight track, he wouldn't eat or sleep, he'd just smoke and drink. If he needed an ingredient, he would buy the very finest, even though he didn't have a dime. I think that's part of the great con system: You never shoot low. He would walk into the showroom of the best manufacturer of the best equipment and say, 'I want ten of those and ten of these.' If he'd just asked for a couple, they'd have been suspicious, but he would bowl them over with his grand design. I went for it all the time.

"For instance, that great Christmas after he got two grand out of me? Well, he knew I would give him anything. I knew his personality, but I loved the guy. That Christmas he came over and cooked my family Angels on Horseback, which is thick filet mignon with envelopes cut in them. You stuff oysters in the envelopes and broil the whole thing. God! He made onion soup and I realized, *I'm paying for all this!* His generosity was coming from me! But we all knew it. You couldn't help but love the guy, 'cause you knew one of these days that brilliant mind was gonna come up with the real thing . . . if he could only *stay* with it.

"Remember the scam when he wrote to all the fireworks manufacturers internationally, tellin' 'em that he was a U.S. government inspector for quality control? And they sent him samples of everything! He gave me a whole case of first-class British fire-works. China, Britain, France, Germany—everybody sent him fireworks. Cases and cases of 'em. Freebies. But he always shared. He'd bring them over and shoot 'em in the backyard. They were too dangerous to keep around his house, so he'd put 'em in mine.

"But you couldn't turn him down. You wanna say, 'That's pushy, Barry'? You couldn't 'cause he was so harried that you just didn't want to give him another problem. If you asked him how he feels or how are things going at home, he'd say, 'I'm so tired—Jesus—I've been up all night and I'm exhausted, I'm just exhausted.' That was his normal routine: exhausted. And he was. He was like a meteor, burning everybody as he went by. He was just tryin' to burn everything he could. He had candles burning at both ends. I guess he was that compulsive because he knew time was short. He said he would never make forty-one. He missed it by what? Two hours?

"There was several Barrys. That's a cliché, 'cause there are several of all of us, but Barry had a clear demarcation between his costumed role and the man inside there somewhere. I could watch him switch roles, depending upon who appeared on the scene. I took him to the local prison, where I do some volunteer work, because he was unusual and I knew he could talk on any subject and he liked violence and he had a Gothic sense of horror and fear. When he went in, I could see him looking about, waiting for an opening. When I introduced him, it was just like *showtime!* He went right into one of his horror stories about weaponry, the effects of bullets on the body and what kind of shock it goes into when it's hit. . . .

"Now to the idea that he was alone. I think Barry was a very lonely man. He wouldn't let many people in, because if they ever really got close, they would see that he got out of costume now and then. He didn't want anybody to know that. Once anybody really got to know him, he'd move on. 'Cause he knew lots and lots of people and could impress them. But once they knew his whole gig . . . it hadda be a constant renewal of the audience.

"He had a wide variety of friends. Strange combination of people, but all people who could do something for him. We were the closest of friends, and yet I knew he would put a con on me anytime if he were desperate enough.

"I always thought, Wow, when Barry really hits it big, there'll be some trickle-down. It never worked that way, but there was always that potential—that one of these days when Barry made it really big, I would be included. I knew Barry would say, 'I'm worth a mil and a half and I want you to come with me,' but I wouldn't have been surprised if he didn't. Especially if a woman appeared. If you were drowning and he had you by the hand and he was about to save you when a woman appeared, he might very likely let go. Getcha later if you made it. You could be treading water up to your lower lip in liquid shit and he'd let you float. 'You can handle it,' he'd say.

"He presented a mask of not needing anybody or anything. He didn't want to show that high emotion—well, because that's the snake image. The unemotional, cold-blooded effect. He would have loved to have been a poisonous snake.

"Is this an understatement? He was a compulsively secret person. Always had to have secrets. That secret room, for Christ's sake. I knew what was in there. When he moved out of Hill House to the secret house, the last one, I moved every stick of stuff into that house. It should have been obvious to him that I knew what was in there. But he had an Odyssean protective coloration in lying. He lied the way Odysseus lied, the way Huck Finn lied. When you're in a hostile environment, ya lie till ya find out if it's safe to come out, till you find out who the friendlies are. It was a reflex to lie. 'Where were you last night? You look beat.' 'Well, I was on a job and, y'know, I was outside a motel all night and a guy came out and poked a gun in the window and I had to kill him.'

"And you're saying, 'Jesus, Dawn told me you fell asleep on the couch.' But I wouldn't say that, 'cause I knew he needed to have that lie, that little when-in-doubt-brazen-it-out. Lie to cover your tracks in case anybody wants to know. Even when I was covering for him, when judges were looking for him and calling me 'cause he was using my phone. Even then he wouldn't tell me what it was about, he'd make up some sort of lie.

"He'd get on the phone and call somebody and blatantly lie. He'd be on the phone and say, 'Look, I'm in Millville. . . .' I'd say, 'But you don't—you're not in Millville, you're in my house.' But he couldn't tell 'em where he was, where the phone call was coming from. I think one of his fascinations with the phone was that the one on the other end never knows where you're calling from. There was a certain joy in that for him.

"He *had* to call people at all hours of the night. He was the Howard Hughes of the Hard-on. *Had* to get on the phone and talk to women. Mostly he would complain how difficult his life had been, like, 'I'm really *exhausted.*' That was the opening line of any conversation we ever had. I'm *exhausted.* Jesus. I been here, I been there, I gotta do this. I gotta do that . . . got an assignment tonight. . . .' Completely exhausted. That's all he'd say. How exhausted he was.

"Here was a guy who loved the telephone. Had one in his car —but nobody to call! He'd call the operator just to get the phone working!

"It was no good unless it was secret. If we were gonna meet for breakfast at a diner, we'd be coming from the same direction, but we couldn't ride in the same car. He'd have to circle around once and come in from another direction. In broad daylight at ten o'clock in the morning on a nice sunny day, he hadda go around and back in. He'd often back in so nobody could see his license plates. But, hell, you could spot that dirt-track racer a mile away. Nobody had a car that filthy. He'd park it under a tree and it would go away, you couldn't find it again, it would sort of blend in with the terrain.

"*Nobody knows where I'm living.* I've heard your father say that how many times? *I don't want anybody to know.* He would say, 'Look, I'm only gonna let you in on this, because if anybody else finds out where I'm living, the phone company'll be after me and the CIA and several Mafiosos and a couple women's husbands . . . so nobody can know where I live.' So I button my lip and don't ever betray the secret, till I find out that about sixteen other people know. *Nobody can possibly know where I live. . . .*

"He had great eyes. Very sensitive and sort of deep. But the poetry and the danger and the black—if a motorcycle hood had done that, it would have been silly. But somehow Mr. Death and the Silver Serpent—he actually wrote poetry to one woman and signed it The Silver Serpent. He had that silver ring with the serpent on it, and the gold one with the grotesque crucifix and skull and octopus arms. That stuff always seemed theatrical to me.

"Barry could have been a devil-worshiper. But he wouldn't have taken it seriously, he couldn't have carried it off. He was too bright for that, but he saw the appeal.

"If he could have had an affair with a cripple, he would have. Don't you think? I can see him with a quadriplegic. He would have taken her to a masked ball. Or a picnic in the park where they play volleyball and track races and Frisbee.

"He had that incredible theatrical need. And yet, he could have had the power to do things the right way, the normal way, if he had been consistent and stayed in his business. He should have been wealthy. There was no excuse for that man not being rich. He had all of the ability. But it was fragmented, he couldn't sustain it. And the body would give out 'cause he'd get exhausted and couldn't give up the women. Women mattered most of all.

"One night at Rubble Ranch, a whole bunch of students showed up. The house was crawling with teen-agers, but it was crawling with just about everything else, too. You'd have to step over ammo boxes in the living room. Barry and Dawn would always lay down and talk on that couch that Dawn made—the Iron Maiden. Remember that couch? An orthopedic sadist designed that thing, with the coffee table covered with crumpled cartons of Marlboro. There was a typewriter in the back that hadn't worked in years, and bills piled up everywhere that he was gonna get to any minute now. Huge bookcase filled with Marquis de Sade's work—he had a whole collection of all kinds of classy porno, along with a lot of Freud, a lot of herpetological and geological books that he would spend a lot of money on. 'Cause I don't think he could steal those. Camera equipment, along with ticking bombs and hand grenades with the pins half out. It was always a very exciting evening, no matter when you were there.

"Anyway, a whole bunch of teen-agers showed up one night. He gave 'em his crack-of-doom talk, about the fact that there are a hundred tons of Gravel mines in crates somewhere and all the nerve-gas canisters are corroding and he calculates that by 1980 they will all corrode and we'll all be . . .

"He killed 'em. They were fascinated. He went on and on and

on. I'd heard some of the routines before, but he got me every time. 'Cause he could give you the facts, the times and the places, all from *Scientific American*. He was sure that everybody had got *The Devil's Diary*. Wasn't that the problem? That it was written for the Green Berets, written at a third-grade level, and was supposed to be secret? It wasn't supposed to get into the hands of the Black Panthers, but it did? Or some revolutionary organization? Wasn't it designed exclusively for the Green Berets as a secret field manual but everybody knew what was in it?

"He even gave talks in town here, to the police—all on how you could go to your local drugstore and hardware store and make a devastating weapon out of common elements, things you could buy anywhere, that any household would have. The combinations were so devastating. Again, show business. Mr. Death. Even the cops were impressed.

"You could always see him go into his number, like when that *Playboy* guy appeared. Barry regaled him, just destroyed the guy with stories. Barry impressed him with his fireworks, really gave him all his best shots about guns and intrigue and international spies and covert assassinations and CIA and the Mafia. . . . Barry wanted the notoriety. He was a showman, and the idea of *Playboy* listening to this—because *Playboy* means pussy. . . . Barry was meant for *Playboy*. He could've been the Jewish Hugh Hefner.

"We did some fireworks through the back door—the storm door with no glass in it, so all you had to do was light the fuse from inside and toss it out. I think that *Playboy* guy actually *lived* at Hubble House for a couple days! Can you imagine a guy makin' the bucks he was makin' and lookin' the way he did— what kind of place he musta had in Chicago—to come there and live in *squalor?* Mildew Manor! Can you imagine? He must've been serious about the interview, 'cause where would you sleep?

"He always had that weltschmerz—that trouble in his eyes. The *regret*. The *horror*. When he got finished, you were whipped! Wrung out!

"He showed me the original interview before it got edited and edited out. That's another example of knowing if it were published the way it was taped, a lot of people would get hurt—he among

them. Doesn't it sound like a last hurrah? It sounded like somebody whose tide was going out, if you catch my drift. How was
he gonna face some of those people? It didn't matter at that
moment. What mattered was the drama. If you hadda embellish
or change a date or a fact . . . It was his crowning achievement!
Mr. Death! Hah! Can you beat it? He *loved* it! He never saw it
in print, did he? No, never saw it."

His Toys

(LITTLE GIRLS)

"Is there a why in there worth pursuing? Or is that something we
just can't understand? Why does anybody have a little aberrant
desire like that? I never could quite get it. I don't understand a
gambler either. I don't understand an alcoholic or drug addict.
I don't understand why they can't say no. But the little girls—
that was absolutely an obsession. It was not a now-and-then thing,
it was constant. The films. All that money. He didn't try to get a
bargain, it was retail all the way. I don't know if there was something you may have uncovered in his childhood or if that's an
endless search. . . .

"A grown woman had difficulty with that enormous engine. A
mature cow would have had trouble with that enormous engine.
How—what—did the little girls do with it? They could swing
on it. But they certainly couldn't hide it in any of their bodily
apertures. Not that thing.

"When Zapcap, his toy firework, was really gonna take off,
according to Barry they needed a plant and the best place to put
the plant seemed to be Puerto Rico. So he hadda make several
trips to Puerto Rico. He was always tryin' to fly off somewhere
and I'd eat my heart out 'cause he was always flyin' first class
to L.A., to Vegas, to the Playboy Club in Chicago.

"He kept telling me he was going down to Puerto Rico again
to scout a site for the plant. That made sense until, after a couple

of times, I started thinking, He can't keep making those trips without finding a site. On such a tiny island, he hasn't found anything yet?

"It wasn't until later that he told me there was a kiddy brothel —no, it was a private person, a father who sold his daughters. There was several of them and the guy wanted a hundred and a half up front for a couple of hours. This girl was not an infant, which was his real goal. This girl was twelve or thirteen. Mature for him. I don't know if you want to publicize it, but he told me about several children—I mean real *children,* like three, four, five. I mean, I don't know for sure, these are just what he told me. I don't know where, could have been anywhere. . . .

"I think he knew the family and he seduced the little girl, but he was amazed 'cause she knew a lot. She'd already been trained by her father. He talked about at least two cases like that, which is astonishing, unbelievable to me. When it came to the kiddy stuff, he was *verrrry* private. I don't know who else was involved. I never met anybody. I met a lot of people with him, but I don't know if they were into that or not.

"He corresponded with people who were into it. There were even meetings, actual conventions, of people into kiddy porn. 'Cause not many people would handle that stuff. The police won't bother you much for regular stuff, but for that they get angry. Here's a quote: 'There are a lot of 'em around, but they cost big bucks, and I haven't got 'em. If I had the money . . .' But he *had* 'em. 'Cause he'd rather get films than eat. My guess is they cost seventy-five dollars a reel, and how many hundreds did he have?

"Then he'd give 'em away, unless he could sell 'em. I don't know how big an operation it was, or if it was just on a friendly basis, but he would get them with the idea of looking at 'em all, and then selling them.

"You never found out about the cache of flicks? That he had when he died? Well, they were there in that funny little room. It was just packed. The room that nobody could get into.

"He kept the alligator out in the pond on the front lawn, for Christ's sake. He was like a goddamn pet. He'd call the alligator out of the water and feed him and then the gator would run back into the pond. He had the only pond around with goddamn gators in it. What was the gator's name? Wally the Gator, yeah. Jesus. I mean to sit in front of this idyllic goddamn pond and he'd go *click click click* and the fuckin' alligator would come out of the pond at you. You'd expect maybe a frog, but not an *alligator!* Wally the Gator! Isn't that unbelievable?

"Well, he raised him from a pup or whatever they are when they're little. And the sucker kept gettin' bigger and bigger. Can you imagine what was going on in the mind of that alligator when he got tossed into the freshwater pond and nobody'd ever been there before? He must have thought, Don't throw me in that briar patch. Can you imagine all the tadpoles and frogs in that pond who had never seen an alligator before? It must have been chowdown time for the alligator. Must have looked like a log floatin' in that pond. Eatin' everything in sight. The sucker grew about four feet when Barry threw him in there. 'Course then he also had the snake room in that other house, after he left Dawn the last time. We had to move all the snakes into that one little room. When he closed the door, the smell was unbelievable.

"He had an absolute need for young girls—young, young, *young!* He was as sensual as a child. Nothing was beyond him. He wanted to explore everything. Anyone female who hung around him more than an hour was fair game. But from the beginning, he knew I knew, or had guessed. It must have been a year before the subject ever came up. He'd talk about it, but he'd never say exactly where or when.

"His sensuality was very honest. You do it, that's all. I don't think Barry ever felt immoral. It was an erotic expression, and he had an incredible appetite, incredible instincts for it. And of course he had a vulnerability that helped people relax around him. Even in his stories of making assassination weapons and being a covert agent for all sorts of violent organizations, he showed himself as the victim of it. He had the brains to do the technical work, but he was victimized. The immorality offended him. He made it clear that's why he left those organizations.

"But that morality didn't carry over into sex. There was morality, and there was sex. Morality had no bearing on it. When he talked about experiences with a—with a—with a five-year-old, there was never any thought that maybe that was not a nice thing to do. He gave the impression that everybody does it but it's just not very well known. That particular five-year-old had been prepared by her father, even before Barry got there. He could look over a kindergarten class and tell which ones knew. Some people don't get it till they're fifteen. Some get it when they're eight. He could always tell the ones. That *look*. They knew.

"I don't think he had any agenda for pursuing that in real life. I don't think he went places or did things—is there a Kiddy Club somewhere? I don't know. I don't know if he ever manifestly went out looking. When the occasion arose, he'd act on it. But I don't think he went out and solicited clients—except for the Puerto Rico thing.

"I'm sure if there had been a Pamper Room brothel somewhere, he'd have been rappin' on the door at eight o'clock in the morning. But I don't know if there ever was one or if he ever did it.

"He would go there for a three-day weekend, with that express purpose of going to that particular place. I know he went at least twice, maybe three times. Maybe a helluva lot more, because, as covert as he was, he may have been there a whole lot more. He enjoyed secrets so much that I'm sure he hid lots from me.

"I can't key into the kiddy stuff—except if you're as gifted as he was, the element of surprise would have been titillating. The effect on a small child of that enormous organ . . . the disparity. If he were a dwarfy little person, you could say, Well, he went to little people 'cause he was a little person. Barry was a little person but unbelievably equipped. . . . I don't know if that irony had something to do with it.

"You know that suntan-lotion ad of the girl having her pants pulled down by the dog? *That* turned him on incredibly. Don't give him porno. Don't give him *Playboy* centerfolds, with big jugs and all that hair. *That* hit the spot. *That* was erotic. Can you believe it?

"It was an area where we just didn't understand each other. I didn't approve or disapprove. It was like being Republican. He was my friend, and I respected him and he had a great deal of respect for me. I never questioned him about it. Kidded him about it. A man of his intellect and power . . . it didn't matter. It was like a wart on his nose. Do I disapprove of his wart?

"It never seemed dangerous with him. He could talk on one level one minute about making some hideous destructive device for murder, and you didn't get offended at Barry; you got offended at the system that would hire him to perfect it. The same obtained with his inclination. I always thought it was harmless. I remember him saying there had been episodes early on, long before I knew him, and while I knew him I didn't think any were going on, till he told me about Puerto Rico. It was an aberration and a bit kinky—we joked about it, and it didn't seem like anything to worry about. If he were busily at it all the time, traveling here and there, then it might have been something to think about. But it seemed harmless, like a fantasy that wasn't gonna happen anyway.

"You didn't question anything with Barry. I would not have been surprised if he pulled up in his shaggy Buick Riviera with a very large, colorful snake on a leash, saying, 'We just got married in Boston.' I could handle it. 'I have found my true love and we're gonna be happy forever after making little snakes together.' "

His Toys
(P o r n o)

"I often wondered why he wasn't interested in performing for porno flicks. I think he tried it with video. Would be interesting to retrieve those from the secret archives. I don't know if there are any, but he mentioned it, 'cause he was doin' switchies in a club. The term was 'swingers' in those days. He belonged to a club in a nice residential neighborhood where you partied in one room and everybody paired off and went to other rooms. Apparently they had closed-circuit TV. I don't know if any of that's extant, but that, too, would be interesting, no? Just to see that skinny white ass lookin' like a little boy carryin' an ax handle.

"I don't know how much bearing that had on his demise, but it surely hadda be a stress on his pump. To engorge that thing took four quarts of blood. It hadda do damage to the rest of him— starve your brain for a while, wouldn't it? And your limbs, your extremities—'cause where was he gonna get all that blood? That's probably where the skin on his ass went. I used to kid him that he had taken a drug earlier in his career and he oughtta sue the pharmaceutical companies. The drug must have been called noasitol, 'cause he didn't have any.

"I understand why he was fascinated by porno, 'cause we talked about it. Porno was his sexual will made manifest. But I think that's fairly common: All women are wanton and acrobatic and they always lie in bed naked masturbating and dial the phone and Barry appears knocking at the door in a plumber's uniform.

"He could totally immerse himself in it. Infinite capacity. He could watch fifteen reels of film—what are they, about fifteen minutes apiece? That's a whole night watching, and after a while he was runnin' the film on the floor until you were up to your hips in tangled film. I'm sure the reason he needed so much of it is that his own imagination was the best possible pornography. He kept looking at more and more films, always new films, always looking at films, hoping that one of them would be the one that could match his imagination. But they never did and he was always contemptuous that they always missed the point.

"The filmmakers forget that closer isn't always better. It always looks like an esophagus when they zoom in. There's no foreplay, it's all just pump'n'jump. I think he kept saying, 'One of these days I'm gonna find one that does it all, that does it just right. I'll see the woman who is my fantasy woman and someone who looks like me who is doing what I want to do and the woman will perform the way I wish all women would.'

"At one time he could remember the titles of six hundred reels. That doesn't include all the ones that are just spliced together and reprinted with no title. The titled films were the only ones he cared about, the only ones he could document. Remember, he was gonna write a book on the history of porno films, but like so many other things . . .

"His real joy was in porno. Not the real ladies. I don't think they ever really measured up.

"It's funny, but he had one real quirk. Imagine saying Barry had one quirk. What the hell were the others?

"As close as we were—we shared everything; I can't think of a more tight friend that I ever had—we shared the most intimate secrets and longings and fears—but he kept that one room in his most recent place locked up. It was always the place where you were not allowed to go. He had to have at least one secret from everybody. No one person could ever know all there was to know about Barry. And it was that compulsive secret, that idea that everybody was out to get him . . . the CIA were watching him . . . the Mafia were trying to get him to make silencers and special weapons for 'em . . . there were people lurking in the woods and real-estate agents were really government agents in disguise . . . Mafia people were gonna blow up his stuff . . . it was constant. Constantly changing his telephone number because bills would not get paid. Lawyers would write to me and judges would summon Barry through me because he'd use my phone. He couldn't get a phone in his own name because he'd ruined his credit with the phone company forever.

"But he was so tight that nobody could ever see the porn he had locked in that room. He'd rent hotel rooms just to be alone. With the projector."

His Toys

(W E A P O N S)

"He would let the gun be seen. Somethin' about pullin' off your shoulder holster or your boot holster and poppin' it on the bureau . . . certainly a dash of drama in that. "You a cop, or what?" she'd say. "Wellll, I'm, uh, *undercover*. . . ." For all I knew, he never was, but wanted to believe it.

"Of course Barry was a little man. I don't know if the Jewish thing is important or not. There is a Jewish paranoia—it comes with the territory. I think it might have been exacerbated by the fact that he was green and bald and had no ass and knees that buckled in the wrong direction. So guns were kind of an assistant power, leveling device. Was he really good at weapons? We fired 'em a couple times . . . on the shooting range in back of Hovel House, and he couldn't hit a damn thing with 'em. I couldn't either, but . . . well, I don't think he could see that far. Not more than three trees away. He was more interested in the effect of the bullet than accuracy. I guess he was otherworldly about those things, too.

"The CIA was out to get him, the Treasury, police in general. Most of the time it was true. All sorts of plots and subplots. He didn't trust anybody, including me. I don't know if he trusted anybody completely. He loved intrigue and Machiavellian machinations, things that were turning and twisting. An ordinary transaction had to be somehow covert. He just couldn't go buy a gun from somebody. It had to be under the cover of darkness and somehow it hadda be a barter. He just couldn't *pay* the guy —it hadda be a trade. And he was fascinated by right-wing fascist types, or maybe it was because they were the ones who had the guns.

"And yet he didn't keep them. He didn't put a whole lot of value in things. He'd give them away. When he inherited all that camera equipment, it appealed to him for a while because suddenly he had to understand optics. I'm sure he totally immersed himself in optics and cameras as soon as he could, and when his studies were complete, he didn't care about 'em anymore.

"Now in matters of making bombs, one part of him loved the totally objective scientific approach. He complained so many times that he found the CIA totally unethical. He said on many occasions that the Mafia was a lot nicer to deal with than the CIA. You could trust them more. At least the Mafia had a code, there were some rules, whereas with the CIA he felt they were totally amoral. No rules whatever except rules that they were making up at the moment.

"Yeats said that sex and death are the only two subjects worth thinking about, worth giving serious thought. Barry would have hit it off with Yeats.

"There was an objectivity about him with children, too, even his own. He had little time for children. I don't know how that affected you, but I have some photographs of him holding a baby, and it didn't look right. He just didn't know how to deal with that. It was a funny little wriggly creature he had there. He couldn't wait for them to become adults.

"I'm not sure where the rock collecting came in, why he got caught up with it or how . . . do you know when the first rock appeared? Obviously rocks are eternal and enduring, but when he went to study rocks, he had to know all there was to know about them. He was a superb amateur when it came to studying something. Not a geologist, but he might as well have been one. I'm sure he could have held his own with anybody as a geologist. There was a great deal of intellectual pride in Barry—to know all there was to know about something.

"If I had to pick the fields he was an expert in, I would say he was a herpetologist, a geologist, a pyrotechnic expert. He spoke a great deal about toxicology, though it's hard to test him on that. He was one of the few people I know who could study *Scientific American* each month and really grasp it. If it was a matter of astrophysics, he could reach out and deal with it. If he was gonna know something, he wanted to know all of it.

"I've always suspected that Barry's personality would not let him study gerbils or birds. They had to be *reptiles*. The dangerous, slinky, slippery kind of creature, the one that everybody fears. . . . There was something about Barry that wanted to be deadly, that wanted to be fearsome. I never quite bought the whole act, because there was a great kindness and decency about him, and understanding and compassion. I loved that about him, but there had to always be a tincture of drama in everything.

"I was working for a contractor doing cement work, workin' my ass off. The guy couldn't collect some bills from some people he had done a lot of work for—heavy-equipment builders—and he wanted to know if Barry could think of something. In a wink, Barry designed a little packet that looked like a tea bag, a little Gravel mine that didn't explode—it was supposed to get petroleum. He said you unscrew the fuel cap of one of those big diesel cabs and drop the whole packet in the gas tank. 'Cause it dissolves and turns all the fuel to Jell-O, which clogs all the fuel systems but doesn't hurt them. You then have to take it all apart to clean it out. It's not damaged in any way, except it will not run. Did you ever hear of that?

"He also suggested putting gnat larvae in the guys' house. He had a little scheme for getting into the guy's house and just depositing a hundred and forty billion gnat larvae in a little capsule about the size of a cigarette butt. Just turn 'em loose. He said you'd never be able to live in the house again. And he also suggested gases that would make the place unlivable.

"But that thing for jelling petroleum, that made a lot of sense. There'd be a lot of uses for it, but there'd be no noise, no sign, no evidence. It's just that nothing will run. You never heard of that?

"If he would meet a woman and take her to a motel or just be alone with her, he'd very carefully—never blatantly—but always let her know that he was carrying heat. Like put it under the pillow, or on the table next to the Gideon's Bible, or shoot out a light in the parking lot. He knew a primeval secret: most women like to feel a little threatened. 'Whose side is he on? Is he working for himself or The Organization? What is he?' It was all very sexy for him.

"And her."

His Toys
(FIREWORKS)

"There was a great deal of the child in Barry. That's one of his charms. You're supposed to grow out of fireworks. They always have a fascination, but Barry's just kept growing and growing— because it's a show. If he went to a flower show, the only thing that could possibly interest him would be the venus flytrap or some flower that had a toxic aroma. Or a plant that ate dogs and children.

"Well, I had visions of that look into pandemonium during a fireworks show. Remember he used to shoot those shows? How we'd all be watching up on the hill . . . show business, absolute show business, although you don't have to perform with fireworks, because they do the performing for you. They're violent and colorful and loud, all the good things that Barry liked. I still have visions of this little Jewish gnome down there with his funny turned-up shoes and his knees bent backwards, running, going *zzzttt! zzzttt!* It was Mephistophelian in the smoke and haze and the brilliant red flashes to see this little dark figment lighting things off. It looked otherworldly. And he had a glow. . . .

"He had incredible patience for wiring up goddamn explosives. What an incredible amount of care. But the effect was what he wanted. Were you there the Fourth of July night out at Western Weapons when he set off an incredible amount of extra material? He just dug a big pit and put all the extra shit he could find, all the leftover explosives, and mixed it and threw it all in the big pit. He had a hundred thousand whizzers, and when he set those off, you thought it was the end of the world. Women were dropping babies and running and screaming, we were all ducking under trees, and finally when the final blast arrived, when the grand finale came and he set off the pit, cars were toppled, windows were knocked out of second-story windows, and miles away the highway lights went out. The explosion was so brilliant it told the highway lamps that it was dawn and they all went out. A mushroom cloud came out of that sucker. He just had to have the biggest bang of all."

His Possessions

(HIS BODY)

"It's just a shame that nature or whoever supplied him with that kind of a brain and put it into that body. If he'd had a better life-support system, he would've been trouble for the world.

"He looked like a slug—something you might find under a wet rock. When he peeled his clothes off, you hadda look the other way. It was almost as if nature had counterbalanced him. His ass fascinated me. How couldja have no ass at all? How can you walk? That's what powers your movement. It was like somebody had wadded it all up front. He was proud of his vasectomy, too. Didn't wanna have any more kids.

"He had an enormous capacity, though. He used to stroke it off vigilante-style—takin' matters into your own hands. He used to say he'd stroke that big sucker off a couple of times a day just to keep the pain down. I used to find that unbelievable 'cause I was never sure he could reach all the way up and back. Used to tell him to go buy a little black boy to run up and down and get the job done right.

"Barry was what? Five foot nine and a half? A balding, green-skinned Jew. Looked like a vampire. You remember how he had a *green* complexion? And a balding head with funny bulgy eyes? The guy was a *disaster!* And yet he had such power over people.

"Barry had so many peculiarities—like his backward knees. Anthropologists are gonna find those bones somewhere and figure they've been wrong all these years: The apes descended from *us*. If Dr. Leakey found his footprints in the sand behind Rubble Manor, he'd never figure out which direction this fucker was goin'. Here we have the first Homo Erectus whose knees revolved three hundred and sixty degrees. Good for climbing trees and parking small cars. Do you remember his knees? They were unnatural. They were hinged backwards. He'd lock them and stand in your living room like some undiscovered species of carnivore.

"Now it may have been that he was the most unathletic human being since the beginning of man. Ever since we came out of the trees, I don't think there's been anybody less inclined to athletics than Barry, although he could have been a hell of a long jumper with those knees. They would never know which end he'd be jumping from. If he could have developed that knee power, he could have done things that are awesome to think about.

"Of course he dressed stagewise, he dressed for effect. His jewelry was somethin' else. Upside-down crucifix on a chain around his neck and snake rings, and he'd wear those goddamn little black shoes. Do you remember the gnome shoes? Those little fuckin' gnome boots? With the curling-up toes. The goddamn boots were so big for him that he looked like a Jewish Mickey Mouse. They were terribly worn out. Looked like glove leather by the time he got through with 'em. Also wore the black pants, black shirt, black socks, black belt . . . but that was all part of his disguise. It was the same reason Mark Twain wore white —showmanship.

"The orderliness of his mind was reflected in the disorder of his life. You remember Hilltop House or Mill Road House? You couldn't get the *Star Wars* crew to make rubble look like that. If you gave them three million dollars and said, 'Create a house and fill it with rubble, they couldn't come up with enough rubble to match that house.

"Do you remember how you'd have to step over piles of little white things on the floor, which were really frozen white mice tails that break off when you take them out of the freezer for snake food? The faucet leaked for as long as I knew him, and the dishwasher was melted, frozen shut. It was only a storage bin anyway. There were dishes in there that Dr. Leakey would have loved to have found.

"And the time he was making thermite grenades in the refrigerator? They went critical and melted his brand-new refrigerator. I had never seen a limp refrigerator before, and I hope I never do again. I used to bring a coffee cup with me 'cause you wouldn't dare drink out of whatever was there—even if you could find something in that archeological wonder of the dishwasher.

"I used to tell Barry that they should find the architect and builders and arrest them immediately. First of all, they built the wrong kind of house for that hill, and then they faced it the wrong way. The house was backwards. Was not meant for human beings to function in. Didn't it look like a large gerbil cage? A hamster habitat? There was no way to get from one room to the next. 'Course you could always look ever his estate from that balcony on the back porch if you were a naked jockey and could squeeze out the back door.

"Well, I did find his house that first night. Unbelievable. It took me about two hours to find it. Climbed the hill and I had the feeling there was no way to get in, because the back door, which should have been the front door, was actually the side

door. It was Christmas and very cold and the storm door had
no glass in it, which I thought was bizarre 'cause it was locked.

"Then I met Dawn and I wasn't prepared for that one either.
Here is this green-complexioned little Jewish vampire type and
in walks a very robust black lady who is introduced as '*my wife.*'
Then three little black children emerge from the woodwork.

"After that, we just got very very tight. He told me about his
fireworks and his work with the CIA and the Institute. There
was a certain excitement about him. You knew that whatever
was happening to him could not possibly be dull. At the very
least, it would be bizarre.

"I finally got into the upstairs bedroom. I don't know if you've
ever seen it, but it could have been a horror-movie still life. It
could have been a horror movie all by itself, 'cause you open the
door and there was something resembling a bed, but clearly all
the way up to the box spring was film, long loops of film. The
projector was on the nightstand, and then there were mountains
of crumpled empty Marlboro boxes. They'd be ankle-deep on
the near side, and on the far side of the room was laundry.

"Now I say that without really defining it. It *looked* a lot like
laundry. It was very well-worn laundry which had been disposed
of, discarded, and had never made it to any kind of washing
device. Apparently he and Dawn would watch films for hours at
night. One time he didn't hang up a take-up reel, so it just
ran through and never rewound again. Film all over the floor
in big confetti piles.

"And yet, if he went somewhere, he had to have the best hotel
room and it had to be immaculate. He was very particular about
towels, the soap, the cleaniness of the bathroom, while he lived in
squalor! Do you remember that little powder room? Unbelievable. And the rug in the sitting room that molded into the floorboards. Looked like a fossil.

"When he wanted to build a fire, he'd bring in firewood that
was usually moldy. Old firewood with rats and bugs crawlin' all
over it. He had no patience with fire—fire had to be very quick.
I forget what kind of pyrotechnic he used, but the fire would
suddenly ignite into full blossom.

"Well, you know the backyard looked like Armageddon, right?

Remember all the fuckin' trees were withered? Looked like a goddamn atomic bomb had struck. Remember bullet holes in the trees and bark ripped off everything? Years' worth of fireworks and debris were right there—nobody ever picked anything up.

"Of course there was the greenhouse without any glass in it. Half the windows were knocked out in the real house. Goddamn rain forest in the basement. Smellin' like mouse shit everywhere.

"Twice when he left Dawn he took his snakes with him. Can you imagine that? And I had to go down that cellar each time and carry those big cases out with the snakes in 'em! I'm at the bottom 'cause Barry didn't have two muscles that would ever work together at the same time, so he's carryin' the light end of the case and I'm carryin' the heavy end and there're all sorts of wriggling creatures in there. My gonads are straining and the goddamn glass door slides open and I'm lookin' in at all these little reptilian creatures just lookin' at me as if I'm good to eat. Of course I can't let go of the cases, and Barry's sayin' 'It's okay' and calling them by names. 'Down, Rover!' We had to carry all the snakes over to his other house. Do you believe that?

"And the car—the Buick Riviera that had wrappers and packages from McDonald's when their hamburgers were nineteen cents? You'd try to get in the car, but first you'd have to shove forty pounds of debris out of the way. You knew there was a seat under there somewhere, but just couldn't be sure where. I used to tell him he had the only Buick Riviera with mice.

"He used to haul munitions in that poor car. Food wrappers of all kinds, cans of soda, but as long as there was room for him, he didn't care about anybody else being able to find any.

"Barry always leased his cars, and after he did, Dawn and I took the car back to the dealer. Of course he never put oil in it. The last Buick he had for two years and he never put a drop of oil in it. It was running on who knows what. But we took it back to the dealer. . . . I've never seen a grown man cry. You couldn't drive it. No one would ever look at it. It looked like a dirt-track racer that had lost every race—had dents everywhere, headlights were hanging off. Then you looked inside, and you thought he had accidently parked it at a shopping market and the shoppers thought it was a Goodwill bin, 'cause it was full of clothes, old shoes that he hadn't worn in years, munitions, frozen mice, fire-crackers, and about seven hundred cartons of sparklers. It looked like a scene from a bad science-fiction movie!

"If he had been more athletic, he probably would have driven a weapons carrier. Don't you think? With machine-gun ports on both sides? But he was so unathletic, he couldn't have handled it. He had to have a car that was as automatic as possible. Couldn't see worth a damn. And he drove like José Greco dances. Bangin' on the gas pedal. You'd get seasick just riding with that sonofa-bitch. And then he would forget he was supposed to be going to Canfield and would end up in Marlinburg."

His Women

"Time and again I'd hear from the women. We would have a conversation about somebody, and Barry would say, 'Oh, can't . . . boring, dull, dull . . . I can't take the bayberry candles.' And then I would talk to the woman, and she'd say, 'Oh, Barry was over last night, the night before, the night before he was here twice during the day, he called, he sent flowers.' Wait a minute! It didn't add up! He had to tell me he didn't care, she bored him, and he was not there, or he saw her maybe a week ago. And then I'd talk to her and he was there overnight three nights, every morning he called her at six for a Romeo wake-up call . . . I don't know why it had to be that way. I wouldn't mind. Yet all our friendship long, I never once called him on it. It was too blatant. Why would you want to call him on it?

"Only once do I remember . . . I'd introduced him to some-one and the very next day he showed up there. When I heard about it, I said, 'Gee, I was just a little bothered that it happened so quick.' 'Cause usually he takes a little time and smoothes it around and does a couple business trips, the whole machinery of intrigue. She mentioned to him that I was a little bit bothered, and he sought me out like it was an emergency. Drove out of his way, found me, had to talk to me immediately. 'You know, I thought it was all right and I would never never betray our friendship or anything like that.' If he had any more qualms, he never stopped. Each time he'd do the old backdoor routine. It's in the blood, he couldn't stop. I guess it was because his need was enormous.

"Barry tried never to show enthusiasm, except for fireworks. I'm a gusher. If I see a great movie, I'll kill it, I'm gonna oversell it to you. He hadda pick out the bad points first, talk about what was wrong with it. He would do that with women, too: 'Well, a little dumpy,' or 'Not very smart. . . .' He didn't talk with women in sex. It was pantomime. I like to talk. He talked afterwards and before, not during. 'Cause I think he got into himself. The woman was everything before and everything after, but I think in the middle it was his time to concentrate on the ultimate orgasm.

"I think that's one of the reasons he had private houses. He was afraid of motels, although he'd rent 'em with money that nobody knew where he got. He couldn't be tacky—maybe Holiday Inn was as low as he could possibly go—'cause money really didn't matter at any one moment, even if he didn't have it. If there was gonna be a scene of some sort, he'd buy the best booze, get the best place. And he liked to order food from Room Service. Always the best. Here's the guy who almost got arrested for not paying the telephone bill. He's like a drunk—when the party's rollin' nothin' else matters but that moment. He'd leave exhausted.

"When he'd leave a woman, when he just tore it up, shredded it, beat it, killed it . . . it could be three o'clock in the morning and he would have to go on an assignment. He had to tell you he was beat but he was driving on. You wanted to say, 'Well, sleep some. You burned? Relax, get some food, and go to bed.' 'No, hey, there's too much to do. There's a—I gotta pick up a package somewhere that's coming in by worm train. And I gotta meet a guy in Schenectady in the morning. Got six telephone calls. . . .'

"I was his bird dog. I didn't really have a method, because that's infinite. No one-liners or any of that shit. It's instinct. It's something you can't learn. It's something he didn't have much of. He was not a good bird dog. He couldn't get 'em outta the bush. But once he got *into* the bush, he was king of the mountain.

"We were soul brothers. He was very sensual and mysterious

and appealing—after you got through the outer layer. I can't picture Barry in a bar cruising for chicks, checkin' out some chicks
on a cunt hunt. It couldn't happen that way. He had to have an
entrée. He was great after step two, but step one was beyond
him. So if I met a woman, an interesting thing to do would be to
introduce her to my weird and unusual friend.

"I'd say: 'I'd like you to meet Connie,' and he would be—
distant but warm—*reserved*—until I could draw him out. He
knew I would do it with leading questions, like: Are you still
working on this? And how about that? Did the *Playboy* interview
come through yet? Then he would . . . reluctantly come out—
and then get rolling.

"He had a sense of what would impress a woman, and he
would go through his death-and-destruction and covert-mystery
bits, *very* convincingly. Christ, I heard it fifty or sixty times, and
I was hangin' on every word. He had that ability to make you
go for it.

"He also had a sense of timing. If a young lady and I were
interested in an erotic activity, Barry knew when to leave. But
more importantly, when to return. Pacing up and down, waiting
and wondering when to appear. He could. And did. Only by
invitation, of course.

"Then, when the action got started, he'd whip out that incredible member—it was astonishing to behold. There were times
when I was deeply involved with the lady, and I'd look over my
shoulder as Barry was preparing himself, stroking that thing, and
I'd say—pardon the pun, but I'd done all the legwork—I'd say,
'Are you ready yet?' 'No,' he'd mumble, 'not quite yet.' You're
thinking: Good God! What happens when he's ready? Awesome,
awesome sight.

"He was incredibly gentle with a woman. Very, *verrrry* considerate. Deep, *deeply* committed to her at that moment. At that
moment, she was Queen of the May. He had an enormous power
of concentration, so when he was with a woman, she had one
hundred percent of his attention. It was so convincing that you
would think that no one had ever mattered to him before that
moment. Of course he could push a button somewhere and it
would be completely different. But at that moment, he could
convince her that nothing else mattered to him but her. I think

that was his talent. He was a marathoner and I was a sprinter. I was in the short races, the quick ones, but he went for the looooonnnnggggger ones.

"How did it get started, the two-man-saw team? I guess it was at Rubbleville—Hill House—when he said he'd share. After the event, he said, 'Doc, this is a rare compliment,' and I knew there was a good deal of trust in that. Like every other dealing we ever had, it was all my turn after that. Twenty ladies later, we hadn't broken even yet. His theory was he just couldn't do it, didn't know how.

"I don't think Barry was a womanizer. Maybe he and I had a Swiss-cheese morality when it came to that, but—there are people who take advantage, but he was not one of them. You know the difference? There are lots of people who don't understand what it's really about. You know the slick Italian stud in the disco? He can only think in terms of his next orgasm. *That's* not it. There's so much more to it, and Barry understood that. The pursuit was all-important. . . .

"He radiated a kind of danger, and, without that, it really is kind of pedestrian. I've always known that most women want to feel a bit threatened. Not that you're not predictable, or that, good God, this could get out of hand any minute. He understood that, too. Always flowers, always poetry, always incredible attention, flattering attention. I don't know anybody he didn't get that I sent his way.

"See, he had very little confidence in his bird-dogging ability. He hadda have somebody get through that first reserve. But once he sat down talking with them, that was the end. Then they would be his. It was a passion. It happened over and over and over and over and over again. I think it was that flattering, all-out attention that got 'em. They never forgot him and they were always available. The poetry got 'em, too. He could whip it out whenever he needed it. And he always spent money on 'em. 'Cause money didn't matter at that point. It was just a means to an end.

"He'd be involved in a conversation with a new lady and then have to make a clandestine telephone call. There were times when I suspected there was nobody on the other end, that it was just important to get the effect.

"His winged chariot was always harrying near, and I suspect

that he knew it. So he hadda get a lot done, and he knew it was killing him, he knew chasing all those women and the all-night drives to do the hat trick—he took great pride in that hat trick. Three in one twenty-four-hour period. Three different ladies. He was very proud of that. I kept awarding him the trophy. Kept asking when he was gonna retire. But it meant many miles. . . .

"He didn't seem to have many specifications for his women. He wasn't for the tall, thin, little, round, black, yellow, or green— but if they had small young daughters . . . That was definitely a pattern there. But I can't see what else. Age didn't seem to matter. There was some talk that he had a sixty-five-year-old woman, very attractive and well preserved, with lots of bucks. Again, I never met her, but it was probably because it was un- usual. Not many people are hittin' a prune. But apparently she was good head, and that mattered to Barry, because I don't know if he got that very often with that astonishing weaponry.

"There was one woman in particular who used to come—she was supposedly Dawn's friend and then became Barry's friend, but I guess was both of their friend. She was boring beyond belief and homely as mud. Tall, angular, not a good feature on her body. Boring but generous. Bring food, bring ham, cook any- thing, and they used to both complain that she was deadly boring and would stay endlessly. I suggested to Barry, 'Are you, hmm . . . she's not that horrible *not* to.' 'Hey, not a chance,' he said.

"I found out later he'd been tyin' her up and whippin' her and the whole bizarre sex thing with her for years—taught her every- thing. He was seeing her till the very end. She was always on the back burner. Not a beauty, but very pliable. I don't think she was les, but I think whatever Barry said was worth doing and I'm pretty sure he whipped up on her. Although he really didn't go for that most of the time, he was so unphysical.

"When it came time, he wouldn't dare wrestle. I don't really think he'd whip up on somebody unless somebody else tied her up. I don't think Barry really got into that. He'd *talk* about it. There may have been some—I'm not sure about this at all—but he may have gone in for English massage himself. It would be a sensation . . . I think a domineering woman could've really turned him on. Spike heels and leather. Barry could've gotten into that. I don't know if he ever did, though. 'Cause he could also be very smooth, serpentine, wiggle around into oral. When he really got down to it, he could be a hundred and sixty pounds of tongue. Really bring it all to bear on that one spot.

"He was a great back-rubber. It's hard to believe anybody would fall for the ole back-rub trick, but he was so goddamned good at it. He got *into* it. After a while you're thinking, God, maybe that's all he wants. Infinite patience. Nothing was hurried. He'd rub your back—I mean he'd rub *her* back—for—how long? Hour?

"He didn't talk much. I'd really like to give you some memorable lines. Dredging my memory . . . I can't think of any . . . except *one*—how could I forget? I'll call her Sherry. She was a new catch, and I brought her to Monster Manor. We went through the usual intro bit, and then she and I went off to the so-called den to do our thing. At the preordained moment, Barry walks in wearing his usual black outfit. He sits down on her side of the bed, puts his hand on her ass very gently, but before he has a chance to go further, she turns to him with this serene look and proclaims: 'I'm sorry, but I wouldn't want to come between two friends.' And he leaves like a whipped puppy, with his clothes trailing behind him.

"That's odd, because that particular woman ended up really loving him. He gave her one hundred percent of his attention, but at first sight . . . Barry could set ya back a couple feet. He was weird to look at when he was dressed, but when he was *naked—yuck*—please, not while I'm eating!

"But, see, even with that particular lady, the door had been opened. Then he just laid one of his assaults. I'm not even sure how he did it. But, boy, he did it. He got her. Love! She was absolutely crushed.

"He was relentless. Once he set his sight on a woman, there was no hope. He was like a snake. He would charm them. They knew it was gonna happen and he would just get them.

"I know he went to California once and picked up a black girl, a hooker. Took her to his room and called out dinner. Then he said he was going to Vegas, and she said, 'Take me with you— and my sister, too.' She called her sister and she appeared, and they flew to Las Vegas and got a suite . . . Of course he threw his gun on the table when he got there, and stayed with them for a couple days.

"Did you know he was thinking of running a line of girls in this area? He had it all set up. All the plans were laid, as it were, to take over for some guy who was—*retiring*. He was gonna service the local communities with five or eight girls—and of course the suggestion was always, 'Hey, but for *friends!*' But that never came off either. He woulda gone broke anyway. Couldn't push 'em around, but he'd be eatin' all the goods, all the profits.

"He did have a hooker, you know. Paid occasionally. She was in that group. That's how he knew about 'em. She was from Millville. I never met her or the guy, but he'd talk about her once in a while.

"I think that last girl, the one we used to call Betty Jean Number Two, because her name was also Betty Jean—I think she really did him in. *Physically* did him in. 'Cause then he didn't need the porn. It bothered me that she didn't even attempt to understand the guy. At the funeral, she was telling me about all the money he spent on her and all the places he took her. I'm sayin' to myself, Oh, God! I know where a lotta that money came from! He was buying her little-girl dresses from someplace out in the Midwest. Buying her little pinafores and nighties . . . I'm thinkin', Jesus, she didn't know what kinda man she had. She didn't know what the expenses were, how much it was costing him. Just a mindless little chick.

"Here's a quote. I don't remember which of us said it first, but it was a running theme song: If they didn't fuck, we'd have to put a bounty on 'em."

His Death

"His deepest secret? That's the important one. I know his deepest fear was death, and not so much the end of consciousness—which was real for him because he was an intellectual—but he lived so much in the physical . . . even though he didn't have much body to work with. He didn't sky dive and he obviously didn't go in for physical culture, but I know he thought of the body as a life-support system for his intellect. Fear resided in the fact that the life-support system would give out and all that stored-up brain power would go with it.

"It's funny, but you can't think of an old Barry, can you? He was almost doomed. I can't think of a sixty-five-year-old Barry. No way he was gonna make that trip. But even at his death, we know there was a great deal of money spent on brochures for Tahiti. I mean, is that hokey? To escape to Tahiti? Didn't he have all sorts of brochures and letters of correspondence with travel agents and government agencies? He was gonna escape to Tahiti, probably with the little girl, the Betty Jean Numero Dos. . . . You know, the little one—yeah.

"She was not very smart. A real groupie. How could I put it? Really taken with herself. And she was just a skinny little chick. Not all that pretty. But she looked twelve. And could look ten. And Barry worked at eight. She told me that he bought her little-girl costumes. Sent away to a special kinky house that sold that sort of thing. Little baby nighties and little jammies and little costumes when he was supposed to be broke, when he was desperate to get the product off the ground. That's why I gave him the money. I had to take a loan. I didn't have any money. I'm still paying it back. She told me that he took her into town to exclusive ritzy hotels. The idea was to walk into the hotel with her on his arm, probably in costume. Stunning. Attention-getter.

"Yep. She was scheduled to go with him. It was gonna be a mutual flight. I think he had found the little girl he'd been look-ing for all his life, since he was a little boy. And I think she had the mentality of a twelve-year-old. You wouldn't want to talk with her very long, 'cause she was so taken with herself. Coy. Teen-ager kind of cutesy. Not a woman who would understand what she had to offer, but cutesy little kid who knew *something* was valuable but wasn't quite sure what it was. She was the femme fatale. If it hadn't been for her . . .

"There were always hints that he thought somebody was tryin' to assassinate him with poisons that he himself had helped to design. One of them was a heart-attack poison. A slow-acting heart-attack thing to give you a massive cardiac infarction—and that's what he had.

"You know about the fireworks-factory explosion, don't you? It was the one in Crystal Springs. If you're gonna build a fireworks factory, that's where you'd build it.

"He had developed a modular system for snapping together rockets and other fireworks, instead of all that handwrapping that fireworkers have been doing for centuries. It was the first time in two thousand years that anybody had designed a different way of putting rockets together, and apparently all the Italian fireworks manufacturers who have been doing it by hand—when they *had* hands—were angry as hell at him because he was gonna put everybody out of business.

"I saw him the morning of the explosion. He left to go to the factory, but he was late. When he got there, he sat down at his desk and started working, but then he remembered he had left something important at home. He excused himself, told his foreman he'd be back shortly, and left to go home. He was out the gate about a mile down the road when the factory went up. He went back and there was debris everywhere and people injured, but fortunately nobody was killed.

"He couldn't understand it because he had followed all the rules for safety. You gotta believe him when he says that you're only allowed to have so much powder around at any one time, and it's gotta be in bunkers separated from all the other units and the stuff's gotta be kept in boxcars way out of range. He said he had followed all the rules, but when the government men came—all of whom Barry knew, was sort of friends with—when they finally did their examination, they found that it was his filing cabinet that blew up. Right next to his desk. Which was fairly convincing evidence that it was a bomb to get him, that it was set to go off when he would normally be at his desk.

"As he told it, they found out who did it, and Barry explained in some sinister obliquity that the guy met an untimely end—with no details given. Barry liked to be dramatic like that. The suggestion was fairly clear that he had done the guy in. I don't know if he did, though. Do you think? He had enough to scare them, anyway.

"He always had forebodings, and they were especially acute right before he died. The night before, we talked on the phone at least an hour, and I kept saying, 'Barry, you've always had those feelings. This is nothing new. Tomorrow morning we're gonna have breakfast as usual at the Kountry Kitchen. No big thing.' He says, 'No, they're comin', they're comin' to get me, the monsters, fears, forebodings, and horror. . . .'

"He had an absolute Gothic sense of horror. He had no Lucretian sense of material—the roman poet Lucretius, the one who lived from ninety to fifty-five B.C. and said, 'Everything is part of everything, so why fear death? It's just the disintegration of matter, the same as everything else.' Barry had incredible fear, inordinate fear of corruption and demons and horror, and he had it particularly the night before he died. I kept saying, 'Tomorrow morning we will have our usual breakfast and it will all be fine.' But they'd been getting worse and worse. . . .

"I had seen him on the weekend before the Tuesday that he died. If I didn't see Barry four times a week, it was a strange week. Then we'd be on the phone at odd hours, talking like two middle-aged women, complaining about our marriages, our health, the weather. . . . I always thought, of all the friends he had, I was the one that counted the most, because I gave him everything and asked for nothing back.

"We had met that weekend, but, before that, he had been talking about his nightmares of dying, of the horrors. *Grim.* He was obsessed with them. For months beforehand, he'd say he had dreams last night that were terrible—this doom, corruption, horror, horror, horror. He would get teary-eyed from the terror. I would always try to downplay it: We all have those; you're almost forty-one, it's that time of life when you get a sense of mortality.

"He'd say, 'Oh, my heart, I'm overdoing things, I better take care of myself.' I knew *that!* The whole world knew *that!* And I'd tell him: You're courting disaster all the time. But he was always frantic, always busy, busy, busy, hadda be movin', cuttin' it, movin' on.

"He called me during the day on that Tuesday. We were scheduled to have breakfast at the Kountry Kitchen on Wednesday morning. He was talking about the doom thing again, the death fear; premonitions were very real, up-front, intense. I was saying, 'It's all right. I know you're having them, but they don't mean much more than the fact that you're having them. . . . We'll have breakfast tomorrow as usual, you'll see.' He said, 'No. I'll be forty-one tonight, and I'm programmed not to be forty-one, not to make it that far.' 'Yo, Bar,' I said. 'Come on! This is a typical Barry drama! It's just drama!'

"I listened—I didn't ridicule him—because he was so deadly serious this time. I tried to reassure him that tomorrow morning would come. . . .

"On that particular Tuesday night, he said he had to take Dawn to a doctor's appointment because she wrecked her car and had no way to get there. So he said he had to take her at eight that night. I said, 'Okay, see you in the morning, we'll talk it out.'

"The following morning, Dawn called. Said he had taken her to the doctor, left her there . . . said he was gonna go out and get some eggs and butter and other groceries for her. Then he was gonna pick her up afterwards. But he came back ten minutes later—in pain—and collapsed there in the office. Dawn said she just wiped the froth from his mouth and tried to breathe into his mouth, but he was already dying.

"We had talked hours before and he was dead by ten o'clock that evening. Two hours before his forty-first birthday.

"He was hooked up somewhere, to something, that normal mortals are not hooked up to. You and I won't know, but *he* knew. That's why I wouldn't be surprised if he walked through that door right now. I wouldn't even take a deep breath if he came in and his green was gone and he had a tan, he's been in Tahiti all this time."

16

Ms. Death

July 1974. I have made my annual pilgrimage to be with my father on the Fourth of July, to celebrate our ritual of fire. As usual, these are the happiest days of my year. Some tribal, violent voodoo hoedown of a ritual that has evolved over the years because of my father's fiery obsession. He doesn't know it but he is giving me more in these few days than most fathers give their sons in a lifetime. He is giving me a sense of the mystery of life and death without teaching, without preaching, without going one step out of his way, without doing anything extraordinary, without thinking twice. It will be a blessing and a curse, but more of a blessing than a curse.

A few days after Independence Day, I go with him for a ride, supposedly to do some errands. Actually he *is* going to do some errands, but not what I thought he had in mind.

First he stops at some nondescript row house and picks up a manila envelope containing "some films." I am a little too naïve to know exactly what he's talking about, never having seen a real smoker, a blue movie, but I get the drift that there is something illegal in the transaction. That's cool. I'm up for it. Into it.

Then he stops at a local K-Mart. This I can't believe. If there's anything my father hates, if there's anything *I* hate, it's this prime example of late-twentieth-century American mediocrity. But he's doing it, for real, and since I never know what to expect from him, I don't question. Who knows what he's got up his sleeve this time? Could be an even more clandestine transaction! Hope springs eternal, even at K-Mart.

He walks in like he knows exactly where he's going. "I just want to say hello to a friend," he turns to me and says as we're entering the Cosmetics Department. "I'd like you to meet her, too."

She's beautiful, and I would like to die right now so I don't have to talk to her, so I don't have to make up an interesting conversation about myself. What could I say to a woman this gorgeous that would hold her interest for more than two seconds?

She's not gorgeous like a movie star or fashion model or dancer. She's gorgeous like a waitress is gorgeous, like a nurse is gorgeous, like the lady who cuts your hair is gorgeous, like the clerk at the supermarket in the fruit section is gorgeous, like the girl next door when you're seventeen is gorgeous, like every girl who works on a farm is gorgeous and every girl who doesn't get asked out is gorgeous. She's got a radiance—an utterly blond radiance, a blinding blond radiance—that is so bright it actually hurts my eyes and I have to turn away. I already want her in some deep hard corner of my tender young manhood. It hurts so bad that I just want to get out of here, away from her, away from all this heat and light and dizziness.

At first I don't understand why he wanted me to meet her, but later I do. He's showing me off. He's teasing her. He's trying to set us up and I don't even know it. I'm too damn young and dumb and full of come to know when my old man is pulling a fast one on me. There's more than a little masculine brag in my father and I'm too shy to see past my own self-consciousness. I just want to get out of here and I let him know it.

They talk about this and that for a few minutes while I drift off, away from this cosmetics counter, away from these terrible new sensations, away from the lights swimming in my head. Then he says to me, "Let's go." He's obviously angry with me, but I know we'll never talk about this incident because I won't have the guts to bring it up.

"On June 5, 1973, Ian took me up to Hill House to meet Barry. It was in the evening. It was a peak time in my life when I look

back on it now. I felt really good, looked better than I'd looked
in years.

"Barry and Dawn had some friends over. They were sitting in
the kitchen at a round table having something to eat. The kitchen
cabinets were open, there was disarray all over. I'd never been in
a house like that before. We walked through papers and books
that must have been ankle-deep. Passed by something I later
found out was Barry's desk, then into a room that had no windows, through the kitchen, and ended up in the living room or
den. The only rule of the house applied to that room: No children
allowed. It was a comfortable room to the extent that I liked the
mineral and crystal display in the glass case. A beautiful piece of
quartz up above the fireplace. Really huge. Really struck me.

"After dinner, Barry and Dawn came in and talked with Ian
and I. I don't know what happened to the people at the table.
We talked for a while . . . I don't know why Ian took me there.
Later I found out he did that often to flaunt his catches in front
of Barry. I know they shared girls and women from the college—
I guess they were really girls, not women—so maybe that was in
the back of O'Hennessey's mind because our relationship was
new and he didn't really know who I was.

"We stood talking long past dusk. Maybe nine o'clock. Must've
been fog that night. Really misty. The play *Steambath* had been
on public television the night before. Ian hadn't seen it, but
Barry and I had. That was our first thing in common. That's when
I felt the first attraction to him. We had really similar viewpoints
on the play. I can remember standing there discussing the finer
points with Barry, and I think Ian was really taken aback because
I don't think he ever thought I would think a profound thought
and be able to vocalize it. And not only that, but capture his
friend's mind for just a moment and make it work. I still remember the white shirt he was wearing. It had a little pistol em-
broidered over his heart.

"I can see him standing there. His voice was one of the most
masculine, soft voices I'd ever heard. I thought him a really
strange man and I was also aware of my attraction for him. Then
Ian and I left because Ian became impatient.

"Maybe a week later, Ian called to tell me that Barry was attracted to me and would I be interested in seeing him? I said

no, I wouldn't be. I kind of joked it off that I wasn't interested; not to try to set me up; that I would take care of my own romances. I was still married and it was all I could do to handle my first affair and trying to decide what to do with my marriage. I was going to school, working, keeping house, taking care of three children and a husband. It was awful. So I didn't see Barry anymore that summer.

"In the beginning of October, Barry called and asked me to go to lunch. I was really okay with that. I didn't think about it any more than maybe finding something out about this man that I was attracted to. It was more than sexual. I liked his mind. I liked the way he thought. He was the first man I'd ever known who had similar thoughts to mine. It was reinforcing to me to know that someone else was thinking in ways that I was familiar with, that I was just beginning to know within myself. Or accept.

"We had lunch in a place that's torn down now. It was near the Music Fair. I had been in town for the day. I was gonna do some modeling and had just gone to an interview to try to make some extra money. I looked really good. I was thin, still tan from the summer.

"He had eggs Benedict. He was probably broke. When I think about it now, I don't even know how he had the money to take me to lunch. But he did.

"I had to go see the lawyer, who was finally doing something about the divorce. I remember the dress I wore that day. It was brown plaid with a white collar and cuffs. Your father really liked it. He liked young-schoolgirl-type dresses. At least on me, that really turned him on. He liked white collars and cuffs. I had a couple of those outfits. They must've been popular then, or maybe I was into looking like a little girl, or younger than I was. Certainly not a woman at that stage, except maybe in bed. Maybe not even there.

"I met him back at Hill House. Dawn was in school. Kids were in school. I took my camera 'cause he said why don't you bring your camera and I'll show you how to take some good pictures. I still have one we took of that big tree on the front lawn, or whatever you could call it—it wasn't really a lawn, it was more like a junkyard.

"We walked up behind the house and down the hill. He told me about the geodes that he had had dumped next to the house, and how his little business of selling them was going. I started to learn something about him.

"The house was in shambles. Oh, my God. I don't know why it didn't turn my stomach, because I was Miss Spic and Span. I was gung-ho cleaning. But he just accepted what was around him and I guess I did, too.

"I felt intuitively that he had an explosive nature. I was inquisitive. Curious. I guess I wanted to make some kind of contact with him. I can remember standing in the room with no windows. That was where he first kissed me. Right in the doorway. I said that I wasn't going to make love, and he seemed to accept that. He didn't pressure, he just seemed to accept it. So I left.

"Maybe psychologically he manipulated me, because he knew if he pushed himself too far that day I would run away disgusted with the whole thing. Maybe it was manipulation from the very start. And I was sucked right in.

"He called faithfully to see how I was. I was going through a terrible time trying to find a place to live. Apartments wouldn't take me because I was divorced with three young children. I didn't have any education, didn't have a decent job, no one wanted to take a chance on me. Except Clearmont Apartments. So I paid an exorbitant rent and found my way to Crystal Springs. It was really convenient for him later, because it was only a mile or two from Hill House. Just a few minutes away.

"I moved into Clearmont in the beginning of November. The first time we made love was in that apartment. He helped me christen two apartments. On the floor. Clothes were on the floor.

"It was a time that I don't remember very well because I wasn't into the relationship for sexual satisfaction. Wasn't why I wanted to know him. Sex was secondary. I gave that part of me so I could have a part of him that I wanted. The first time we made love was nothing super. It really didn't have to be. Because he was already giving me all kinds of emotional support during a really rough time.

"He told me he wasn't possessive, but I don't believe that now. In the beginning, he was so convinced that he had something more powerful than what Ian had to offer me that it really didn't bother him at all, the idea that I would see him and also make love to Ian.

"He told me that he could not just have a relationship with anyone. Just bodies were not important. That he needed to be inside my head. No one ever said that to me before. That just clinched more things for me. I thought, Oh, my goodness, you mean there's actually a man who cares for me other than fucking every once in a while, or often?

"And I really did let him inside my head more than any other person I'd ever known. And he really did help. We spent hours and hours on the phone talking. He talked about some of the things he had been through, and I believed them all. It was hide and seek, seek and find. It never even dawned on me to doubt the things he told me. No matter how incredible or how out-landish or how totally almost ridiculous—a lot of it bordered on the absurd—I accepted it. It fit his voice. As long as he said those words with his voice, it was okay.

"It never occurred to me to get out of the relationship. I think of it now and I think something like that would scare me a million miles away if I were confronting it. I would say, Whoa, wait a minute, something is really—twisted? Twisted. Get me out of here.

"By then I was seeing O'Hennessey every once in a while and I was seeing Barry three, four, five times a week. In the morning I wouldn't have to be at work till ten, and sometimes he would just come and have coffee. He'd collapse. Sometimes he'd take me to bed for a short while. He would meet me for lunch. Then he'd come out to K-Mart's at the mall an hour and a half or two hours later and I'd see him again. There were a lot of evenings that I got to see him, too.

"He needed money that Christmas and I gave it to him for the first time. Just a few hundred. He thought the settlement from my house was a lot greater than it was. What was he going after? I don't know. Maybe I do know.

"My children didn't know yet that I was seeing him. I always managed to work around that. They didn't know he existed. Nor Ian. But there was a reason. Barry was entirely different from my relationship with Ian.

"Later he told me he was running from bill collectors, that he was haunted by phone calls. I began to learn how deeply in debt he was.

"His first heart attack—both were on the same day, July twenty-sixth, my birthday. Or at least that's what he said.

"During this time I really think Barry felt okay about our relationship. I never had a sense that he was seeing any other women. Now when I look back I think it's highly possible, but I didn't at the time. I felt him completely faithful to me.

"When he talked about making bombs that blew people apart, or going to—I think it may have been Mexico—someplace in South America—and blowing people apart—sometimes he would talk about it with regret. Sometimes he was just matter-of-fact about the whole thing. I would just listen. And none of it ever really stunned me. I accepted it.

"He started talking about the CIA and the men that he had worked with, and I had no reason to doubt any of that. This was all beginning to happen in December and January. I'd known him since October. It just seemed perfectly natural that he was getting used to being with me and trusting me and needed someplace to pour that energy and I was the target. Maybe he got some kind of kicks from being able to tell a story again. I didn't think it at the time, I didn't question it. We would make love and then he would talk about killing people. He would touch me and tell me about his sexual fantasies, and that's when I began to learn about his mind, what it was capable of. He craved a film that showed a man making love to a pregnant woman. He finally got one.

"In the beginning when we made love, it was more of an attempt to get inside my head, as he would say. To know what I was thinking. That came first. So that by the time that he was talking sex and death it was perfectly acceptable to me. I just thought it was his turn. His stories were better than mine anyway.

"This must've been spring of '74. Can it be that long ago? In March, K-Mart's sent me to New York for a seminar for a week. That was when I met a man named Daryl Phelps. I was sitting in the lobby waiting for a couple of women who were in the seminar with me. We were gonna go to dinner together because it was my last night in New York. A man came in. He just stood there waiting, too, and eventually he came over to me and said, 'Would you like to have a drink?' I said no. He was very insistent, and I said no. I said, 'I'm waiting for someone and then I'm gonna leave,' and he said, 'I'll tell ya what, come and stand and have a drink.' There was a bar adjacent to the hotel lobby and he said, 'You can stand and watch for your friends and talk to me at the same time.' I said, 'Okay, fine, all right, I'll have a drink.'

"So we talked for a few minutes. My friends came in. I introduced them to him, and he was very insistent and still wanted to take us out to eat. I said no again and we left.

"When I came back, there was a business card in my mailbox. He was one of the presidents of a large clothing manufacturer. His name was in the bottom right corner, and that was all. Except his telephone number.

"I called the next day. I wanted to know if he was really one of the presidents or was he just a salesman trying to make a good impression 'cause he had the same last name as one of the real presidents. Well, he was *the* president.

"I ended up having cocktails with him at the Saint Regis before I left to get the Metroliner home. From the Saint Regis at five-thirty he took me to a little apartment on Park Avenue. Very insistent about wanting to go to bed and, if I didn't go to bed, wanting to take me to Beverly Hills. He offered to put me up in Beverly Hills for a week. I said no, I wasn't gonna have any part of that; I had someone waiting for me back home.

"He couldn't believe that somebody was turning an offer like that down. I was a little lady from the country and why wasn't I impressed with this big-city president of a corporation who was offering to send me to California and to a lovely hotel, buy me clothes if I needed them? But he put me on the next Metroliner and he told me he would be in touch with me.

"When I got home, Barry was waiting to hear about the trip. I think that was when he began to love me. And at the same time, I'm sure that dollar signs slipped into his head when I told him I had just met this big-city corporate president. At that point he was beginning to work on Zapcap and he needed funding. He would make insinuations or inquiries as far as 'Do you think you could get him interested in financing my idea?' He would have used me if I played into it. I know he wanted to. I played dumb about it all. I played as if I didn't see what he was trying to do.

"It was in March. Every once in a while I would see O'Hennessey. Barry spent a lot of Friday nights at my place. The children would stay at their father's for the weekend, so I'd have my weekends free. Sometimes on Sunday afternoons Barry would be so worn out that he would come to my place and fall asleep on the sofa. He was very tired. A lot. He was tired.

"It was the same time that he was also trying to work at the Farmer's Market. He had that kind of paper that bookies use, so I think about numbers. I know he drove contraband across the borders of three states and brought it into Massachusetts. I really only thought of it in terms of cigarettes and booze. I knew guns were a possibility, although I didn't ask him. Porno was another. I preferred to think of it in terms of cigarettes and booze, rather than porno and guns. The more he opened up, the more I could see how much it took out of him. I guess he felt he could trust me.

"He said something in February of that year that really blew me away. He said that I was the first woman he had ever really wanted to give a child to. It became part of what we had when we made love, on his side. If that was a form of manipulating me, it worked, psychologically it worked. He was a very bright man if he used that in that way—because with that, I thoroughly believed that he loved me. Supporting me in all the emotional turmoil I was in, and demanding very little except a place to hide, to escape to. My house was fairly straight. I generally had food. Warm blankets on the bed. He retreated there.

"Sometimes he talked about the drugs that he took to stay alive—at least that's how he put it—and how he hated to swallow them, he hated to be that dependent on pills for his life. He would have to have blood tests every once in a while. . . . He suffered terribly from phlebitis. Was it phlebitis? What is that when the joints get inflamed? Gout? Oh, I'd forgotten. I haven't heard that word since then. I'm certain it was excruciating for him. I don't know what it's like because I've never known anyone else with gout, but he would joke about it by saying it was the disease of all men that are geniuses. That was his plight.

"This is the first time I've thought of that in a long time. His feet would be so sore. His hands. I can remember how he said he tried to work in spite of it . . . I felt sympathy for him. I felt sympathy. I guess I returned to him some of what he gave me when I felt so weak. It was amazing to see how weak he could become when he let go. On the other hand, he could be so violent. I didn't know his violence directly, but he certainly talked about it. It was there.

"He wanted me to shave—I'll let your imagination do the rest. And I did. I'd never done it before and I've never done it since, but I did then. For him. And I'm certain it had something to do with his fetish as far as young girls were concerned. He loved the idea of taking a young girl. The younger the better. And I did all of it soooo willingly, so accepting. And graciously. And gladly. There was no limit.

"He wore black. Black turtlenecks, black pants, black shoes. I bought him a beautiful sweater for Christmas, a white fisherman's knit sweater. And I never gave it to him. I don't even know what happened to it.

"I remember being at his house when he took me down to the basement to show me his collection of creatures. He had the iguana and the snakes and Wally the alligator. I couldn't believe my eyes! Then we walked over to the other side of the basement, where he had some geodes. It was all new to me. I had never known what a geode was until he explained to me how they were formed and fossilized. That's where I got my collection downstairs. They're all pieces that he gave me.

"I was completely enthralled with his gifts. To me they were very precious. To him, I don't think they meant very much. I don't think I ever conveyed to him just how much they meant. By the time I could have said something like that, it was too late, because the relationship had changed.

"He was such a strange combination of a person. A lover who took me to bed and a man who kept an alligator in his basement. I mean really. And he talked about a vulture or a hawk that he nursed in the bathroom? The powder room? I can't remember all that stuff, it was so crazy, but I remember there was a greenhouse in back of the house where this vulture or hawk supposedly

lived after Barry nursed it back to health. I had been married
to a guy who had been a schoolteacher and was into education
and corporate images, and then this man comes into my life with
alligators and snakes and vultures . . . I couldn't believe it.

"His books, his writing. He had so much potential. He stunned
me a lot of times, literally stunned me. Blew me away.

"Sometimes he could be so *potent*. I'd been married to a man
that in ten years of marriage only made love at night. And that
was it, once. He'd turn over and go to sleep and so would I.
Nothing beyond that. Maybe the whole thing took half an hour,
an hour at the most. That was the beginning of the end. Here
was this man who could take me to bed and spend *hours*. I often
wondered if the drugs that he took for his heart had something to
do with that. I couldn't understand his potency, I really couldn't.
He would tell me that I turned him on, but I found it hard to
believe that I had anything to do with it.

"He would run himself ragged—I think that's the way he also
described it. I think he used . . . it wasn't 'treadmill' . . . it wasn't
'vicious circle' . . . I'm trying to think of how he would explain
his life sometimes. Can't remember. Can't remember. . . .

"Those first six months, from October to April, were really good
months. I think he was talking to Japan, at least he said he was
talking to Japan, because his phone bills were terrible. He was
trying to work out a deal where he would go over and see how
they put their fireworks displays together. I never understood the
connection, I never asked about his life as a fireworker. I think
it had a lot to do with his anger. Have the fireworks explode
instead of Barry explode. He exploded with each one, I'll bet.

"In April of 1974 I visited Hill House with my children. It
was a Sunday afternoon. Barry wanted me to bring them. He
was excited about it—he enjoyed children, at a distance. It was
very strange for my children to see three black children with this
very Jewish man inside that upside-down house. I wanted them
to *see* this person who had meant so much to me. There was no
way my children could know the place that he had had in my
life—and my heart?—for six months. But I wanted them to see
the difference between their father and someone like Barry. I
wanted them to know that those differences exist.

"I remember the beginning of *A Tale of Two Cities*: 'It was the best of times, it was the worst of times, it was the age of wisdom, it was the age of foolishness. . . .' The first six or eight months that I knew Barry are described right there in those words. I come from an upper-middle-class sterility. Barry was so fertile, he was a social outcast, and I loved it. I loved it. I loved him for it. The fact that I could entertain him never ceased to amaze me, that I could hold his attention.

"And so I wanted the children to know something about this man, to see where and how he lived, and also that I could care for someone who was very different from anything or anyone they had ever known. From their father. . . .

"We'd meet at eleven o'clock in the morning for a cup of coffee, and he'd be on his way to make one of his 'pickups' or 'deliveries,' which is what he called them. Eventually I found out those trips had something to do with porno, but I didn't know how heavily he was into it for quite a while. Then I remember he said he was selling his own guns because he needed the money. I often wondered about drugs, although I never asked him questions about any of it.

"It wasn't till I'd known him for more than a year that he brought that bookie paper over and burned it in front of the children. I'm certain he wanted that to be a lead-in for me to question him, and I didn't. I didn't ask him why he had it or what he was doing with it. Didn't touch it.

"He would always talk about being tired because of all the driving he was doing at night. He talked about driving big cars to certain places and making changes—'switchies,' he called them. Driving trucks full of 'contraband'—that was also his word. It all seemed very strange because I couldn't see Barry driving any kind of truck, but I never questioned him about that either. He talked about putting mud on his license plate so it couldn't be read. I only questioned him about things like that a couple times, and that was too much, because he'd get really bothered. So I quit that.

"He used to bake bread at home—I think it was black pumper-

nickel—and sometimes he would bring me a loaf or two. He'd
come walking in with a loaf under each arm, fresh out of the oven.
He'd put them in the refrigerator and then he'd take out his gun
and put it on top of the refrigerator. He had to do that. Couldn't
bring me bread without bringing his gun, too.

"He really appreciated beautiful things—that was the other
side of him. He enjoyed beauty in nature: the formations of
minerals, knowing about a tiny insect in a pond and how they
mate or sting. That was a really beautiful side of him. That's what
I concentrated on.

"I don't know what was in the house that he rented after he
left Dawn for the last time, but I had a feeling that that house
was alive. The few times I saw it, it was bare to my sight: no
furniture, no bookcases. Just a lot of snake cages all over the
living-room floor. He got all these white hospital sheets from
someplace, so he had tons of clean white sheets. I can remember
him chuckling about how clean his dreams would be from now
on.

"He played so innocent with my friend Sara. He played the
mild-mannered reporter. It was incredible. I don't think she ever
had any idea of his explosive nature. Some women are unbelievably slow. He was always playing games with me, but I don't
think I was ever completely blind to them. I may not have
questioned or confronted him, but I think I was perceptive
enough to feel it.

"I wonder at what point I started questioning what was really
going on. If you're in a play, you don't question the lines at all.
Then suddenly the act stops and you wonder if it was really a
play or only a dream. Then you wonder because some dreams are
so real, more real than something you experienced.

"I could divide our relationship into three sections. The first
went from October 1973 to August of '74. Then September '74 to
January of '75. And from February of '75 until December '75. We
had three entirely separate relationships.

"During the first months, he was highly supportive of me because I was going through a lot of trauma with my divorce, very

much a rescuer. That was the tender, gentle side of him, the one
who enjoyed walking down the lane and sitting beside a pond,
talking about insects and spiders and snakes, the beauty of a
geode, the age of a plant. He brought me tokens of this—this—
this love, which reiterated what I saw in him. I had never experienced those things before. He had a real feeling for them, and I
had never known what a geode was. And the idea that he had an
iguana in the basement amused and entertained me. It really
touched me, too.

"That period lasted roughly until I began to suspect that he had
an inkling that maybe I had some money and he could use it. He
suggested that the money would be used to promote his fire-
workings. I don't know if that was true. Could've been to pay
debts, or to buy more contraband. I know he bought stones—he
was especially fond of quartz. He bought all kinds of cut gems. I
still have two or three of them. They've never been set—a moonstone, a piece of amethyst. He *gave* these to me. I don't even
know if he ever paid for them. He was really kind at that time, at
least that's what I saw.

"Then I met the guy from New York, the corporate president.
It was such a freak accident—little girl from Small Town, U.S.A.,
goes to New York, meets a corporate president who owns one of
the largest retail clothing houses in the country . . . the whole
thing was like something you read about in a novel. Harold
Robbins. The *National Enquirer*.

"He started it and I continued it, I played the game, even
though I knew I'd never see him again. At the same time, Barry
knew where I was.

"But I did see him again. In June I had to go to the courthouse
to sign papers which would take my ex-husband to court for child
support. It was really an unnerving day, one of the worst days of
my life. I had planned on having dinner with Mr. President in
Boston that night. We had a very expensive dinner in a very fancy
restaurant and then went to a hotel afterward. It was like I was
in a trance, I was just numb to everything. No excuse, but that's
how I was. He ended up asking me for money to take a cab to
catch his Metro! I had money and he didn't! This guy's a million-
aire I don't know how many times over. His wallet probably cost
more than the clothes I had on. I ended up giving him ten dollars

so he could catch his train on time . . . I have it in my journal. Needless to say, when we made love, it was all of forty minutes. I went home and he went home. Still boggles my mind.

"During the six weeks that followed, Barry was the only one who knew I was pregnant, and he really stood by me. It was a really bad time because I was going through a lot of problems with my ex-husband. I had to get out of my apartment, I knew I couldn't really keep my job, and where were we gonna live, and the kids would have to change schools and it was July. Plus being pregnant by Mr. President.

"The day that I went into Boston and had the abortion, Barry wanted to go with me. I wanted no part of it. Go by myself. It was awful, the absurdity of the whole thing. Afterward he met me at the train station where I parked my car. I got off the train and threw up. That was how I felt about the whole situation. He cooked dinner for the kids. He was really sweet.

"Then I turned around and did something really awful. That was the end of anything good that we had.

"Of course, for the first few days after the abortion, I thought I was gonna bleed to death. It was really bad. There were complications. There wasn't anybody to call—I was alone at night and having really bad contractions and internal bleeding. I was afraid I was gonna pass out and nobody would've known, because I'd arranged for the children to be away. None of my friends wanted to be bothered or else I didn't want them to know. One of those days was my birthday. What a way to turn twenty-seven.

"Barry was the only one who stood by me. He found a drugstore that was open that Sunday and got me medications. He was really kind. He literally came and sat with me through a raging fever. That went on for a week or ten days.

"The first night I went out was to meet Barry and Ian. Barry had driven his car and Ian had his and I had mine. We met and had a drink—I'm not exactly sure why—I think Barry called and said why don't you come out and have a drink with us, it would do you good to get out. We just talked for a while. Had a really good time. When we went out to leave, Barry went to his car and came back with a bunch of red roses for me. They were really beautiful. And I thanked him. And I've gone over in my mind a million times why I did what I did, how awful it was. When I said goodnight to him, I got in the car with Ian. That was such a slap in his face. To this day I don't know why. I don't know why.

"Later, I think I paid for it because Barry treated my best friend as a temporary lover. I think that was the return slap in my face. And it worked. That was the end of our relationship.

"So you see, here was a man who was perfectly capable of violence, evil, cruelty. And he had not been that way with me. Still, he got slapped really hard for putting himself out on the line. I think when that happens repeatedly to a person, how that twists . . . they're never the same again. I think for him that marked the end of the kind of relationship he had with me. I don't think any of the women he knew after me—I don't think it was like what we had had, I don't think he wanted it. He certainly didn't have it with Sara and didn't have it with either Betty Jean. I think he was even less tolerant with Dawn. I don't know that it was so much me as it was just another action, just the slow process of destroying a human being.

"A lot of the time he tried to pretend that things didn't hurt him, which was really strange because you'd think this hard shell of a man, this brutal man—but that wasn't always true. He didn't want his vulnerability or his weakness to show, especially to a woman, to me. He wanted to be tough. And maybe sometimes he really meant what he said, like when he'd say, 'I really want you to do what's good for you. If you wanna see Ian, that's really okay.'

"In reality I don't know that he felt that at all. I think it ripped him up into little pieces each time I said I'd just seen Ian, or Ian mentioned to him that he'd just seen me. Of course Ian had no idea that Barry and I were having a relationship. He didn't know till spring of '75. It came as a total shock to him. That was a slap in Ian's face. I'm sure I'll never forget that night either.

"If Barry had told Ian about us at the beginning, it would've been so much better. But he couldn't do that. As much of a man as he was—as much courage or whatever he had—he didn't have that simple ability to let people in, to really touch. Directly. He was about to let me touch, but I didn't want it.

"And it's no wonder. If you have too many of those incidents—like that night when I thought so little of his red roses . . .

"He had a lot to offer, but it wasn't sexual, it was something else. The gloom-and-doom talk was discounted by many people, but . . .

"We were riding high at that time. Inflation hadn't caught up with us yet. Vietnam seemed far away and unreal. All we knew was that we had more money than we had ever had.

"Barry was just a man beyond his time. I think we—meaning the people who knew him—accepted him as an important individual even though we didn't hear what he was saying. We heard what was there for the moment, but I think there was more to him than that. He was many personalities, he could be many people. But there's this one basic man that most people did not get to see. I think I had insight into some of him without even being aware of it at the time. The reasons that he enjoyed weaponry . . . he had a flip side that despised it. He knew that that weaponry was necessary. It was like a miniature game for him.

"On the other side, he knew the destruction. I think that's why he swung the other way toward the end of his life, toward fireworks and butterflies. Nature. That wasn't anything new to him, but that's what he chose to maximize near the end, to make the most of.

"He knew how close his own end was. I believe that life killed him, and not that he destroyed it in himself. He was a victim.

"I did not see him as a sexual creature. It's natural for many men to see him that way, because that mirrors so much of themselves. But he was not totally that creature. He was a creature of a very certain design. There was a mind capable of anything. Sex was only an asset. It was higher developed than in most because he was honest with it. But I don't think that's all there was. I know that's not all there was. I think he had more answers than I was capable of seeing. I don't know what—I can't put my finger on particulars—but I think those answers are related very little to sex.

"A lot of his loneliness was because he didn't find a way to communicate his deepest thoughts and wisdom. Don't ask me why, but he didn't really search it out either.

"He was hoping for added time, for a chance to go beyond his loneliness. But first a woman had to get past his armor, and that was pretty thick. But he really wanted a woman to get past his shell. If he had any hope, that was his hope. That was the void he was always trying to fill. And of course he always tried to fill it through sex. All kinds. Anytime. All ways. And I think it was a conscious choice, just as much as he was conscious of his loneliness.

"I don't think he knew where he wanted to go after leaving Dawn. Except death. He knew that. That was a final relief. When you think about it, that was a release from many burdens, and I think sex was one of them. He couldn't hold up the mask any longer. That's why he was so tired all the time. He *chose* not to do it any longer.

"On those tapes you played for me, Ian makes reference to Barry's size constantly. To me, as a woman, to whom that should have been important, it was not. That was not—I repeat—the primary reason for my relationship with Barry. It was not because he had a—it was not—because he was well equipped. It's true! Turn that thing off for a minute! . . .

"I wonder about the other women, and if that was really important to them. Or if that's just a man thinking that those things are important to a woman. Maybe they're important to other men, but how important is it to the woman? Or the girls? The Puerto Ricans? If you are a young girl and you've never seen one before, how do you have anything to compare it with? Maybe it's smaller! Right? Right. That's a good point. One of the more important ones we've discussed. What virgin would know that his was bigger than your average Joe's? Only another man who has been around would know, to comment on it so often.

"I didn't have the courage to look as far as I was capable of seeing. Others may talk about his attractiveness in or out of bed. I wonder how many of them saw him as a man. You can run a test, because by now you're getting a pretty complete picture of the person. You should know by now if he's real or if this was all such a facade that he didn't have anything inside him. Only *you* know the answer. I'm really going out on a limb exposing myself, by revealing my thoughts about who he was as a man, not just a cock in bed. Or on the sofa. Or the floor.

"He was a unique individual that our world killed. That's how I feel it. I was just as much responsible for his death as anybody else. And it starts way back when he was young. It's no one's singular fault, it's just how things turned out. It's up to you to decide whether or not I'm close to the truth—it's not a question of right or wrong, it's a question of the truth. Telling the truth about a man's life. That he didn't have time to tell."

17

Freedom of Misinformation

COPY TO:	1–USA, EDMA (AAT: AUSA DOMINICK X. DI ROCCO)
REPORT OF:	(DELETED) Offices: Boston, MA.
DATES:	AUG 2 1961
FIELD OFFICE FILE NOS:	175–6834 Bureau nos: 175–3834
TITLES:	(DELETED)
CHARACTER:	INTERSTATE TRANSPORTATION OF OBSCENE MATTER
SYNOPSIS:	Barry Rothman, Boston, Massachusetts, advised he purchased two reels of obscene film from subject. (DELETED) interviewed and was uncooperative. Subject appeared before Judge LEO B. RAFAEL, EDMA, on 7/6/61, for sentencing; postponed to 7/20/61. Subject appeared before Judge WALTER BROCKHORSEN, EDMA, on 7/20/61, and sentenced to custody of AG. for one year and a day.

By communication dated June 27,
1961, the Boston Office advised of
the following investigation:

On June 12, 1961, the Boston Telephone Directory was
reviewed and revealed that Barry Rothman had listed his
telephone at 7075 Rising Sun Avenue. This telephone is
(DELETED) and was in addition to the telephone ROTH-
MAN had listed at his apartment, 491 North 12th Street.

On June 12, 1961 the information concerning ROTHMAN
and his connection with the subject was discussed with
Boston Police Inspector (DELETED) at which time he
advised he had no definite information that ROTHMAN was
a dealer in obscene matters; however, he had heard rumors
to that effect in the past. He stated he would immediately
institute a surveillance on ROTHMAN's apartment and, if
this surveillance determined there was a possibility that
ROTHMAN was involved, a search and seizure warrant
would be obtained.

On June 19, 1961, Inspector (DELETED) telephonically
contacted SA (DELETED) and advised a search and
seizure warrant had been obtained and that the men sur-
veilling ROTHMAN's apartment would enter this apartment
with this warrant as soon as it was determined that ROTH-
MAN was in the apartment.

On the evening of June 19, 1961, SA (DELETED) was
telephonically contacted by Patrolman (DELETED) Inspector (DELETED) Squad, at which time he advised
ROTHMAN's apartment had been searched and therein was
found numerous obscene photographs, books, and six reels
of film. He advised that ROTHMAN had also been arrested
and at the time of ROTHMAN's arrest, he was in the
company of one (DELETED).

The material obtained by Patrolman (DELETED) from
ROTHMAN's apartment was reviewed and revealed a telephone bill for ROTHMAN which indicated that he made a
telephone call to (DELETED), Paterson, New Jersey, on
May 1, 1961, and telephone call to (DELETED), Baltimore,

Maryland, on May 8, 1961. It is to be noted that the Paterson, New Jersey, numbers are contact numbers for (DELETED).

Interview of (DELETED) indicated that she was a business acquaintance of ROTHMAN, who is employed (DELETED). Her address is (DELETED) . . . telephone . . . (DELETED) She is a (DELETED).

Material obtained from ROTHMAN's apartment was carefully reviewed on June 22, 1961, and revealed four reels of 8 mm film entitled "Fireside Lights," "Sherry's Hideaway," "For Pete's Sake," and "Kutchur Balzoff"; and two 16 mm reels of film entitled "Miss Park Avenue" and "El Satario" (The Devil). All film was definitely obscene. A total of 295 photographs and negatives, the majority of which were obscene, were also obtained by the Boston Police Department and eight obscene books were also obtained. This material has been sent to the FBI Laboratory in an attempt to determine its source.

On June 20, 1961, ROTHMAN appeared before a Boston Magistrate, at which time he was held under $800 bail for court. He has made bail and is presently awaiting court.

BARRY ROTHMAN, Apartment (DELETED), 491 North 12th Street, Boston, Mass., was interviewed in the office of Boston Police Inspector (DELETED). After being advised that he did not have to make any statement, any statement he made could be used against him in a court of law, and he had the right to obtain the services of an attorney prior to interview, ROTHMAN advised as follows:

ROTHMAN advised he was formerly married to (DELETED), but had recently obtained a divorce. ROTH-MAN advised he was employed as a Laboratory Associate with the Lincoln Institute, and had been employed there for nine and one-half years. He stated that in his job at the Lincoln Institute, in approximately 1956, he was involved in an explosion during an experiment and, as a result of this

explosion, he was made sterile. He stated that because of his
sterility he subsequently began having sexual problems with
his wife which he believed to be his fault. He stated that he
had formed a "psychotic neurosis" towards his sexual problem with his wife and with anyone for that matter, and
because of these problems he began collecting pornographic
material. He continued that after living with his wife under
these conditions for approximately three years, he and his
wife separated and recently divorced.

ROTHMAN advised that approximately six to eight
months prior to interview he attended a photographic
exhibition in New York City and while at this exhibition he
had met (DELETED). He stated that during conversations
with (DELETED) he realized that both of them had a
personal interest in pornographic material and since his
return to Boston he had talked with (DELETED) on the
telephone on numerous occasions. He stated that during
April 1960 (DELETED) called him on the telephone and
made arrangements to meet him in Boston at which time
(DELETED) was to bring two reels of obscene film for
him. He stated that during their previous telephone conversations, he believed that (DELETED) was attempting to
set him up as a distributor for this obscene material in the
Boston area and he frankly admitted that he willingly let
(DELETED) think this for he believed in this way he could
obtain the film from (DELETED) at a wholesale price.
ROTHMAN advised that he arranged for (DELETED) to
bring two reels of film to him and that he had met
(DELETED) at the Oak House, a restaurant located on the
corner of 26th and Oak Street, just a few blocks from his
apartment house. He advised that (DELETED) indicated
to him that he had just driven up to Boston from Trenton,
New Jersey, and appeared to be in a hurry to depart because
of the necessity of driving back to his home in New Jersey.
He stated the time of the meeting was approximately 8 or
8:30 PM and occurred in April during a very cold spell in
Boston. He advised that (DELETED) was driving an auto-

mobile of an unknown make, but that he did recall that the automobile was either light brown or beige in color. He stated that to the best of his knowledge he paid (DELETED) $16.00 for the two reels of film or $8.00 per reel.

ROTHMAN stated that (DELETED) spoke often of obtaining more film from "the factory" and because of this he did not believe that (DELETED) himself was making the film, but was obtaining it from another party.

When questioned regarding the source of the other material found in his possession, ROTHMAN stated that he sincerely could not recall any names from whom the material was obtained, but that it had been obtained from chance acquaintances who learned that he was interested in pornographic material. He denied that he had ever transported such material across a state line or that he had ever exhibited this material to anyone other than himself. When questioned regarding the telephone calls made to (DELETED), he advised that he usually called (DELETED) at (DELETED) which he understood to be his home, but had been told on occasion to call (DELETED) at (DELETED) because he did not believe (DELETED's) wife knew too much about his obscene matters activities.

ROTHMAN gave the following description of (DELETED):

Race	(DELETED)
Sex	(DELETED)
Height	(DELETED)
Weight	(DELETED)
Build	(DELETED)
Age	(DELETED)
Hair	(DELETED)
Complexion	(DELETED)
Eyes	(DELETED)
Characteristics	(DELETED)

The following description of ROTHMAN was obtained during interview:

Race	White
Sex	Male
Born	January 14, 1935, Boston
Height	5′ 10″
Weight	155 lbs.
Build	Medium
Complexion	Dark
Hair	Black, straight, receding hairline
Eyes	Dark brown
Scars and marks	Cross-cut scar on left thumb; X-ray burn over left eye
Marital status	Divorced from (DELETED)
Education	Graduate high school; attends night classes (DELETED) University
Employment	Laboratory Associate, Lincoln Institute
Residence	491 North 12th Street, Apt. 3–L telephone (DELETED)

On July 5, 1961, Assistant United States Attorney (AUSA) DOMINICK DI ROCCO, Eastern District of Massachusetts (EDMA), was advised of the investigation in Boston pertaining to BARRY ROTHMAN. He advised that since (DELETED) was to be sentenced on July 6, 1961, he would ask JUDGE RAFAEL to postpone sentencing of the subject in order that (DELETED) could be interviewed concerning ROTHMAN.

On July 5, 1961, (DELETED) Federal Probation Officer, Brooklyn, New York, was advised of the investigation in Boston pertaining to BARRY ROTHMAN and the subject. This Probation Officer was called in because of (DELETED's) previous arrest record in that borough.

On July 6, 1961, subject appeared before Judge LEO X. RAFAEL, EDMA, for sentencing. Judge RAFAEL postponed sentencing to July 20, 1961.

Three pages withheld entirely at this location in the file. Deleted under exemption(s) B7C, B7D, with no segregable material available for release.

On July 20, 1961, subject appeared before Judge WALTER BROCKHORSEN, EDMA, and was sentenced to the custody of the Attorney General of the United States for a period of a year and a day for violation of Section 1465, Title 18, United States Code.

On July 20, AUSA DI ROCCO advised that the obscene films and reels found in the subject's automobile could be destroyed.

On July 28, 1961, (DELETED), Federal House of Detention, New York City, advised that (DELETED) was still assigned to this institution.

18

Black Widow

There is more to be said by this black widow, much more. But how to get it out of her? If I push too hard, I may never be able to consult her again. But I must try. I must. I have no choice.

When we meet for the second interview, she tells me she would have canceled this morning if she had been able to get hold of me earlier. She doesn't know it but I purposely didn't offer her a number where I could be reached, for just this reason.

"Business is crazy as usual," she says.

I suggest that we could make this interview shorter than the last, if that would help ease her work load.

"No, we'll do it right this time. This should about do it anyway."

I feel an instant tightening: She's trying to make her stand against my attempts to make her open up and remember. But I don't say anything, don't plead. I don't tell her how much it means to me to have more time with her. I let the conversation unfold, figuring I'll have my best chance if I get her to soften and recall some of that past she loved, the man she loved.

And it works. Is it odd that she softens most when talking about his sex and the weapons projects they worked on together in the lab at Western Weapons? Is it mysterious that she laughs most heartily when recalling his trips to Puerto Rico to buy little girls, when he would come back with a serious case of crabs? There is a loving tone in her voice when she describes how he would come home frayed at the edges and weary of the world, exhausted from his sexual adventures and misadventures in business. "Home for a little medication," she says, grinning. Her voice is feminine, maternal, tender, giving. I feel him dragging himself home, knowing she will agree to stay together one more time. They share a chuckle while she warms his bones and feeds him a hot meal. Then, when he's well enough, she sends him out of the cave and back into the raging world.

I begin our second interview by trying to narrow the circles that can be drawn around her knowledge of him. I am aiming for the inner circle.

"It started as a sexual relationship, a mutual attraction. Curiosity, I think, for both of us. Very quickly we both recognized that we had something to give to each other that we wanted. I was rather dependent then, as I was later on in our relationship, and he wanted that, he needed that. So it was mutually satisfying for both of us. We were fulfilling a need for one another.

"He was a good lover, period. *Period.* All those things he was later, he was then. Very attentive . . . I think more attentive to my needs earlier than later on. Later it became very internal, it became different for him, he went into a world all by himself as a lover. He remained that way till the end. Really fulfilling his own needs entirely. Self-stroking. He could lose himself in sex, he *needed* to lose himself in sex. Sex was his only escape. As he got more and more frightened, he indulged himself more and more.

"He tried various things and they just fell apart. His vocational ideas got more and more strange and far out, and nothing ever materialized. I think he became more insecure and frightened and turned to sex more often for more superficial reasons. More stroking.

"He couldn't see himself as an ordinary guy out of work. So his solutions couldn't be ordinary. The notion of finding another job was unthinkable. When he was initially out of work, it was, 'Now I have time to do all those projects I've been wanting to do.' The fantasy developed that he could be an entrepreneur and a free wheeler and dealer and piece it all together 'cause I'm good at wheeling and dealing and I'm a good salesman, although I couldn't really be a salesman for a company, but that's one of my talents and I can put it to work.

"There was nothing to say that wasn't a possibility—some of the things he was doing were very real and could have worked, if some of the other things were there, but they weren't. He didn't have the strength to stick with things and do all the sensible things that go into making a business succeed. Take care of details and make sure all the pieces are fitting.

"Well, the fireworks factory was one of his ideas. He always wanted to do fireworks. He always wanted to make a better firecracker than the Chinese. He wanted to make a different pattern in the sky. He noticed that all aerial fireworks are just variations on one pattern. He figured he could sell that to somebody in the States, because it was getting tougher and tougher to import them and costing more money with more federal restrictions, etc., etc., and that's when he talked somebody in New Mexico into backing his fireworks inventions.

"I forget a lot of the details. But anyhow, he came to them with his ideas about a bigger and better fireworks display, and they thought it was rather interesting and they paid for him to go down there and fiddle around. He made a few at home, took 'em down there, and some of them worked. There was something wrong with the ignition system, so they paid for him to go down there again and work on the ignition system, which he did to no avail. It really wasn't getting off the ground in any big way.

"But lo and behold they had an accident, not due to any of his stuff, and they suffered a great deal of loss. They had a big inventory that just went up in smoke. And so that deal petered out. But he was still in the firecracker race.

"After the accident, he went to talk with some fireworks guy in Virginia who was making sparklers. Took the same idea to him. He managed to talk the guy into backing the factory he had over in Crystal Springs, just a few miles from here. It didn't make any money either, but it had promises of getting off the ground. Which it did, literally, because they had an accident there, too. Really rotten luck. But that's what happens in that kind of business. And there was money lost and money missing, although

Barry didn't put any money into it. The employees weren't paid after that accident, which soured a few people on fireworks.

"Then he went into making M-80s and working on the Zapcap, for which he got money from a patent attorney, so that's where the funding came for that. Which he did not use for Zapcap. That never got off the ground either. He was talking to a couple of people about marketing . . . the patent came through for Zapcap a few weeks after he died, and the patent attorney, of course, owns the rights to that patent.

"There were times when I questioned whether it was a sincere endeavor or if he was just going from person to person collecting money to do his thing, staving them off as long as he could, because he did collect money from an awful lot of people. There was the patent attorney, the two doctors, and on and on. On and on and on and on. All those people were supporting his ship that was coming in. Sooner or later, probably sooner. I couldn't even guess how much money was involved. I'm sure it was thousands and thousands over those last few years.

"The relationship was disintegrating at the same rate that everything else was. Just plain disintegrating. I made up my mind to do my thing while he did his. There was no growing going on. We lost interest in talking to each other and seeing what was missing. It was a dependence. He depended on me as much as I depended on him. There were certain ways in which we would not let each other down. There was a genuine caring and a strange type of loving, and we both knew that, but there wasn't much of anything else. We couldn't do any more for each other. I stopped trying. I could not be anything for him except someone to feed that ego that needed to be fed, and I had become so disillusioned I couldn't pretend to do that anymore, just feed him.

"He went to a shrink several times prior to the end. Even the shrink told him he needed to decide whether he was going to stop playing games or get on with real life. The shrink asked him if he wanted to be here, and he did not. The shrink said, 'Then there's nothing I can do for you until you want me to do it for you.' He asked Barry why he came to see him, and Barry's general response was he was curious to see if the shrink could tell him more than he already knew. Just more game-playing. He'd try to fool the shrink as much as he could. So there wasn't any reason for me to try or be interested, because he wasn't interested. He was interested in stroking. It superseded everything. *Everything.*

"I guess deep down inside I always felt some miracle would happen, or eventually, sooner or later, or something like that. I really, really felt that. That's one of the sorrows I felt when he died, that there was no chance for that miracle. There was no more chance for him to become a happier person, 'cause he really wasn't happy. I think he was even afraid of being happy.

"That race that he ran really wasn't him. You know what I mean. That runnin' around, taking trips, doing this and that, the women. Those things never made him happy before we met. He wasn't like that. He needed the book in the bed and somebody to hear him and feel comfortable and let him wear his pants down around his knees. Not that people don't change, but I don't believe that stuff made him happy for a minute. That was only his way of escaping. I don't think that's how he wanted to live. Of course, whatever he did was part of him, but I don't think that was his ideal, what made him feel comfortable and at home with himself.

"He fooled a lot of people about who he was, and it takes a bit of energy to do that. He didn't want anybody to know a lot about him, that he was as frightened as he was.

"Sex meant something different for Barry than for me. The more he could do it, the better he felt—that people were attracted—that females were attracted to him—and I don't think he had an awful lot of that in his lifetime. He also did a lot of using in sex, a *lot* of using. I could see it literally and physically, see it, feel it emotionally. I could hear it when he talked about it with someone else. So it must have meant a great deal. I don't know what all those things were, but it certainly was different from what I felt when it came to sex.

"I don't think it was there in the beginning, not that I could detect. Later on it gave him great pleasure to inflict pain during sex. That grew to be more and more important in every sexual encounter he had. Anally, orally, choking, holding. He did that a lot with a certain close friend of ours. She must have needed a lot of that. She needed a lot of everything. That's fine. So before he started going out with an awful lot of women, he would literally use her for that reason.

"I just wouldn't indulge if that's the way it had to be. I wouldn't allow him to use me like that. But he was built for it. What can I say? A little foolin' around's okay if you have a little to fool around with—but, gee. *God!*

"Little girls must have happened long before I knew him. I don't think it just cropped up overnight. Started coming out with movies, pictures, stuff he had. He used to correspond with a couple people who were into it, too, and he used to tell me he was getting stuff for them. It sort of became a joke between us, when I found out it was part of his fetish. We'd talk about it as if in fantasy, but then I realized it wasn't just fantasy. I never condemned him for it. Never. But I was always terribly frightened that he'd get in *serious, serious* trouble.

"Puerto Rico? I think that was purely a lust trip. Oh, shit. One of his jaunts with somebody's cash. I don't know who in the hell's turn it was to pay for that trip, but I'm pretty sure it had to do with little girls. At that point I didn't want to know. Didn't try to find out and didn't ask any questions. Really did not want to know. I was totally disinterested. O'Hennessey may know—they were close at that time. I know he came back with a helluva dose of crabs. Times like that he'd crawl home. '*I got da crabs!*' Ah, Jeez. Exhausted. Totally burned out. Came home for medication. I'd hose'm down in the backyard, then send'm back at it again.

"I have no idea how he set it up. He just told me he had a splendifero time. Whores were as thick as flies, I do believe he said. And you could buy any age you wanted. I never really asked, I guess due to a lack of interest. I think something in the back of my head consciously prevented me from pursuing it. By then it was getting pretty painful.

"I don't know if it was more than lust. The pretense at first was a business trip. But I really have my doubts. In fact, I'm pretty certain it had nothing to do with business. That was part of my not even pursuing it, because I knew better. I'd hear him talking to other people about the business trip and I knew better. Warm weather. I don't remember when. I think only once. All I remember is that he told somebody he was going someplace exotic, but, again, that turned out to be Chicago.

"Don't look at me like that! I don't know! I don't know why that sticks, but I think he only went once to Puerto Rico. The other times were to Trenton or Maryland or Baltimore or some weird place, *weird* place. There was this weird character that was really a slime who came to Hill House. Lived out in California and came to visit his mother who lived in Trenton or Baltimore or someplace like that, and he had a whole setup there, wherever it was. Barry went down there once, but mostly it was local material he was dealing with. O'Hennessey knew. He may be the only person that knows.

"The slime is dead, incidentally, so don't try to interview him. He had some weird disease, which doesn't surprise me. He just kicked the bucket about eight or nine months after I met him. He willed me his camera. That's how come I remember. Isn't that weird? Really weird. He came to visit for an afternoon and brought flowers from his mother's garden and put them in a jar on our dining-room table. What can I say? He was into photography and he liked me. If you're into that, I guess you'd better learn, huh? . . .

"I have no idea how much of himself Barry shared with the other women. He mentioned that it was nice to have someone in love with him. He was referring to one of the Betty Jeans. He needed that. I never pursued that with him either. He'd come over and tell me about some record that one of them bought for him. He'd play it and ask me if I ever heard . . . He really did need that, and I certainly couldn't give it to him."

I wait a couple of weeks so she knows my mission is serious, and then call her at work with a new idea: How about finishing the interview on the phone, since I only have a few more questions? I'm taking a risk, but I'm hoping my chances of hitting the target will be better instead of worse if we talk through a machine. She won't have to go through the ritual of rescheduling meetings, taking off from work, driving to the park. She won't have time to think before she speaks, to plan her defenses. She'll have to jump from one world to the other. Maybe some of her inhibitions will stay behind. Talking on the phone is part of her normal day. Every spy knows that the best way to steal secrets is to make the theft part of the victim's routine.

It works like a charm. She's all for it. We set a date for later in the week when she'll be able to hold off the hordes for at least an hour. I tell her I probably won't even need that much. Do I hear a silent sigh of relief?

Before I dial her number, I review my notes and my last questions. I make a list in order of intimacy. I try to think of the ones that will open her, the ones that will help her find her humor, that will get her out of that office and back to Hill House. I take one last stab at trying to unlock her secret heart. I list a dozen questions, and halfway through the conversation I am shocked to discover that she has offered the answers to half of them before I've had a chance to ask.

"Do you remember anything he said about me or his relationship with me?"

"His regrets were expressed a number of times, for not having a chance to know you very well. Then, when he became aware of your capabilities and talents, he had a feeling of pride and satisfaction. That's the flavor of any comments he would make in a conversation when he would be asked if he had kids and how they were doing. He'd say, 'He's a bright boy, following in his father's footsteps. . . .' I can't remember anything more specific than that."

"Can you recall the various weapons that went through the house over the years?"

"Let's see. There was the M-3. That's a black semiautomatic gun that was used in Vietnam. It was made to look like a machine-gun type of affair. It was one of the newest guns that was produced for Vietnam. Had a plastic stock, all black. He played with it out at Western. Had it home for a long time and played with it up on the shooting range. I doubt he took it back to work. Probably sold it.

"He had a Fonteuse, which is a French shotgun. The Number Ten Riot Gun, the kind the cops use to start or stop riots. He used to shoot cinder blocks with it up on the range. Sundry pistols. The Walther. The .45 with 'Destroyer of All Worlds' engraved in gold Sanskrit on the stock. A Smith and Wesson .38 that he gave to me for one of my birthdays. A few Colts. I think there were some other guns, rifle types, but that was so early in our relationship, during the Western days, that they were disposed of one way or another early in the game. The ones I've mentioned were the only ones he maintained for any length of time."

"How about explosives and other choice incendiaries?"

"My God, you name it. From C-4 to black powder to lycopodium to silver fulminate. Wait a minute. I don't think he ever brought home any silver fulminate. Sundry ammunition. I think the C-4 was the most powerful stuff he ever had at home. He had some grenades. Old collector's items, but one was armed. Couple of tear-gas bombs. Miscellaneous stuff like that. That's about it. Course that's enough for anybody. That could be enough to ruin anybody's day."

"What did you think of his taste for collectables?"

"Very well put. Wouldn't be the kinda thing I'd like to have to explain away at a tea party or to the Welcome Wagon or to baby-sitters. That, coupled with frozen rats, was about enough to make my job well-nigh impossible. I used to wanna send a résumé to people before they came to visit for the first time. Or tell 'em we're only renting this house furnished."

"How did you explain it to visitors?"

"Didn't. But that wasn't really a problem, because most of the people we were friendly with were weird in their own way, if not the same way."

"Did you ever have to deal with very straight people who came to the house?"

"Baby-sitters. Whenever we needed one, it always made me realize how weird we really were. And I had a woman who came to do some ironing while I was working. It hadn't occurred to me that she might be a little wary of the household. Later I found out she was terrified. She finally got the courage up to say she didn't want to do the ironing anymore. I guess she was even afraid to say that, thinking we might blow her head off or force her to eat a dead rat. It must be terrible to be in that situation and even be afraid to try to get out of it. For that, the poor lady got my sympathy. . . .

"I don't care how old a person is, but just about everybody is curious when they shouldn't be. Gettin' into stuff that's none of their business. Can you imagine runnin' the sweeper and comin' across a grenade under the sofa? Get into the closet and four dildoes fall on you? Then go down to the freezer in the basement looking for something to munch on and find a bag full of dead rats? And an albino snake in a plastic bag? Does that give you the picture? I was getting so weird, I didn't even notice it after a while.

"On top of that, we always had pregnant cats. We always got females for some stupid reason. We had three litters at one time. All these little live things runnin' around, getting under your feet. It was pretty bizarre."

"What did you love about him most?"

"I was fascinated with his curiosity about things. He was an interesting person, no matter what viewpoint you're coming from. He was very passionate. He was passionate sexually, but he was passionate about things, too. Stop or violent with his living. That's kind of nice when it's directed in the right directions. I think his sensitivity really established my love. Sensitive to people, animals, plant life, life in general. Sensitive to the motivations of people, their inner worlds. Responsively sensitive."

"As opposed to . . ."

"As opposed to being blasé, unaware, taking things for granted, not thinking about underlying realities. He didn't take anything for granted. Always looked beyond the obvious. I'm sure there were other things, but those are the basics . . . his spontaneity really clinched our personalities. We were impulsive in the same ways, got bored very quickly. That changed when he started going inward and focusing on his fears. His impulsiveness became stymied, he wouldn't venture out because he was afraid."

"Why did he become so afraid to venture outward?"

"His sicknesses, afraid of dying. That fear comes from feeling helpless. Afraid that there's not going to be help. Afraid of getting on a plane or going on a cruise because there's not going to be a hospital in the middle of the ocean.

"When things started going wrong, they went wrong all over the place, which didn't help. That just added to his fear of not being able to control his surroundings. Those fears manifested themselves in many ways. When parts of him became stymied, it made him even more insecure. It went against what he liked to conceive of himself. That's a round robin, a vicious circle. Your fear makes you more afraid, and then you're more afraid of your fear, and you lose track of what it is and how to solve it."

"Did he know what it was or how to stop it?"

"I'm sure he did. We talked about it. He knew what it was, he knew what was happening. He wasn't sure he could stop it . . . he didn't feel he could help it, nor did he want to help it. He established those ways of dealing with it because he felt he couldn't deal with it any other way. If it worked for him, that's what he was going to do. He did not want professional help. Did not want a professional person to see that side of him because he didn't want to see it either. He had his solutions and he wasn't ready for any others. Didn't even want any others."

"How much of it was being able to and wanting to?"

"Wanting to was the bigger portion. He did not want to heal himself. He did not want to have to admit that he needed to work some things out and therefore 'I'll find this way to deal with it and that's what I'll do.' Sometimes he'd say he was too old to change, or 'If it works, that's what's important.' He simply did not want to change."

"But he must have known that was a dead end."

"Oh, yeah. That's what was so masochistic about the whole situation. That was the sad part."

"How did he express that? Would he just come out and say he wanted to die? Or, 'I don't care if I die'?"

"No. He'd say, 'This is what I wanna do. I don't think I'm gonna live that long.' He had terrible fears of dying and when. Premonitions of an early death. He knew that, he felt it. He didn't feel any other way of life was worthwhile. When he'd get sick, he'd be terribly frightened that he wasn't gonna make it through this one. As soon as he felt better, he'd push it harder, knowing that that was exactly what was destroying him."

"What are your earliest memories of those premonitions?"

"The second heart attack, which would've been the summer of '69. They were a year apart almost to the day. That's when he started talking about his mortality."

"Had he ever expressed that before?"

"I think he thought a lot about it but didn't talk a lot about it. He wasn't even very hypochondriacal before that second heart attack. But afterwards, he became very hypochondriacal. He started paying a whole lot more attention to his inner workings than was healthy. Listening to his own heartbeat. Not being able to sleep because he kept hearing it. Making it race harder because he couldn't hear it, and then being afraid because that didn't sound right."

"That must've been very hard on you."

"Oh, yeah. There was a changed man. Wasn't even a gradual change. Looking back—I didn't realize it then, but now I see that the hardest thing was at that point where he became so preoccupied with dying and his health and death and finding an escape, there came an end to our ability to grow together as a couple in any way. We were still there for each other, but there was almost a lack of a future. No need to make plans. It was never spoken out loud, but, in retrospect, those were the feelings coming from me and him, too. And that's sad. If I could've identified that more clearly at the time, I probably could've done better for both of us, but I couldn't, I didn't see it."

"When did you start to see that fear rising in him?"

"Maybe a year after the second heart attack. I started to see it in my guts but not really identify it. Just before I went back to school, I was able to identify it. That was part of why I went back to school. I felt I had to do something. Which he was quite agreeable to. Supported me all the way—I feel very fortunate for that and a lot of the experiences I had with Barry. Verrry fortunate. But it was not a *we* thing that either one of us lived up to. It was also unspoken, but the *we* gradually went away in anything of any real importance, any real growth or future plans.

We served each other's purpose and gave to each other. And maybe that's enough for anybody. Or maybe that's all there is. But at the time, even now, I need and needed more than that. I needed those subtle, underlying feelings of we're in this together . . . we'll get out of each other and grow into something else, something bigger and better. . . ."

"Can you re-create his last days?"

"There was something a little more settled about him. He wasn't as edgy. He seemed to be more at peace. He was doing more things that he enjoyed over at his other house, as opposed to going to rock concerts. We were having dinner more often. Talking calmly, casually. He seemed a lot more giving. Not that he wasn't a giving person, but it was just easier for him.

"I'm not certain that it was really like that or if I just want to think that. He was doing more peaceful things. He'd talk to me about this or that plan. I don't know where he was with his other affairs, but they didn't seem to be on his mind. Before, he used to talk about them. But it seemed that something stronger was on his mind. What to do with his life.

"As soon as he died, he just called me for help. That was terrible, terrible. That'll never go away. That image will just never go."

"Can you describe it? If you don't want to, that's okay."

"I don't even know if I can put my finger on it or find any words. It was a real reaching out. I can't describe it. I can't. He was going out to the store for me. He was closer to a hospital than he was to getting back to me. He left the car in the middle of the road and just rushed in. I can't describe it. There's no sense in even guessing why it happened that way.

"I never did believe he died until they actually came and told me. I just did not believe it. I guess I really knew he was pretty close to it, if not dead, while we were on the way to the hospital. But I just figured some miracle would happen. Something. They would revive him. I just did not believe it.

"That whole image is still very raw. I'm sure you can understand. I still think about it very frequently. I don't think a week goes by when I don't think about him. There was just so much unfinished business."

Sunday, Jan. 19th, '75

Dawn—

Quiet here now. I took the kids over to the skating rink at the Motor Lodge. I needed the (short) span of peace and quiet. I spent most of last night with Paradise Plastic's lawyers hammering out specifics of a contract. It was grueling, mostly because lawyers say ten words for every one that is needed. It went, I believe, well & I should have a draft of it in the next week or so.

I am faced with an enormous work load for the next two weeks. You see, I *must* locate a place and people and accurately determine the production costs of Zapcap. I am about convinced that it cannot be done in the U.S., which means I must establish a foreign source and prices for same within two weeks. Paradise wants to offer Zapcaps to the market at the annual Toy Fair in New York—which is on Feb. 10th. Since they can't quote prices until they know how much the damned things will cost to make, etc, they must have the information in two weeks. I fervently hope I can get all that done—it will no doubt mean infinite phone calls and probably some running to various consulates, Banks, etc, in N.Y. and D.C.

I am not too down, tonight, as I seem to have been for the past two weeks. Although I am honestly scared about the work ahead of me, I am glad that it is something I can finally sink my teeth into with purpose. I am *very* lonely, my love. Although I know I could call Jeanie to keep me company I have not. I am peculiarly empty without you. The simple truth is that I am *in* love with you (yes, still!). I have, in the course of these singularly empty nights since you've left, stared up at the ceiling in the small slow hours trying to pin down just what the hold is you have on me. I cannot, as my over-analytical mind is wont to do, sieve, separate, isolate, or even define why I am less than whole, frequently depressed and downright unhappy-miserable when you're out of reach. It's not just the super sex that seems to get joyously better—even with momentary halts and hurts—or even the heavy, heavy investment of tears and pain and finding of ourselves and each other over the past ten years. I am frustrated—there is no definable essence, no ultimate nitty-gritty thing, touch, smell, solid, tangible *anything* that I can grasp. You are so close to the naked me that you are orgasm and agony simultaneously, a flower with petals of fire.

You have enabled me, for the first time in my life, to love and be loved. The catalytic, self-sustaining need that we generate in each other has stripped both of us of lifelong armor plate. So we tread on each other's souls, rub naked old wounds with salt. You snarl and curse me and lash out with acid venom, like the night before you left. And I have barricaded from you, pushed you away, exploded my anger grenades in my own frenzied fashion. Why? Because two entities cannot occupy the same space at the same time. And because our need for each other is so intense, and because we are what we are, we will always, as long as we live, try to mate our shadows. We are, I think, beginning to learn this. . . . And all of the above tortured words are my way, tonight, of telling you that no one, no one will ever hate you or need you or love you as much as I.

B.

19

Memorial Day

I will never forget that last fireworks display. It seemed we had more fireworks assembled in one small field that I had seen in my life. We had aerial shells from most major fireworks-producing countries in the world—China, Britain, France, Japan, Brazil, and on and on and on. We had thousands of bottle rockets, hundreds of packs of firecrackers. We had more bombs and flashes than I could have fired in an entire summer, and here we were burning it all in one night.

Exactly which July was it? . . . I don't remember. It doesn't matter. What matters is that my father told me there was a guy here from *Scientific American*, a photographer, who was doing some preliminary shooting of his own. *Scientific American* was interested in the possibility of profiling my father in a future issue they were planning on fireworks. They would bill him as a "vanishing species."

He loved that phrase. I heard him say it two or three times, which for him was exceptional. He rarely overdid a joke. Or, when he chose to overdo it, he went all the way, told it over and over until his puns got so sickening you'd do anything just for him to shut up. But now was different. It was a special, private joke that wasn't a joke at all. We all knew it. He let us know it. It—whatever *it* was—was in his voice.

So here I am back again at the home of Dr. William Walton, patron of the pyrotechnic arts, and my father's urologist. Urology must be good business, because the good doctor owns a huge

Colonial stone house that he and his family have lived in for a quarter of a century. ·

Dr. Walton stands about five nine, balding, liver spots on his scalp, gray hair flying out in all directions. His face is open, friendly, midwestern stock. His voice is thin, high, raspy. He looks as if he plays a lot of tennis.

Walt, his twenty-two-year-old son, looks like a young clone of his dad. He's got the same sharp nose, the same nasal voice, the same open, friendly facial structure. He's also got a black belt in karate. He tells me he's probably proficient with every hand-held weapon ever invented by man, including the crossbow, musket, dart gun, samurai sword.

Mrs. Lucy Walton could pass for any mother down at the supermarket. Straw-colored hair, green eyes, puffed face, a lazy slouch in her voice. I get the feeling the bottle is one of her closest companions. I like her. I like them all. But very quickly I realize that here is an opportunity to replay the past, his past. Play some of his games. See how far I can sink the hook. So I play dumb, just to see if they're awake.

Dr. Walton is walking across the driveway toward us. Walt and I are sitting in lounge chairs on the veranda overlooking a small pond and the surrounding fields and woods. Those fields are where my father and I and the rest of the gang shot our last big fireworks display. Dr. Walton and I shake hands. It's a bright, sunny, hot Memorial Day. We're remembering.

DR. WALTON: You're looking more and more like Barry.
DAVID: Thank you. I take that as a compliment.
WALT WALTON: I forgot to tell you I could play the young Barry Rothman in the movie version of this epic. But don't let me interrupt you and dad.
DAVID: When did you meet him?
DR. WALTON: I guess I met your dad at the rock shop he used to have on Main Street.
WALT WALTON: Got a lotta rocks. In fact I'll show 'em to you later.
DR. WALTON: There used to be kids coming in for fifteen-cent geodes, there were kids coming in for the twenty-five-cent geodes,

there were kids coming in for the seventy-five-cent geodes. He had a pretty good idea which ones might contain amethyst crystals, but he told everybody to buy five or six at a time, take your choice, then bring 'em home and hit 'em with a big hammer. Crack 'em and see what you'd find inside.

Eventually this got so popular among the children in town, especially the teen-agers, that he started mail-ordering larger and larger amounts of geodes. He would have these huge piles of geodes in his back room. Every now and then somebody would come in and say they found amethyst crystals inside, which are these beautiful, very valuable purple crystals.

He also had a lot that he cracked himself, and would sell as amethyst geodes. This got to be such a big thing that he finally sent away and got this big cracker. It was a beastly-looking torture instrument with a big chain that would fit around a geode. It had this lever and it would actually crack geodes like you'd crack a walnut with a nutcracker. He used to crack 'em right there in the store for people. He'd say, "Pick out half a dozen and I'll crack 'em for ya."

In that period I remember going over to your house and seeing his wife struggling with probably a ton of geodes. She was trying to move them or unload them. Just a tremendous pile of geodes that must've been three feet high.

Then he got a couple of polishing wheels. He got a crude polisher and then he would also do some fancy polishing. So if you found a nice geode, he would polish the face of it, so you'd see the agate lines or other crystals.

Later he even got a diamond saw so he could cut geodes instead of cracking them. If it turned out to be something nice, then he'd polish the face of it. We have one or two of those, as well as a set of bookends he made. They're made out of calcite from a Mexican cave.

He started to have more and more beautiful pieces in the store. Fine minerals. Probably we should've invested in 'em, because a lot of 'em are, I'm sure, rare and valuable things. Huge—

WALT WALTON: We have that one big feldspar in the living room.

DR. WALTON: So this was my first exposure to your dad. I don't know how our talk drifted, but he mentioned that he was interested in snakes, and I said I had always been interested in snakes. He invited me over one time to see his assortment of snakes. He had a dozen snakes, an American alligator, and a crocodile. The American alligator was about three and a half or four feet long. He had raised it from a little tiny fella. The snakes that intrigued me most were—

[Somebody shouts from the house that there's a huge snapping turtle cruising in the middle of the pond. Its shell appears to be at least a foot long. It resembles a large log looking for something to eat.]

—a pair of bird-catching snakes from Korea.

WALT WALTON: It just went under.

LUCY WALTON: Do you think that's the one that's been eating the geese?

WALT WALTON: *[To his mother]* Yeah, probably. *[To me]* Some of our geese have been decapitated recently. Either some psycho is wandering around these woods chomping on baby geese heads or that snapper has been pigging out on some aristocratic chow. Maybe I should go get the rifle.

DR. WALTON: The baby geese must've been diving for food and the snapper caught 'em in the act.

LUCY WALTON: How are you, Barry? Nice to see you.

DAVID: Nice to see you, too.

WALT WALTON: Where'd it go?

DR. WALTON: It just went under. That thing that just looked like a destroyer has a thing for baby geese. Did you ever meet our daughter Ginny?

[If I've met your daughter, doc, I've got an awfully bad memory. A young lady appears to my right wearing a bright blue bikini top and a towel sort of wrapped around the rest. She has to choose this moment on this day to undo her straps. Smiling in the sun. Already tanned. Torture time.]

DAVID: No, I don't think we've met. Hello.

GINNY WALTON: Hi.

DR. WALTON: What experience did you ever have with Barry? Barry here is asking for reminiscences about his dad.

GINNY WALTON: Oh, yeah? That's great. Your father was a blast.

DR. WALTON: Sit down, sit down. Say what you can recall of Barry. Did you buy any minerals from him?

GINNY WALTON: I didn't buy any minerals. He came over a couple times, I guess. The only thing I really remember was that Fourth of July and the fireworks display that he did. That was the most spectacular I've ever seen, and I live in New York and I go to the Macy's show every year. His was just put together more creatively. What I really remember is that he set them off about five feet from us. *[Everyone laughs.]* It was a little disconcerting, but it definitely added to the total effect. He was a real fireworks whiz.

DR. WALTON: I guess I went to three of his shows.

WALT WALTON: The best one was at the Western Weapons factory.

DR. WALTON: The best one was at the Western Weapons factory. They had a couple of these sewer tiles sunk in the ground that they used as launching pits.

WALT WALTON: Mortar tubes.

DR. WALTON: I went over to see one of the rockets go out of the tubes, and at just that time the rocket I picked decided to go up about twelve feet in the air. Fantastic! *Whooooshh!*

WALT WALTON: The neatest thing about that display was that he had—

DR. WALTON: Two displays.

WALT WALTON: Yeah, but he had the end fixed up so that about a thousand bottle rockets went off at once. Remember that?

DR. WALTON: No. He told me. *Twelve thousand bottle rockets went off in two minutes.* For about two weeks prior to the Fourth of July, he got permission to get the girls at Western to wire his bottle rockets. It was the most fantastic—

WALT WALTON: Percussion—

DR. WALTON: No, no. A curtain of rising fire. It was fantastic. It was spread out over maybe fifty feet. Then, at the end, he said, "Now we're going to set off our plastic explosive display." When he set off the plastic explosive display, he moved it back another fifty yards, but he also suggested that we move back another fifty yards. Walt was just a little tiny kid, maybe eight or ten, and he was standing in front of me, and the concussion, the shock wave, just knocked him right back against me. This tremendous roar went off—

WALT WALTON: It was somethin'!

DR. WALTON: The next day it was discovered that many, many windows had been removed from the Western building. After that, Barry's favor with the Western Weapons folk got a little tenuous. [Grins slyly]

WALT WALTON: As soon as that plastic explosive charge went off . . . it was interesting because you thought the bottle rockets were the grand finale . . . it was the biggest explosion, the closest to me, that I've ever seen. It was really interesting because the shock wave put out all the lights in the Western plant. You could see the lights die. . . .

DR. WALTON: The building was back another forty or fifty yards behind us.

LUCY WALTON: Were you there that day?

DAVID: Yeah, I helped make the show.

LUCY WALTON: Oh, then you do know how to make fireworks. You'll have to team up with Walter!

DR. WALTON: Since then, Walt has learned to mix chemicals so that he can make, say, charges of different colors go off.

WALT WALTON: Yeah. Stars.

DR. WALTON: I'm trying to think what I can tell you about your dad.

WALT WALTON: He was definitely just an interesting person. He could talk on arcane subjects—

DR. WALTON: He was interested in music, he was interested in good books, he was interested in wildlife, he was interested in minerals and science and fireworks, and then he was—

WALT WALTON: A basic naturalist.

DR. WALTON: —he prob'ly shoulda been a naturalist, really. But then he also had these CIA attachments. That also made him fascinating. He never said much about that part of his life and I never pried, never asked him exactly what his attachments or detachments were. Except he told me once, "I'm sure that ever since I left the CIA my phone has been tapped. I'm sure my phone will always be tapped." That's the only thing he ever said about the CIA.

WALT WALTON: The only other thing I remember him saying . . . I forget who it was at the time, but someone had just died in an air crash and he said, "CIA." A couple political-type deaths he said were, you know, definitely CIA. *[Casually as if discussing baseball scores]* But other than that . . .

DR. WALTON: I don't think he left the CIA with any great love. Other things I know . . . he had a lot to do with developing these flare shotgun shells that the navy used—

WALT WALTON: Made them for the Penguin Company.

DR. WALTON: —to try to frighten the gannets, the boobies, off of—which island is it? Midway? Guam? Where the navy has a base and they had so much trouble with all these seabirds on the runway that they were afraid that they were gonna get sucked into the intake of the jets and cause crashes. They constantly had to clear the runway. They didn't wanna murder all these birds and they felt if they could only scare them off the runway, that would be enough. So Barry developed these tracer shotgun shells which they used for that purpose. Did you know that?

DAVID: No, I didn't.

DR. WALTON: Well, he's the guy who developed that.

WALT WALTON: Remember those little red flares he also invented for the Penguin Company? I still have some upstairs.

DR. WALTON: It is the same flare which has since been used—

WALT WALTON: Emergency distress flares.

DR. WALTON: Yeah, you can buy them in sporting-goods stores. Hunters buy lots of 'em. They come in twelve-gauge, sixteen-, and twenty-gauge, and there's even a rifle size for a lost hunter who can shoot three flares into the air. I think fellas that hunt in big woods areas should prob'ly carry them. Your dad is the one who developed that. What else can I tell you about him?

WALT WALTON: He was always a great source for fireworks.

DR. WALTON: One real screwball. Had a great sense of humor.

WALT WALTON: Yeah. He could really—

DR. WALTON: He definitely qualified as a dirty old man. Sex was high on his list of interesting subjects and avocations. No question about that. We had a few little talks about that, which— *[getting awkward for first time]*—which might add a little ginger to his life story, but I don't think—

WALT WALTON: *[Speaking at same time]* Maybe it's better left a mystery. *[Laughs]*

DR. WALTON: We won't expand on it. We won't take that away

from Barry. That was—that was—he admitted, one of the high
points of his life, but, uh, we'll just, uh, not expand upon it.

WALT WALTON: How 'bout that time Dawn got bit by the snake?
That was kinda interesting. Or maybe not. [Laughs] I don't
know.

DR. WALTON: Yeah, well—

DAVID: Tell me what he told you about his sex. [Long pause,
broken by Walt's short laugh]

DR. WALTON: I just gathered he was always, uh—

WALT WALTON: Game.

DR. WALTON: He was always ready. Heh-heh. Always ready and
always interested. What I'm trying to think about is the timing
of his heart attacks. He had one heart attack on the Fourth of
July. And his next heart attack was on the Fourth of July a year
later. His second heart attack. I knew that the Fourth of July was
one of the high points in his life because he was always getting
himself all ready for one of these grand affairs. Fireworks affairs.
He got so excited that he had a heart attack on the Fourth of
July. And his next heart attack was again on the Fourth of July,
one year later. One year following that he was a little bit appre-
hensive as the Fourth of July approached, but nevertheless he
weathered it and nothing happened. [Chuckles gaily] He was
very happy.

Do you have any recollection of a story he may have told you
when you were a youngster about how he got bit with a copper-
head?

DAVID: No. I don't remember that one.

DR. WALTON: Well, he was born and raised in New York, wasn't
he?

DAVID: Actually, I don't know where he was born and raised.
[I happen to glance out to the pond. A large creature is gliding
across the surface of the water.] Is that a turtle or a snake?

DR. WALTON: That's a water snake. He was born and raised in
New York, wasn't he?

DAVID: I'm not sure. I haven't been able to verify it. It's either
Boston or New York.

DR. WALTON: I believe it was New York. Are either of his parents alive who could help you with this?

DAVID: Uh, no.

DR. WALTON: Well, I'll tell ya another side of your dad that always kinda upset me. And that was he struggled so much to try to make a financial success of his interest in fireworks. He felt that there was a real future in being able to provide fireworks displays for national holidays, baseball games, political rallies—that sort of thing. Special events that occur, especially in the summertime. Events that are celebrated in various parks and ball fields and so forth where a fireworks display would be safe and interesting and certainly lucrative for the person who knew how to put on a good display. He felt that if he could only get *known* and get a couple of decent contracts, he could make a damn comfortable living putting on displays.

He succeeded several times in landing contracts, but he never had enough money to actually come up with all the fireworks to meet his own contractual obligations. He always felt so frustrated. He said he had a chance to shoot a show for the opening game for the Philadelphia Phillies down in Philadelphia. There was gonna be another doubleheader on a certain Sunday night on Labor Day or something like that. He said, "If I had enough money to have enough fireworks *at hand,* I could've had those damn contracts."

This was a matter of great frustration. He looked forward to the Bicentennial. He felt the year of the Bicentennial he oughtta be able to make fifty or a hundred thousand dollars if he could land enough contracts and set off enough fireworks displays. Somehow, because he didn't have enough financial backing, all of these things folded up. I think those things folding up had just as much to do with him having heart attacks as anything. His intense frustration over not being able to get it off the ground.

Finally, toward the end of his life, he came up with this neat little invention which he felt that every schoolchild would wanna play with, which was completely safe. It was a noisemaking thing—

WALT WALTON: Did you ever see one? It was an improved version of a Snapcap. It was a cylinder with a little explosive charge of ammonium triiodide. He called it Zapcap, and it was based on something called Biribas, which were imported from Brazil. Biribas were sperm-shaped paper twists filled with sand crystals painted with ammonium triiodide. You threw it on the ground and the friction provided by the impact would cause the ammonium triiodide to explode.

Dr. Walton: But you could feel the little pellets of sand stinging you on the legs or face. This could put out somebody's eye. He said he could make it safe. Go ahead, Walt.

Walt Walton: He made Zapcaps out of tiny cardboard tubes. The explosive charge was in the front, the tube was folded in the middle, and there was an iris diaphragm at the other end. When the pressure built up in the front half, it would open up at the back end because of the iris diaphragm. It wouldn't allow any flying pellets. It would just make a loud *poooff*.

Dr. Walton: You set the things off on the palm of your hand. You could set them off on the coffee table, right in front of people. They'd make a neat little pop and a neat little flash, but it was completely harmless. There was no way anybody could swallow it, eat it, or harm themselves in any way. In fact, Barry told me he even put a couple in his mouth and bit down on them and set 'em off inside his own mouth, and they were completely harmless. He said, "We oughtta be able to sell these by the millions. Kids would love to play with 'em." You could have a handful of 'em and just throw 'em down on the sidewalk for kicks.

Walt Walton: He was hoping to develop some sort of little gun that could shoot them so they'd explode on impact.

Dr. Walton: He was gonna have these made in a factory in—

Walt Walton: Puerto Rico.

Dr. Walton: Exactly. Labor costs were too much here in the United States, but he figured he could get these little tubes carefully wrapped in Puerto Rico. And he was all for it. Some toy company was even all set to help him, but Barry didn't have enough money to do it. He was despondent. I gave him five hundred bucks, and two months later he was dead. I said, "Barry, what'll it take to do it?" He said, "Five hundred bucks." I said, "Here. Take it. Go for it." Two months later.

Walt Walton: Well. Who knows. Can't win 'em all.

Dr. Walton: As soon as he was gone, there was nobody to grab the patent or push or continue the idea.

WALT WALTON: *[Speaking at same time as his father]* Hey, dad, let's make some money! But, no, I guess you've got first rights.

DR. WALTON: Isn't it down on paper?

WALT WALTON: Aren't patent rights hereditary? Perhaps not. It's seven years to renew them.

DR. WALTON: But the kinda person Barry is—that gives a doctor the opportunity to treat a python bite. How many doctors in these United States ever get to treat a python bite?

WALT WALTON: Hey, yeah! Remember that time he got hold of a Russian Coast Guard flare pistol? He shot it off in the backyard of his house up there on the hill, and it was much more powerful than he suspected, because the Unionville Police showed up. *[Cool and casual]* Evidently he was always doing things like that.

DR. WALTON: I can tell you two other things about your dad. He told me once that he had a friend in Africa who sent him a postcard: "I'M SENDING YOU A PRESENT IN THE MAIL." Remember this story?

DAVID: No. But it sounds right.

DR. WALTON: This package came and he thought it was just gonna be some new mineral or crystal. But it was an empty Rothman's cigarette carton wrapped in brown paper. He shook it and it rattled. He thought it might be some sort of plant. So he turned it over and dumped it out. Out popped a seven-inch black scorpion. The only kind of scorpion that is—

WALT WALTON: *[Speaking over his father]* An African rock scorpion.

DR. WALTON: *[Not missing a beat]* —supposed to be highly poisonous or even fatal to man. Alive! *[Laughs heartily]*

WALT WALTON: I remember once he told us he had a cobra loose in his basement and he had to chase it around down there with—

DR. WALTON: Oh, yes! He had to succeed in catching the cobra!

WALT WALTON: A big cobra!

DR. WALTON: *[Speaking over his son]* The cobra actually turned on him and cornered him. He was able to eventually—

WALT WALTON: —subdue it with a badminton net or something ridiculous. Some kinda pole.

DAVID: *[Hearty laugh]*

DR. WALTON: What was the other thing I was gonna tell you?

WALT WALTON: Gee, I don't know—I think you're losing your mind. No, evidently he was playing around in the cellar with a seven-foot cobra or whatnot.

DR. WALTON: [Mumbling to himself] This wasn't a snake story....

WALT WALTON: The first one was the bite.

DR. WALTON: I just had another incident on my mind....

WALT WALTON: He always had those dogs running around the house. Especially that big dog?

DR. WALTON: He had dogs that galloped right through the screen door. [Makes loud, sharp whistling sound] They would leap through at full speed.

WALT WALTON: He had the biggest Doberman pinscher I ever saw. Attila. Jesus. That was a big mean dog.

DR. WALTON: That was a helluva magnificent dog. Whatever happened to Attila?

DAVID: Dawn sold him to the folks who bought Hill House after she moved out, a few months after my father's death. Eventually they shot him because they said he turned vicious.

WALT WALTON: That was prob'ly a hundred-and-fifty-pound Doberman pinscher.

DR. WALTON: He said that the father of that dog had been weighed at something like a hundred and thirty-five pounds. And this dog was equal to that and maybe bigger. The thing was he seemed to be very good-natured.

WALT WALTON: But, boy, he looked *mean!*

DR. WALTON: That was the most impressive Doberman I ever saw in my life.

WALT WALTON: Real big Doberman. Neat dog.

DR. WALTON: He had an Afghan too. And that Afghan had the Doberman buffaloed. 'Cause he was older, he had it bluffed. The prime spot on the overstuffed chair belonged to the Afghan rather than to the Doberman.

I was gonna tell you another ... the tarantula ... the snake ...

DAVID: You didn't tell me about a tarantula.

DR. WALTON: He was always gettin' them in the mail. From the Southwest. He had some fool down there send 'em to him. I've got one up in my room now. *[Laughs nervously]* What else was I gonna tell you?

WALT WALTON: Remember when he said he had what he thought was a scarlet king snake when it was really a coral snake? He didn't think it was poisonous, but it was.

DR. WALTON: Oh, I wish I could think of this other story, 'cause it was a great typical Barry story. It's like the scorpion in the box . . . I forget now if it was a gun story or a fireworks story. . . . You know, when he was in high school he was a great one for salting all the toilets with this ammonium iodide.

WALT WALTON: Yeah, ammonium triiodide. As soon as you apply any pressure or friction—*boomm!!*

DR. WALTON: Or even if a person sits on it. The friction of your body—*whap!!*

WALT WALTON: He told me he used to flush Knox gelatin down the toilets. Evidently it would make some unusual sucking noise that would reverberate through the pipes. That's a Barry trip.

He'd get the most interesting fireworks that you'd never see again. Stuff from Macao, Brazil, any country that had a fireworks industry.

DR. WALTON: He apparently corresponded with people in many countries about fireworks. And he obtained samples from them. I guess he was one of the last fireworks people to obtain fireworks from China.

WALT WALTON: Before Nixon reopened trade with the Yellow Peril. In other words, when it was very illegal to be corresponding with the Reds.

DR. WALTON: In fact we have some Chinese things stuck on the wall going down to the cellar. Some fireworks wrappers. Did you know that in that little greenhouse he used to have on the side of the house that he used to have an assortment of iguanas?

DAVID: I didn't see or hear about a lot of these things because I wasn't there very much. I'd just visit during the summers for a week or two. *[I say this so they don't get suspicious of my supposed ignorance.]*

DR. WALTON: *[Long pause.]* These are all things that you didn't know, aren't they?

DAVID: Right.

WALT WALTON: He died at some sort of weird time, too. When exactly did he die?

DAVID: January 13, 1976. The night before his forty-first birthday.

WALT WALTON: But wasn't something else going on in the news that day? Something weird? I know something was. In a local paper or in a national rag. Something strange that sort of corresponded. I remember saying, "Isn't that strange. That's too bad. Isn't it funny that that just happened and now Barry . . . " You'll have to check that out as a professional journalist.

He was interested in guns. Especially Mausers . . . he got us some of those strange high-velocity Mauser bullets, remember? We shot 'em in that one Mauser we used to have.

I remember he used to have a crossbow rifle on the wall of the living room. Killed some bird out in the backyard that he didn't particularly like. One of those steel jobs that are powerful as hell. And he had a crossbow pistol, too. I guess he also liked crossbows. I remember seeing crossbow bolts lying about the house.

DR. WALTON: He did cause a couple of rather anxious complaints from his neighbors. Because of loud noises at odd hours.

WALT WALTON: The old earthquake bombs. They were pretty neat.

DR. WALTON: He had a thing called an "earthquake bomb." It was a very, very small fragment of a plastic explosive. Barry was well, well beyond the black-powder period. He said he could dig a six-foot hole anywhere he wanted to in a hurry. *[Father and son get a charge out of this.]*

DR. WALTON: Oh, I know the story I wanted to tell you! The best story of all! After he left Western Weapons, he went into the fireworks business. Somewhere around Clarksburg, he leased an old barn. He had several girls—ladies—who worked for him packing fireworks. It wasn't long after he opened that plant that they had an explosion. The interesting thing about it was that, because it was an old wooden barn, all four sides blew out and nobody was hurt. These women could've been killed or burned, but there was just an explosion without any fire. The place was just completely flattened.

But this explosion didn't stop him. He thought he could do better elsewhere, so he leased an abandoned concrete bunker in New Mexico that had been used in the development of the atom bomb. After a while, he really started making some money. It was goin' along great. He had a number of Mexicans working for him. One day on lunch hour, one of these Mexicans was standing outside the bunker smokin' marijuana. As a joke, the guy lit a little bottle rocket that he'd made. He aimed it at the door of the concrete bunker and sent it inside. And the explosion —because it was a contained explosion—killed one or two people. The place wouldn't blow apart like the old wooden barn. *[Chuckles heartily]* That put your dad out of the fireworks business.

WALT WALTON: Evidently that was a concrete bunker that was supposed to be good against, like, nuclear tests, but evidently after that it was ruined. There was so much damage from that explosion that the bunker was useless afterward.

DR. WALTON: Your dad was the kind of a guy who created these little legends. This wasn't an ordinary person who walked through life, goin' to work in the morning and comin' home in the evening and doin' all the things that ordinary people do. He wasn't an ordinary guy. He was a really different guy and an interesting guy. That's what made him fascinating. Just think if he was here to tell us these stories! *[Father and son laugh.]* He'd have so many more! I would only talk with your dad maybe three or four times a year, so I couldn't ever say I was a close associate and knew all the escapades he was involved in. Just think what went on that I didn't know about!

WALT WALTON: Yeah, we were just casual friends!

DR. WALTON: He'd pick up the phone and say, "I got something interesting to show ya." Or, "Can you come over and see a snake?" Or, "Do you think Walt would like to try a new kind of firecracker?" "Okay, Barry, I'll come over right away." He'd sell me a handful and he'd give me an equally large armful. "Well, here, let'm try these."

WALT WALTON: I'm lucky I still have all my hands and feet!

DR. WALTON: He'd load us up with all this stuff.

WALT WALTON: We used to have some interesting battles, too. Billy almost blew off his fingers a couple times. *[Grinning]* Remember the bottle-rocket battles we used to have back by the pool?

DR. WALTON: We used to aim bottle rockets at each other. One person would stand here and another person'd stand over there and you'd shoot them back and forth at each other.

WALT WALTON: Fifty or a hundred feet apart.

DR. WALTON: They're harmless.

WALT WALTON: *[Laughs]* Pretty much.

DR. WALTON: When you think of all the people you know well and you see every day who create no legends, and here's a guy you'd only see, oh, three, four times a year, and still *[rolling laughter]* it was always something memorable. A real nut. A real nut. Last of the great nuts.

WALT WALTON: Yeah. One of the most interesting people I've met.

DR. WALTON: You could *allllwayyys* tell that the wheels were goin' around. He was always thinkin' something.

WALT WALTON: Always *Ooohh, there's an idea! [Laughter]*

DR. WALTON: One thing that makes his legend more interesting is the fact that, because of the number of things he was involved in, he could have been the most delightful bullshitter in the world. But he was not. Everything he ever told ya was the honest-to-God truth. Everything he told me was completely un-glamorized, unglorified. "This happened to so and so. . . . " Yep. And it really happened. He was the kind of guy who could've made his life seem more exciting than it really was, but it wasn't necessary. He never was a BSer. *[Laughing]* He always gave you the straight, unvarnished fact. And it was always the real thing!

WALT WALTON: *[Wistfully]* It's pretty interesting that, considering all the stuff he was into . . . heart attack. You know? Coulda been a snakebite, coulda been a little mistake with the fireworks, coulda been one of his Central American assignments. But, no. Goes of a plain old ordinary heart attack. Personally, I think he would've preferred to go out with a bang.

DR. WALTON: He got very tense and excited as the Fourth of July approached that third year. He said, "I'm gonna have a couple good scotches and enjoy this Fourth of July. The last two almost did me in, but I'm not gonna let it scare me off this time around." He fortified himself with those scotches. He said, "All day long I was tense, but I just kept drinkin' scotch. I got through it."

He had a wonderful collection of books on chemistry, books on physics, books on attack methods, books on fireworks—really rare things on fireworks. And then he had quite a large collection of classic unavailable pornographic literature. I never had the time to go through any of that with him, but I would've liked to have seen it. He had rare erotic books, things that he would obtain in London, Paris, Berlin, Rome . . . the sorts of things that were never printed in the United States. He had quite a collection of—dirty sex material.

WALT WALTON: *[Laughing nervously]* From a connoisseur's viewpoint.

DR. WALTON: He was apparently a connoisseur of very rare erotic books. Every time I went over to visit, I always had my young son along so I never had an opportunity to sit down and study those materials.

WALT WALTON: Uh-huh.

DR. WALTON: So I was always shortchanged on that particular venture. I don't know what happened to them. Dawn should have that whole collection. Are you planning to contact her?

DAVID: Yeah. I haven't asked her yet about the books.

DR. WALTON: Good. Pretend you don't know. Just say, "Could I look through my dad's books" *[Father and son laugh.]* You might be in for a tremendous surprise!

DAVID: What did you think of Dawn?

DR. WALTON: She was always most pleasant, enjoyable, kind. *[Long, uneasy pause]* However, I never got the feeling that she was as deeply sincere as your dad. *[Strange loud electronic noise echoes across the hills from the farm on the other side of the ridge.]* I think the CIA has finally located me! *[Laughs]* He was always so impressive with his honesty and sincerity. He could've been the world's greatest teller of tall tales, but he didn't have to be. He never needed to expand upon real life. His stories were always good enough just the way they were. And the surprising truth was always that this was the way it happened.

I think Dawn was always happy to see me, I was always welcome, but you could sense . . . he was the one with whom the

warm friendship existed. Just the same way a lotta wives tolerate their husband's friends. *[Giggles]* She didn't know whether
I was gonna put good or bad ideas into his head. But I don't
think she looked upon me as a troublemaker.

You ought to contact her and locate those books. I imagine
that some of those foreign printings must be worth a hundred
or two hundred or three hundred bucks *apiece*. If they were the
sort of thing he led me to believe they were. He'd say, "You look
through that stuff sometime. . . . " *[Grinning awkwardly and
looking at the ground]* And I'd say, "Welllll . . . . " I always came
over with little Walt. We were always lookin' at the snakes or
the fireworks or the guns or the earthquake bombs or the guns
. . . so we didn't have time to dwell over the niceties of Parisian
printing. *[Father and son laugh as the familiar echo of dogs bark-
ing replaces the CIA's mysterious locating device. Lucy returns to
us with a platter of sandwiches. He addresses her.]* He's heard
a lot of these things but he wants our impressions, too. How
would you characterize Barry?

LUCY WALTON: Too smart.

DR. WALTON: I think he should go dig up his dad's books.

LUCY WALTON: You mean from whatsername?

DR. WALTON: I don't know where she has 'em.

LUCY WALTON: She said she was storing them in the cellar of
her father's house. Didn't he have a whole lotta books? I asked
to buy one or two and she said I'd have to wait till Barry's son
goes through them. Do you know where the father lives?

DAVID: I could find out.

LUCY WALTON: It would be nice if you could get down in that
cellar. Her father could maybe drop dead or something. *[To
her son, who is eating all the sandwiches]* Save some for Barry
and Bill! You were just eating in the house! Put 'em over here.
[Deposits the platter on top of my tape recorder] At that time
Bill was so busy, it's a shame they didn't get to spend more time
with Barry.

DR. WALTON: I was runnin' my legs off all the time—

LUCY WALTON: *[Speaking over her husband]* Walter always
wanted to go over and see Barry. You never got to go enough,
did ya?

WALT WALTON: I don't know.

LUCY WALTON: I didn't go because he had snakes!

DR. WALTON: Can you imagine that I would come home from work and I'd say to my young son, "Whadda you wanna do?" He'd say, "Do you think you could call Barry? Maybe we could go over and visit him." Realize what kind of an attraction your dad was to a weird-minded little boy.

WALT WALTON: That's a nice thing to say. *[Offended]*

DR. WALTON: It *was* weird!

LUCY WALTON: He always said Barry was a genius. Do you know what his I.Q. was?

DAVID: No.

LUCY WALTON: I guess his mind was above all that.

DR. WALTON: You should push the CIA a little harder and find out what assignments he actually had.

WALT WALTON: You can't push the CIA, dad.

LUCY WALTON: Have the last one, Bar. I have more in the house. You want the last cracker? I got more cheese in the house.

DR. WALTON: *[Speaking over his wife]* They wouldn't have to divulge anything and say he was responsible for bombing this or bombing that. You'd just like them to say he was put on assignment in Nicaragua or Venezuela for two weeks—

WALT WALTON: Anything that happened before last week the CIA will say never occurred. Lookit that duck over there. A mallard. Anything more you'd like to know? Prod us.

DAVID: What were your impressions of Dawn?

WALT WALTON: She was nice and very pleasant and energetic . . . energetic . . . that was her best quality. . . . I don't—God, I don't know what the attraction was. Seemed like a pretty unlikely person to get hooked up with. *[Strange, uncertain tone in his voice that has not appeared before]*

DAVID: Why?

DR. WALTON: She seemed to be interested in minerals. *[As if filling an important gap in the portrait]*

WALT WALTON: To begin with, I couldn't see getting in any sort of relationship with another person who has two kids. But, uh—I don't know—they seemed to get along pretty well together. . . .

DR. WALTON: I know he damn near broke her back luggin' a helluva lotta geodes! *[Chuckling]* I remember seeing her when her hands looked atrocious because she was constantly handling geodes and fitting them into that cracker. She'd crack one, then reach down and put in another one. Pickin' up all the pieces and sorting them out. She had hands on her like a bricklayer. Very callused and hard. Just from handling rocks. Ever see a bricklayer's hands? They have *tremendous* calluses!

LUCY WALTON: He was too good-natured.

DR. WALTON: Very generous. He had nothing, but he was always giving us things.

LUCY WALTON: Did you tell him about that bomb somebody gave Walter?

DR. WALTON: Oh, *that's* the story I wanted to tell! *[Excited]* I took my wife to an antique shop and she bought a couple of pieces of cut glass. Old fella in the back had a cardboard box. Inside were some World War Two military relics.

LUCY WALTON: How old were ya? Ten?

WALT WALTON: Yeah.

DR. WALTON: One of them was some sort of a bomb.

LUCY WALTON: You didn't know it was a bomb. It looked like a torpedo.

DR. WALTON: Right. It was about this big. *[Spreading hands about a foot and a half]* The man said we could have it for three dollars.

LUCY WALTON: *[Speaking over her husband]* I thought he gave it to Walter.

WALT WALTON: *[Speaking over both his parents]* That old swine!

DR. WALTON: Little Walt must've been nine then. He sat in the back seat of the car and we drove home.

WALT WALTON: Me with the bomb on my lap!

DR. WALTON: And he was holding the bomb in his lap. It was about eight or nine months later that I met Barry. He mentioned that he knew about explosives, and so I said, "Would you like to look at a bomb?" Of course he couldn't refuse. When he saw it he absolutely *blanched*. He took it to the Western plant. There was a marine who worked there as an explosives expert and he set it off. It was an antitank grenade and it was one of the most unstable of all World War Two pieces of armament. Barry said if we had just slapped it against your knee, you could easily have set it off. He said it would've gone through the side of

our car and on through somebody's house. Tremendous penetration force! And it was *live! [Chuckling]*

LUCY WALTON: Thank God he took it! *[Joining in the fun]*

DR. WALTON: Barry said he was almost afraid to take it home
in his car! *[Unable to contain himself]*

WALT WALTON: That dumb old man! *[All speaking at same
time]*

LUCY WALTON: I thought he gave it to Walter.

WALT WALTON: Trying to kill me.

DR. WALTON: No. Three bucks. Coulda killed us all. *[Chuck-
ling]*

WALT WALTON: Do you remember anything else cool, Ginny?
*[She had wandered away but now hovers behind me. I try to
ignore her the way a professional interviewer would—looking
at her only when she says something worth acknowledging.]*

GINNY WALTON: *[Faraway look, saying to no one in particular]*
He was the closest thing to James Bond I ever met. He had no
fear. And I remember ashes coming down on my face.

DR. WALTON: *[Responding quickly with a laugh]* That's right!
Ashes were raining down out of the sky! *[Loving laughter]* We
were sitting there in the dark and you kept feeling all this stuff
. . . here we had all these ashes coming down on us!

LUCY WALTON: *[Speaking loud for the first time, over every-
one]* He was a very calm person! He was calm! Just like you.
He'd sit there calm, just like you. Must be nice to be like that.

DR. WALTON: *[Speaking over wife]* All of this debris raining
down on us!

LUCY WALTON: *[Speaking over husband]* I was *concerned!* I
thought we were all gonna catch fire and blow up!

DR. WALTON: Can you imagine going to a fireworks show where
there's so much stuff goin' on up in the air that you can feel
debris raining down on ya? Ashes! *[Loving laughter]*

LUCY WALTON: Was he taking high-blood-pressure medicine?
His heart attacks don't make reason with such a calm nature.

DR. WALTON: No. The only medicine he was taking was alla-
purinol because he had gout. He had a high blood uric acid.
A high blood uric acid, incidentally, is often characteristic of
people who have an abnormally high I.Q. As his urologist, I
knew this firsthand because I prescribed it for him.

LUCY WALTON: Really? *[Amazed, as if this is solid proof of something she suspected all along]* Do you know if his father, your grandfather, died young?

DAVID: Yes, he did.

LUCY WALTON: *[Speaking over mumbling of father, daughter, and son]* I think you should be interested for your health!

DAVID: I am.

20

Farewell to Fireworks

A Made-for-TV Movie

BY

BARRY ROTHMAN

[Opening shots, in sepia, of traffic jams, milling crowds gathered at stadiums, standing in parks]

NARRATOR: Every year millions of Americans brave traffic, heat, and insects to watch a ritual in fire. It is the annual pilgrimage on the Fourth of July to cheer on the traditional spectacle of fireworks.

[CU shots, sepia, of hot-dog vendors, adults mopping brows. Follow with CU shots of adults' and children's faces illuminated by light from fireworks: looks of wonder and surprise.]

NARRATOR: Although virtually every man, woman, and child in this country has seen some form of fireworks, few are aware of the rich history and technology behind them. In the next hour, we will examine the art of fireworks-making, its roots, its unique problems, and its imminent death in the United States.

[Black frame (night sky), background music of steadily beating large kettle drum that increases in intensity until sound of mortar

being fired: followed by aerial explosion of Japanese chrysanthe-mum shell in center of frame. This shot is in slow motion, expands symmetrically to fill frame, then freezes at maximum pattern. Frozen burst moves sharply to rear left frame as title Farewell to Fireworks *sweeps in from lower right to center frame. Slow dissolve into very slow pan shots of cobwebbed alchemical lab-oratory and slow CU pans of glass apparatus, mortar and pestle, and other equipment; all in sepia.]*

NARRATOR: The history of fireworks begins with the invention of gunpowder, probably in China, sometime in the eleventh cen-tury A.D.

[Medium and CU shots of Chinese "alchemist" compounding powder. He pours powder onto plate, center frame, and prepares to light it with wooden splint. Sepia.]

NARRATOR: The invention of gunpowder has been attributed, at various times and by a host of scholars, to a mythical German monk, Alexander the Great, Roger Bacon, and even Moses.

["Alchemist" touches off powder, which explodes, filling frame with dense smoke, providing dissolve to next scene, in sepia.]

NARRATOR: Exactly who discovered that an intimate mixture of potassium nitrate, charcoal, and sulfur would react with unpre-cedented explosive force remains lost in the smoke of antiquity.

[Smoke dissolves to long shot of ancient manuscript, moving in at slow zoom to CU of medieval soldier and cannon, in sepia.]

NARRATOR: Strangely enough, it appears that although the Chi-nese invented gunpowder and rockets, they did *not* invent guns. The oldest known picture of a gun appears in an English manu-script of the fourteenth century.

[Cut to sepia footage of old muzzle-loading cannons being fired, castles being attacked by artillery fire.]

NARRATOR: The social impact of the discovery of gunpowder and guns was figuratively and literally earthshaking. That symbol of implacable power and unchangeable order—the castle fortress—was rendered vulnerable in a matter of hours.

[Medium shot of castle wall crumbling in dust, dissolving to medium-long shot of suit of armor. Zoom in, coordinated with narration for dramatic effect, to bullet hole in breastplate. All in sepia.]

NARRATOR: Perhaps the most meaningful effect on the psyche of men and their nations was the extension of physical power provided by guns and gunpowder. Medieval noblemen bitterly complained that even the lowest slave could kill a highborn armored knight with impunity, and that guns and bombs should only be used against "infidels." That fearful philosophy is still with us.

[Cut to sepia shots of Chinese New Year celebration, with dragons and popping firecrackers. Follow with shots of crackers being used in religious act on Chinese junk.]

NARRATOR: Gunpowder was the atomic bomb of its day. The Chinese learned to live with it first, and diverted its energy to the considerably happier invention of fireworks sometime in the latter half of the eleventh century A.D.

[Cut to sepia shots of Chinese firecracker manufacture on the island of Macao: girls making crackers, braiding them, etc.]

NARRATOR: That venerable, if hazardous, toy, the Chinese firecracker, appeared in China about 1127. Eight hundred years ago Roger Bacon wrote: "A children's toy . . . made in many parts of the world *[is]* as large as a human thumb. From the force of gunpowder, so horrible a sound is produced by the bursting of so small a thing that we perceive it exceeds the roar of strong thunder and the flash exceeds the greatest brilliancy of . . . lightning." A bit exaggerated, but nonetheless the first recorded complaint about noisy fireworks.

Even in the ancient art of fireworks-making, the Chinese cracker is an anachronism. All of its components—from tiny paper tubes to fuse and powder—are entirely handmade, much of it by young girls.

[Medium and CU shots of mountain of finished firecrackers, sepia.]

NARRATOR: The world's supply—hundreds of millions—of these unique little fireworks are made on an isolated section of the island of Macao, off the Chinese mainland. As far as we know, this is the first time this ancient manufacturing process has ever been filmed for public viewing.

[Rapid-sequence shots of cracker labels, packaging and finishing operations, all in sepia.]

NARRATOR: The basic design of fireworks devices has not changed much in nearly a thousand years.

[Cut to sepia zooms and pan of woodcuts illustrating old fireworks.]

NARRATOR: Aerial shells fired from a mortar, rockets, Roman candles, large and small flares, and fire fountains are still the primary elements of any large fireworks show. All were known in China and Europe by the thirteenth century.

[Cut to sepia action shots of rockets, fountains, and wheels.]

NARRATOR: Early fireworks, by modern standards, were limited to rather dull flame, spark, and sound effects. Some variety was achieved by incorporating powdered iron into the gunpowder mixtures, which provides spitting sparks like a grinding wheel.

[Cut to old litho illustrations of royal fireworks shows, in sepia.]

NARRATOR: Limited or not, fireworks sparked religious and public events as early as the fourteenth century. Italy was the birthplace of display fireworks, and it was mainly Italians who later established the art in this country. Queen Elizabeth the First (apparently) initiated royal patronage of fireworks displays in 1572. The idea caught fire, as it were, and in subsequent years enormous and expensive displays were fired in celebration of royal birthdays, weddings, and almost any state occasion.

[Slow zoom into CU's of Green Park display and explosion, in black and white.]

NARRATOR: The fireworks display in London's Green Park in 1742 was ballyhooed as the greatest show of all time. An enormous amount of money and nearly six months were spent in assembling it, and Handel was retained to compose the now famous "Fireworks Music." To quote a contemporary account: "At the appointed hour, King George II, accompanied by an impressive array of aristocracy, paraded to his seat past the huge, excited crowd. . . .

[Speed zoom into explosion area of photograph, black and white.]

NARRATOR: "However, all was not well behind the scenes, for violent arguments had arisen between the English and Italian fireworkers. These disagreements were brought to a dramatic end as an explosion rent the North Pavilion. . . .

[Freeze frame, bleed whole frame to bright red, and long fadeout.]

NARRATOR: ". . . The fire caused widespread alarm, but was eventually brought under control so that the *planned* fireworks could begin. Judging by eyewitness reports, the display was anything but the memorable spectacle that had been promised. Such descriptions as 'pitiful and ill-conceived' and the 'grand whim for posterity to laugh at' were some of the less abusive comments." Truth in advertising seems to have been a problem in 1742 also.

[Fade in to black-and-white lithos of England's Crystal Palace, slow pan of details.]

NARRATOR: If ever there was a Golden Age of fireworks, it embraced the century spanning from about 1840 to 1940. Two basic events stirred sharp development and growth of the art. First, the evolution of the "pleasure garden" resorts, like England's Crystal Palace. . . .

[Cut to black-and-white litho of Tivoli Gardens, CU's of elegant ladies and gentlemen watching fireworks.]

NARRATOR: . . . and Copenhagen's lovely Tivoli Gardens precipitated an enormous and constant demand for fireworks. Gigantic exhibitions were staged for entering and exiting royalty, battle and peace victories, major and minor holidays, and just plain fun. The consumption of fireworks by these and other resorts throughout Europe established a thriving industry, particularly in Britain.

[Cut to black-and-white shots of Brock's Fireworks Ltd., England. Long, medium, and CU shots of buildings and workers, etc.]

NARRATOR: An example is Brock's Fireworks Ltd. in Hemel Hempstead, England. Established in about 1700, this world-famous manufacturer of pyrotechnics thrives to this day. Brock's in particular produced some of the most spectacular fireworks displays of that age of elegance. . . .

[Cut to black-and-white stills of Crystal Palace fire portraits.]

NARRATOR: . . . The lavish shows of those days are difficult to envision now. Some of the fire-portrait pieces, for example, were over two hundred feet long and sixty feet high. . . .

[Cut to black-and-white still of grand finale at Crystal Palace; follow with long fade-out to black screen.]

NARRATOR: . . . And it was not uncommon to witness several *thousand* of the largest-caliber rockets and aerial shells launched in a single, stunning salvo.

[Hold on black screen (night sky), steadily increasing intensity of kettle drum in background.]

NARRATOR: The second major breakthrough in fireworks creation in over seven hundred years occurred in the last half of the nineteenth century. In an odd parallel with the evolution of color television, the advances of chemistry suddenly provided the fireworkers with a palette: For the first time in the history of man, *fire* could be synthesized in brilliant color!

[Drum crescendo: Black screen bursts alive with full color, live shots of multicolored aerial shells, rockets, Roman candles, and exploding bombs.]

NARRATOR: In addition, the availability of the metals aluminum and magnesium added an intensity to fireworks of all sorts that would have delighted the old masters.

[Aerial bursts of aluminum flitter shells and magnesium comets, in slow motion; slow dissolve to views at Ogatsu fireworks factory, Tokyo; long, medium, and MCU establishing shots of buildings and workers.]

NARRATOR: Fireworks-making is a craft that oddly blends some sophisticated technology with techniques and materials that have remained essentially unchanged for centuries. These scenes were filmed at the factory of Marutayama Ogatsu, located thirty miles from Tokyo. This family-owned business has been at the same address and in continuous operation for over three hundred years—if nothing else, a testimony to the durable appeal of fireworks. The manufacture of pyrotechnics combines elements of chemistry, carpentry, ordnance, theatrics, and, not infrequently, utter devotion.

[Medium CU and CU's of Japanese girls making paper shell casings.]

NARRATOR: You are watching the birth of one of the prettiest fireworks ever created: an aerial chrysanthemum shell. This is one of the awesome display fireworks that bursts in the sky with an exquisite, symmetrical pattern of colored lights. Aerial shells are the most varied and spectacular kinds of fireworks. They are also the most difficult and expensive to make, requiring great skill and patience. Typically, the paper casing for the Japanese chrysanthemum shell must be carefully made from special paper and glue. . . .

[CU of time fuse being fitted to shell casing and bursting bag being filled with powder.]

NARRATOR: Here the time fuse, which explodes the shell in the air, is being fitted. The rice-paper bag attached to it is being filled with a specially compounded powerful explosive powder called the "burst charge." This is the explosive that expels the payload of the shell—the payload is usually a quantity of "stars."

[Medium, CU shots of stars, powder mixing, and tableting operations.]

NARRATOR: "Stars" are the apt name for the small tablets that are responsible for much of the beauty of aerial fireworks. A star may be shaped like an aspirin, a rough cube, or a sphere, but is never star-shaped. They are made from semisecret recipes that read like something out of an alchemist's manual. They are devious and dangerous to manufacture.

[Ultra-CU of stars in man's hands, examining them.]

NARRATOR: Casual inspection of unignited stars gives no hint of the magic they contain.

[Cut to rapid sequence of red, white, blue, green, yellow, silver, and splitter star shell bursts, coordinated with narration.]

NARRATOR: There are red, white, blue, green, yellow, silver, and splitter stars, and innumerable combinations, just to name a few types.

[Medium CU and CU shots of girls placing stars into shell, sealing, and wrapping.]

NARRATOR: In the Japanese chrysanthemum shell, the stars are loaded in geometric order over the burst charge. The top half of the shell is emplaced and the sphere is then patiently reinforced with multiple strips of glue-soaked paper.

[CU of lift charge and quick-match emplacement, followed by shot of piece of quick match being burned.]

NARRATOR: After careful drying, a propelling charge of gunpowder is attached to the bottom of the shell, over the time fuse. A second kind of fuse, appropriately called "quick match" since it burns at nearly five hundred *per second,* is then attached to the propelling charge. The shell is now ready to shoot.

[Cut to slow pan of finished shells, ranging from smallest to largest sizes.]

NARRATOR: Shells are made in a wide variety of sizes and complexities, from two-inch-diameter "minis" to custom-made thirty-six-inch monsters, larger than any modern artillery shell.

[Cut to medium and CU shot of shell being loaded into mortar.]

NARRATOR: Here is how the whole unlikely thing works: The shell is lowered into a loose-fitting steel pipe called a "mortar"; the mortar is buried and barricaded with sandbags for safety.

[CU of shooter lighting quick match.]

NARRATOR: The shooter lights the quick match, which flashes instantly down to the packet of gunpowder on the bottom of the shell.

[Long shot of shell firing out of mortar, followed by slow-motion shot of same.]

NARRATOR: The gunpowder explodes, driving the shell into the air at high speed and, at the same time, igniting the time fuse.

[Long shot of large aerial shell bursting.]

NARRATOR: When the shell reaches a specific altitude, the time fuse burns through and ignites the bursting charge. The charge explodes, lighting the stars and propelling them simultaneously.

Earlier we spoke of devotion to the fireworks art: The following sequences were filmed at a typical large display. This, too, as far as we know, is the first time such action has ever been filmed for public viewing.

[Cut to night action shots of shells being fired at display: the scene and shooters eerily illuminated by the flashes from the mortars, fire, and sparks raining down on the firing site, like scene from Dante. Slow dissolve.]

NARRATOR: It was President John Adams who decreed that the Fourth of July "ought to be solemnized with pomp and parade, with shows, games, sports, guns, bells, bonfires, and illuminations, from one end of this continent to the other, from this time forward forevermore." And Americans have been doing just that ever since.

[Dissolve to rapid shots of Fourth of July parades, bands, flags, etc. Cut to scene of backyard family fireworks, children watching cones and sparklers.]

NARRATOR: From miniature family-group backyard displays— legal and otherwise. . . .

[Cut to rapid shots of large display in stadium, cheering crowds.]

NARRATOR: . . . to giant public exhibitions sponsored by committees and clubs. About ninety percent of America's annual fireworks consumption occurs on the Fourth of July, the balance at Christmas in the South and on New Year's Eve.

[Cut to shots of fireworks retail stands in the South.]

NARRATOR: For those of you who like statistics, an estimated fifteen million dollars' worth of fireworks disappears in smoke every year. That includes about five hundred million sparklers and at least two hundred million Chinese firecrackers.

[Cut to CU shots of old fireworks catalogs and comic-book ads.]

NARRATOR: The demand for fireworks in this country increased sharply after the turn of the century, particularly in the relatively heavily populated East. By that time, the industry was well established, via primarily Italian immigrants who arrived here in the late 1840s.

[Cut to long pan of assorted fireworks cones, candles, crackers, etc.]

NARRATOR: An enormous variety of pyrotechnics was available at roadside stands, corner shops, and by mail order.

[Cut to slow zoom onto CU of cherry bomb, fuse burning.]

NARRATOR: The wide availability of really dangerous fireworks, like the infamous "cherry bomb," led to a steady increase in serious injuries, particularly to children.

[Cherry bomb explodes, in ultra-slow motion, filling screen with fire, smoke, and fragments: dissolve out.]

NARRATOR: Perhaps the model of harmony between supply, demand, and common good safety exists in England. The British, after learning that prohibition is at best disastrous, have established a workable system of rapport between fireworks manufacturers, distributors, and supervisory agencies. Rigid safety codes are easily enforced by clear, uniform law and readily accessible modes of transportation. There are strikingly few accidents and no bootleg traffic in Britain.

[Cut to pertinent interview with Mr. Frank Cadman, Brock's Fireworks, London. Cut back to narrator, at desk.]

NARRATOR: An estimated fifteen million dollars' worth of fireworks are used in the United States every year. Public displays, at least, are legal everywhere. Why then is the fireworks industry and, indeed, the entire art dying in this country?

[Cut to slow scan of piles of legal documents and titles.]

NARRATOR: The American fireworks industry is rapidly buckling under legal and economic overload. Legitimate manufacturers and distributors must deal with a bewildering array of federal, state, and local agencies and their regulators. These include the Food and Drug Administration, Department of Transportation, Alcohol, Tobacco, and Firearms Division of the Internal Revenue Service, the Bureau of Explosives, and the counterpart state and even local groups. This maze, frequently vague or contradictory, has literally forced the industry, in many instances, to either ignore the law or perish.

[Cut to pan of NFPA-proposed prohibition in Federal Register.]

NARRATOR: There are a few groups, such as the National Fire Prevention Association, who would *prefer* the industry to die. The NFPA has maintained steady pressure at the federal level to outlaw all consumer-type fireworks across the nation.

[Cut to slow backward zoom, an overhead shot, of imported fireworks spread out on large floor. Final frames reveal a gigantic assortment.]

NARRATOR: In addition, sharply increased labor, material, and operating costs have opened the door to low-priced imported fireworks. In Taiwan, a fireworker makes about forty cents a day. Fireworks imported from the People's Republic of China are based on even lower labor rates. Fully two-thirds of the over-the-counter fireworks sold in this country in the 1972 season were imported. It is ironic that, in these days of grave concern over the balance of trade, an entire industry will soon be completely replaced by foreign competition.

[Cut back to narrator, in living-room set.]

NARRATOR: Less obvious to an outside observer is the *internal* decline of the American fireworks business. Barry Rothman, who may be the last active fireworks designer in the country, had some incisive comments on the matter.

[Interview with Narrator and B. Rothman.]

NARRATOR: Barry, how does one become a fireworks designer?

BR: First, you must have a large streak of masochism. Second, you must apprentice at an early age under a master fireworker for at least five years, then get some formal schooling in chemistry, business, law, and salesmanship for about another ten years. Unfortunately, there are probably less than a dozen masters left in the country and there are no schools that offer courses directly applicable to the art.

NARRATOR: You refer to fireworks-making as an "art." Is it?

BR: My wife, who is an artist, and I have argued that question frequently. *I* think it is an art, albeit an impermanent one. You cannot reexamine a fireworks display like you can a painting. On the other hand, I have what may be the ultimate canvas: the sky. I can paint in three dimensions, with fire-colors and sound. It is an art that requires incredible patience and manual skill.

NARRATOR: Can you give us some idea what you are currently doing?

BR: Mostly research and development aimed at improved safety and major cost reduction.

NARRATOR: Is there much research and development in the fireworks industry?

BR: No. As far as I know, the projects I am directing are the first meaningful research efforts in over fifty years. The industry desperately needs to utilize new materials and techniques for overall improvement. We are competing against staggering odds.

NARRATOR: What kind of odds?

BR: The old apprenticeship system, on which the art and the industry is based, has completely collapsed. There are very few young people in the fireworks business. Who wants to work in a grimy, dangerous job in which there is neither profit nor future? There is an air of impending doom among manufacturers and distributors. Research is discouraged—why invest in a dead future?

NARRATOR: Just how dangerous is the manufacture of fireworks?

[Cut to stills and film clip of plant accidents.]

BR: It is a risky business. Working with explosives can never be totally safe, but accidents can be minimized by strictly enforced, realistic safety regulations. Brock's, for example, has not had a fatal accident in fifty years. Most of the manufacturing accidents occur in older plants where facilities are cramped, obsolete, or sloppy—or all three. Fireworks-plant explosions are morbidly spectacular, like airplane crashes. Unlike airliner disasters, however, they rarely involve more than a few people, and almost never seriously affect anyone outside of the immediate site.

[Cut back to interview.]

NARRATOR: What do you think could be done to save the industry and make everybody happy?

BR: We cannot, first of all, make *everybody* happy. The very vocal groups who call for the total prohibition of consumer fireworks neatly overlook the lessons of history. If we outlaw what the public demands, as we tried with alcohol, we will establish an intractable bootleg trade. I do not believe that organized crime will overlook a fifteen-million-dollar market for long. We will then spend millions of dollars and man-hours trying to enforce unwanted and unpopular legislation. The prohibitionists maintain that the main thrust of their proposal is to eliminate fireworks accidents. Remember poisonous bathtub gin? Well, the same thing will undoubtedly happen with fireworks—and already has in states where they are outlawed entirely. The public demand will be satisfied with bootleg goods made in basement factories. And the result will be a dramatic *increase* in accidents and injuries.

What *would* work to reduce injuries is a national, uniform

fireworks code on the British model. A code that would regulate sale of the safer kinds of fireworks, perhaps with a direct profit to the state.

[Cut to shots of British safety posters and leaflets for children.]

BR: The British manufacturers, with government blessing, have educated their people how to use fireworks and have minimized accidents. Fireworks *are* inherently dangerous, like razor blades, matches, and ice picks. And, like those things, are particularly attractive and hazardous to unsupervised children. Education, then, must be part of such a program.

NARRATOR: What do you think will happen to the fireworks industry if the changes you suggest do *not* take place?

BR: At the current pace, I believe there will be *no* American fireworks within ten years.

[Cut to night shot of family group on lawn. Little girl, as parents show her, then look on, is holding burning sparkler. CU of her face illuminated by sparkler light. Move back in slow reverse zoom. . . .]

NARRATOR: Fireworks are a unique form of entertainment. There is probably no other form of amusement that so universally bridges generation gaps, political, sexual, and racial differences. Fireworks shows have played to audiences for nearly a thousand years and hardly ever get bad reviews—certainly an enviable record. There is nothing that can really replace the sound and fury of soaring skyrockets and the searing beauty of bursting shells. Fireworks evoke a common denominator in all of us, children and adults alike; a kind of wide-eyed wonder that balances you for a dizzying moment between fear and laughter.

[Continue reverse zoom on girl and sparkler, now from treetop height.]

NARRATOR: It is unlikely that there will be a sweeping reform of the fireworks laws in this country. Although a few states may continue to permit public sale of selected fireworks, outright prohibition will probably follow the advance of urbanization. There is little doubt that the American fireworks industry is an endangered species, likely to meet its total demise within a decade. And, like the buffalo, clean air, and pure water, it will be lamented only after it is gone. We do not look forward to the time when the sparkler, the pinwheel, and the razor-sharp excitement of a brilliant fireworks display are mere nostalgia.

When that happens, a rich and spectacular ritual reminder of those fiery energies that founded this country will also be dimmed.

[Continue reverse zoom until only the sparkler is visible as a point of light in center of black screen, with diminishing kettle-drum beat, until both disappear.]

SCREEN CREDITS

END

21

Frags

CLUMSY, UNCYCLED NON-VIRGIN ANSWERED FORM
FOR CLONED SON

1) Business moving along OK. Enuf $ to barely keep
going, but OK nonetheless.

2) Family alive and apart. Dawn & I have split again,
this time it really looks permanent.

3) Wally, Ebony, Creep, GT all ok. Wally is hibernating,
once again demonstrating the essential wisdom of alligators
over man.

END PART THE FIRST
BEGIN THE SECOND PART:

1) Yep, busy as shit with business. Keeps my mind from
turning to total Jello. New products, if all goes well, should
be on market in Spring. Then $, yea.

2) Busy on pyro toys. Have begun to get busy on lovely
young lady of slim design. If she has any sense she will
live & come with me. Maybe.

3) No new scribblin or dribblin of note . . . too busy re-
assembling head for *n*th time this year. Easier this time.
The scars of previous rebuild provide road map.

4) Continue to write to me at the old address . . . all my

mail collected there. Might be a nice idea to drop Dawn
a line.

5) Poor as shit, but getting it together . . .

PauperDad

END EMISSION

Message from Seena

Well, honey, you won't have to sit in a sike-re-attic chair
when you got a grandmother here to help ya along, baby.
You know the rights, you know the wrongs. I don't expect
you to be a saint, honey. But I know you have more pride
now than you ever had . . . in being a Rothman . . . from
the time I met you till now. Because, honey, family is family.
Love your mother, 'cause she needs so much love. She never
really knew what true love was. Honest. So at least her son
can love her. And put up with her. Which you do.

You're not obsessed about your father the way you used
to be. Thank God! You'll never know how much I prayed
for God to free you from his spirit. You see, my grandson,
there are certain unevolved spirits that try to find a weak-
ened body here on this earth-plane to do evil for them.
There *are* evil spirits, Dave! I'm not a spiritualist, no, but
I believe we have to protect ourselves, we have to pray
to God and His holy golden angels for guidance and
protection.

Once there was a beautiful little girl whose uncle died.
The little girl actually took on the facial characteristics of
her uncle—actual facial tension! And no doctor, no psy-
chiatrist, no psychologist could help her. The rabbi had to
come and do what he does to free a person from an evil one.

That's what I think happened to you, my little grandson.
You were obsessed by your father's spirit after he died. But
—thank God—and I don't know how you and He did it—

but I thank God every day that you're finally free of him. Now he'll be able to move on, too.

I hope your father is in heaven. I pray for his soul, honey, his spirit. Maybe up there, Dave, he realizes and maybe someday he'll come and visit you and you'll feel his arms around you, telling you "I'm sorry, son. Why was I such a fool?" I hope that happens. It would help you find the peace you need.

His Last Poem

Time torn free of death:
The sweet sharing
Of two loves'
Dual detonation.

Time wrapped in honey
When you return to me
Ruffled and wet,
Dripping moonstone drops
Still warm from your lover.

I am lying on the floor of my apartment long past midnight. I am calling my father's spirit. I want him to contact me. I want him to prove that death is not really death, but only an illusion of ending; that it is really just another beginning; that life is indestructible.

An uneasy feeling comes over my body. I can't really locate it, except that it seems concentrated in my stomach and head. Gradually the focus is on my head. A deep pain lodges behind my left eye and slowly moves across my skull. It comes to rest behind my right eye, and then disperses.

I close my eyes, and my forehead tightens unconsciously. I couldn't loosen it if I wanted to. I feel my center of consciousness, of thought, is in the center of my forehead. I am aware that this is a common focus for most meditations, but I have never been able to make meditation work for me.

I feel someone pressing a thumb or wide forefinger against my skull. It enters. It presses through to the back of my skull. I relax, and an image and a message come to mind.

I see a hairless, probably Asian face, opening its mouth wide in a gruesome mask of silent agony. There is a large black space where the mouth is open. The head is bloated, enlarged grotesquely, resting precariously on bony, undernourished shoulders. The torture never stops. The mouth opens and closes in terrible pain. It has passed beyond screaming. There are many souls like this one, clutching each other in a desperate, groping, swirling mass.

My father is trying to tell me that he is traveling with and through these souls. They are the ghosts of his victims and he must learn their pain before he can pass on to higher realms. Again and again he must pass through their torture. He won't be free until each of them is free, until he has learned the results of his work on earth.

I see his gun fall away, then little hunks of metal and tools and chemical concoctions. His death toys. He shakes them loose the way a dog rids himself of fleas. He shakes them loose, loosens his grip. Sheds his armor, scale by scale.

He is thanking me. He is thanking me! He is saying that my journey through his life has helped him free himself of what he left behind. He must still pass through this hell of his own creation, but I have shared part of the burden by traveling with him as far as I could. These other souls were killed by other souls much stronger than themselves, but parts of them cannot be killed. That is why he is traveling with them. He must learn eternal responsibility for his actions. Forever. Forever.

The pain returns. The image fades. A spike is pinned through the front to the back of my skull. The pain rises in pitch beyond what it was before. I relax my body. It rises again, then suddenly disappears. My brow unwinds. I sleep.

22

Dancing with Delilah

I've waited so long to tell this story; and now that I'm finally ready, the words don't come in a flood, the scenes don't unfold in *cinéma vérité* the way I thought they would. If they flash before my eyes at all, it's like a cheap porno flick. Lots of action and only a few moments of subtlety. Lots of light and dark, but very little shadow. Too many close-ups and not enough panorama. Where is the mystery? Will I ever recapture that special ache? The danger? The fun?

College was all wrong for me—what I needed was adventure —so when he died, it was almost automatic, predetermined, that I'd stay on. Of course I needed an explanation, and mine went something like "Blah blah a man becomes a man when he's needed, and I'm needed," or "Blah blah blah I have to work this out my way."

Losing a father and gaining a family, losing a father and gaining a lover, losing a father and becoming a father. Talk about hollow, talk about empty, talk about role-playing: There's always a tonic, but there ain't no cure. What did it feel like, what did it mean, to sleep in his beds for a year, to play with his guns when I hoped no one was looking? Forget about symbols. This was the real thing. A piece took the heat of your hand and spit a lovely dragon-fire. Lovely.

. . .

The day after the funeral, three of us go to his house to pack his things, to scavenge. The day is cold and clear, the kind of day that would have made his gout flare up, the kind of day he would have cursed.

The third scavenger is Delilah, Dawn's sister. We'd met once or twice when I was younger, and of course I'd wanted her just as much as I'd wanted Dawn. They had the same walk, the same talk, the same unbelievable ability to put the ax handle in my pants. Dee had been at Hill House a lot the past few years, helping to take care of the kids, a real friend of the family.

It's a crime to unlock this front door without his permission, but I do it anyway while Dawn and Delilah make room in the car for his junk. I walk from room to room, avoiding all this serious excavation, keeping my useless male carcass out of the way of these efficient females. I touch his bureau and open the middle drawer very slowly, with reverence, wondering if it's okay to enter this pocket of his universe. Two switchblades are right there on top of some black socks, and I grab them without telling a soul. Why should I? Women don't need switchblades. Their weapons are much more highly evolved.

I hear mountains being moved in the other rooms. His clothes, his snake cages, his kitchen utensils—all of it must go in half a day. I'm amazed at how many plants he now has, how green they are, how healthy they seem. It's as if they got the best of his love in those last months.

Now the Dynamic Duo is back and these greens are the last to go. Out to the car in boxes, with blankets wrapped around to keep them warm. Dawn says we can take whatever we'd like— something or things that speak to us, that we'd like to remember him by. I'm a little slow. What could I possibly take that would mean more than what I've already got, and I don't mean switch-blades. But there is one thing I'd like, and it's not really a thing, it's a plant, a cactus called "old-man's hair." It stands about five inches, with a diameter of an inch and a half, with long white hair cascading down from its crown. That's another one, I figure. He got this one for more than one reason. This must have been his favorite. This is the one he'd like me to have.

I say to no one in particular that I'd just like the one with the hair. Delilah is giving them all a closer scrutiny over on the other side of the car, and I know she hears me, but she says she'd really like the old-man's hair. She'd really like it, and a couple other cacti. And one of the succulents. And a palm and a fern and one of the hanging plants.

I see her pull the old-man's hair out of the box it was in and put it with the other plants and things she'd like to keep. I see the old-man's hair more from one life to another, I see the old man submit.

I see the young man submit.

Two weeks later, we're sorting through the wreckage back at Hill House, making piles: Here's one for fireworks, here's one for taxes, here's one for the kids, here's one to laugh at, here's one for Dawn, here's one for me. There aren't many for Delilah, though she's staying at Hill House now, helping out as usual. She's in the den downstairs, near the old laundry room where I always sleep. She seems at home at Hill House, among the debris. She knows where everything is. She belongs.

We're in Dawn's bedroom—or is it still *theirs?* I'm sitting on the bed while Dawn stuffs a heap of photos and papers into black plastic trash bags. I'm feeling strange, far away.

"I don't know, Dawn," I say, my voice shaking. "In the last few years I saw him, maybe even a long time ago when I was a kid"—this last one more for Dee than anyone; I want her to know I've buried that kid, I'm a man now—"I had this strange feeling about him. I felt I could somehow see behind his eyes. I could see what was hurting him, that he was losing and couldn't find his life but just had to go on with the game because he couldn't hold on to anything else. I always felt that he knew that I knew, but neither of us ever said anything because we knew if it ever came up, it would shatter him. And then there'd be nothing. He was afraid and so was I. So we protected each other by not intruding on that secret place."

I'm crying quietly. Gradually, while I've been talking, Dawn and Delilah have stopped sorting and disposing. They're really listening. Dee walks over and sits next to me, puts her arm across my shoulder, the way a man is supposed to do for a woman. I can't see too well through my tears, but I know they're both crying, too.

"There were very few people he shared that with," says Dawn.

Dee stays close to me the rest of the night while Dawn resumes her sorting. Sometimes we talk quietly, sometimes we just hold hands. By touching Delilah, I've touched Dawn; and by touching Dawn, I've touched him. I've got her. I've still got him. I'm scared, naturally, not only because we've touched physically but because something deep down is stirring. We can't afford to rush it, I say to myself later, in the laundry room. But of course we do.

The next night we're downstairs in the den. There's a roaring fire going because it's cold outside, wind howling, talking through the high trees. Kids asleep upstairs. Dawn has left us to ourselves, supposedly to visit a girlfriend downtown.

Delilah's had a few drinks and is sitting on the couch to the left of the fireplace, folding laundry and talking, but mostly relaxing. I'm on the other couch, watching her.

The resemblance to Dawn is strong, yet there's a difference, too: not as hard an edge, younger somehow. Even so, when I half close my eyes in the firelit room, Dawn's face takes over.

She must have known what I was thinking when she raised her head and looked at me.

"You know, Barry and I were pretty close . . . you remind me of him a lot."

I can't believe how tender I feel, how sensitive, how alive, how *manly*, possibly for the first time in nineteen years. The wind that is roaring outside through the trees is also roaring through my long hair. The ice in the earth is matched by the fire in my veins.

She says she's getting a headache, and I move to her couch and put her head in my lap so I can massage her scalp. I get hard, and I know she knows, but she doesn't move one way or another. I massage her scalp, neck, shoulders, back, up and down, reaching under her sweater as far as I can without grabbing her tits, taking away her headache and making her very aware of my condition. I don't know what happens next—it's one of those moments when events bend too far too fast—all I know is that she's suddenly trying to rip my zipper open. She's very scared and very drunk.

"Come *on!*" she hollers. "Come on! Take it out, I want to suck it! I want to *suck* it!"

I'm afraid and shocked and guilty because I've never had a girl or woman want to suck me so violently. I've always had to make love to and with her first.

"What happens if the kids come down—"

"They're upstairs and *very* asleep! Come on! I wanna *suck* it! I want it in my throat! Deep!"

With all this commotion, I'm sure they're up by now and about to tap tap tap on the door asking if they can fix themselves a sandwich.

"How about taking me upstairs? They can't just walk in on us then."

"Oh, no! I wonder if I should go all the way!" She's sounding like a drunken little girl, high-pitched and really scared, and we're both laughing so hard we almost roll off the couch. We walk upstairs, holding hands, not looking into each other's eyes. The higher we get, the more one of us shakes, but I can't tell who it is.

Now it's a different story because she's disappeared into the bathroom. I sit on the edge of the bed. We've both got time to think and worry about what we're about to do. She enters the room, climbs over me, and slips underneath the covers, a little cooled off, and says, "If you don't want to, it's all right." And she really means it. Her words are true even through her brain-fog.

"No! I vont to! I vont to!" I try to make her laugh so it's easier for both of us.

I take my red flannel shirt off slowly, like I've done this a thousand times if I've done it once, puffing my chest just a little, trying to feel like an older man to match this older woman, afraid I won't be good enough, shy about my body because she's watching me undress.

It must be one o'clock by now, and we're both pretty tired after a long day's journey into his debris. In order to hide my fear, I go down on her, and see that her hair is just stubble, as if it has been shaved recently. The light is still on, so I look up for just a second.

"Don't ask," she says. "That was one of the things we shared."

I know who she means by *we*. Everywhere I go I see his face; every step I take, I follow in his tracks; every goddamn bed I seek, I find a stain. I could go so many ways with this, it boggles my mind. If only she'd tell me the whole truth, if she'd share it all, down to the goriest detail, even though I don't want to hear a word of it.

Instead of all that, I make a quick lunge for the lamp and dig in for the long run. I'm amazed and relieved when I make her come almost instantly. This is great! I've never know a woman so close to her sexuality, and now I've got one in my hot, strong, nineteen-year-old hands. The taste of her lips, I want it to last all night, partly because I'm afraid I won't be able to fuck her good enough and partly because it's so much fun, so new, I want it to last and last. But after a minute or an hour she pulls me on top of her and I enter her like a whale with a hat on with a friendly hello to the doorman, no sweat, *comprende?* We rock and roll and fuck and suck and by the time we're through the sun is coming up, it's close to eight o'clock, the kids'll be getting up soon to go to school and I have to crawl back to my room. I don't even come in her this first time and what could make me more proud. This is the real thing, yessirree bob. I enter her like a whale with a hat on.

Now it's my turn to be the man of shebangs. Now it's my turn to have to hold to fuck to suck the brown bitch-goddess. I've out-Greeked the Greeks! I'm so high I hardly noticed Dawn crashed out on the couch in the den the morning after. She must have come home to new cries and whispers, screams and moans. . . .

I'm getting much closer to his secrets than I have any right to —I guess you could say that's what this is all about. But how far am I willing to go, how much am I willing to be father to my father, to be father to myself? I remind myself I have a choice, and then I remember I have no choice—what self-respecting ranting stud dude could walk away now when the action's just starting to get hot?

I'm sure Dee must be thinking the same thing; we've been so much alike so far, why be different now? The lease for her apartment in Millville is going to be up in two weeks, and is she going to extend it? Is she going to continue doing temp work for a boring law firm on Main Street, or is she going to do some of the real work of the world up here on this hill? Is she going to be satisfied with a movie on Friday or Saturday night and a date who will never know that all this woman really wants is to go to bed with a mystery? In one or two days she'll ask me, plain and simple, no big deal, if I'll help her move her stuff into that back room that hasn't been occupied for years. Dawn doesn't mind— she can use the help.

"I don't think we'll need a truck," she'll say. "I don't have all that much." The Buick will do just fine.

What a marvelous evolution, what a unique initiation into the ways of the world. Not only following in my father's footsteps, but going higher, about three feet higher, hitting below the belt. Following in his fucking bedsteps!

The first days were cold, full of ice, wind, and snow, huddled up there in Hill House, a house on top of the world, out of everyone's reach and deep into each other and ourselves. Giving all I had and then some, just a wee bit more, giving something of myself wrenched out of bedrock, anchored way down where no woman had ever been before. I call back the memory of that winter and I see myself walking across those hills, all browns and grays and whites and blacks. I'd pull on his McGregor black leather jacket and, with absolute lack of irony, cry out: *"It fits!"* Pull on his old rawhide boots and his black turtleneck and his black kid gloves and head for the hills for a little target practice. I'd unpack his Walther, take a pocketful of shells, and go out shooting nothing in particular. Tuck it in my boot and walk a long stride with that extra weight swinging me along and pulling me down.

There's only one picture of us together in recent years, and one day I found it while rummaging through his things. It was taken by Dawn one Fourth while we were playing up on the target range. The first time I saw it I swore it wasn't me, then I knew it had to be, standing just in back of him. Young, afraid. We each had a handgun and had been blasting away for hours. It got so heavy toward late afternoon that one of the hick neighbors called the state cops, saying, "There's automatic-weapons fire up there. I think you boys better check it out." No doubt a man of war at heart. They had a hard time believing it was just the two of us out for good times, doing our American thing. Doing it hard, yes, sir. Playtime so intense I learned to take five men out with ten shells in about fifteen seconds. Maybe less. Playtime, for sure, only I wasn't so sure.

The last thing in the world he would have wanted was for word to get out that his death was simple as pie, he'd willed it, arranged it since he was ten years old, maybe younger. He wanted us to be angry, but not at him. At God, the world, death itself, anything but him. He wanted everyone who'd ever loved him to feel cheated by his death, to feel it was wrong, a mistake, justice crucified.

He stopped taking his anticoagulant nitroglycerin a month after leaving Dawn for good. It had always been her responsibility to get that prescription refilled, and when she was definitely out of his life, so was the medicine.

We were cleaning out his other house, the secret house where everyone knew he'd moved, and I can still see the contortions her face went through when she found the nitro bottle in his medicine cabinet, half-full, the same bottle she'd bought for him the week before he split. She didn't think I noticed, but I'll never forget.

Dawn and Delilah—how do I compare them? There was this sneaky feeling that Delilah was everything Dawn could have been for him if Dawn had not lived so much in his world, had not been battered by it, had not chosen to share so much of his way. If Dawn had stayed with flowers and snakes and fireworks and not become his dancing partner on the minefield of life, if she had been able to keep more of her straight lines, if

she'd been able to bend with his wind, had had the supple limbs
of a true dancer, the resilience . . . then maybe, just maybe, it
would have worked, they would have gotten along just fine.

But no, she had to have a sister who was not yet cautious, who
wasn't afraid of a little pain in exchange for all that pleasure.
There was the little girl alive and kicking in my Delilah, and
there was the grown woman battling for breath in his Dawn.
There was that gorgeous feeling that Dee had held on to that
little girl with all her might: She brought her to bed and she
took her out for walks; she let her talk on the phone and get
into stupid lovers' quarrels in absurd public places. How many
afternoons did we spend battling it out in K-Mart, in the A&P,
in the drugstore, at the Farmer's Market and the gas station and
the motel? How many rages did I fly into for nothing, and how
many times did she jump right in, both feet forward and her
hard black velvet arms thrown out like vulture's wings? How
many hours did we waste throwing dishes, cursing, slamming
doors, vowing to kill someone if we weren't left alone to think
long and deep, to meditate on the cosmic significance of it all?
I think I must've smashed that Princess phone five or six times
during the heat of an argument when I had to go out of town to
take care of some of my own small-time pyro business or when
she'd promised that she'd walked out for the very last time and
gone back to Millville.

It was absurd, meaningless; we had no reason to be at each
other's throats—we had paradise, what more could we possibly
want? And yet we had to go at it, we had to stand up to each
other and see who could throw the best punch. I knew Dee had
it in her, and she knew I had it in me, and even though Dawn
and he must've fought tooth and nail, even though they must've
been pretty damn good at drawing blood, at making it last much
longer than necessary, there was something different about what
we had—there had to be. Whereas he and Dawn were fighting
for their lives, Dee and I were fighting because we had nothing
better to do, it was the best game in town. There was something
in Delilah that was Dawn when she was seventeen, wide-eyed
and innocent, and at the same time she had the electric sex of
an alley cat in the hottest of midsummer heats. There was a yowl

her body made in sex and her voice made in conversation; it
never failed to make me want to take every square brown inch of
her long brown body and do what I was put here to do.

Do you hear me, love? I'm still counting the ways.

There were days when Delilah was there for the kids, and I
was there for the house. Dawn was in town every morning
settling his debts. One day she came home with the happy news
that he'd forged her signature on a $10,000 bank loan and had
hostaged the house as collateral. I was with Dee when she was
told the story through the closed bathroom door, and I couldn't
resist cracking up, which made it impossible for Delilah not to
bust a gut, which completely demolished Dawn's angry pose.
Pretty soon we were all laughing, until one of the kids yelled
for us to quiet down, they had homework to do.

Days when I would pray for rain so I wouldn't have to dispose
of the ten bottles of concentrated nitric acid he'd stashed on
the front lawn. I guess he figured that was safer than burying
them in canisters in the basement—if they leaked, all it would
kill would be a few ferns and blades of grass; no chance of
reaching the water table, even though our water did come from
our own well.

That particular day, I had to move those bottles, it was on the
agenda; they had to be got rid of or else we'd be sued by a
neighbor whose rabbits would mutate into aliens, the squirrels
would turn vicious, the blue jays would become possessed. As I
proceeded to lug the first box of bottles toward the house, I
heard a crack, and before I could say, "Well, scald my balls,"
my thighs were on fire. I was wearing black bell-bottoms and
the acid left yellow streaks which made them look tie-died, very
much in vogue. But I didn't care about fashion, I just wanted that
fire out, so who did I call away from her household duties to
strip me down and wash me off and stomp those flames?

Days when I shoveled dirt and shoveled shit and couldn't tell
the difference, when I filled whole rooms with poisonous paint
fumes, when the bang of my hammer and chisel echoed up from
the basement and out into the woods, whole days when I'd hear

Delilah singing the blues upstairs, when I couldn't wait to get off work to see my baby.

The time Dee is going down on me in the middle of the driveway, sprawled out there on the gravel at a forty-five-degree angle. Laughing mad at the fat full moon, pinning me to the side of the mountain all night, gravel crawling up our cracks, laughing all the way to the slammer because we know any minute someone might drive by on the road and see some weird goings-on; the kids bailed us out one time, saying *Oh, Mommmm* to Dawn, and not even looking at me or Aunt Delilah. Everybody fails. If they hadn't learned that by now, it was highly unlikely they were going to get away from us unscathed.

We filled those rooms with love so furious that Attila the Hungry would just about attack when we'd rub up against each other in the kitchen, the bathroom, the basement, on the wide Buick hood. The first night it was good—you've never had it so good, I told myself. The next night it was firm and shaky at the same time, but we were committed. And then it got old, old like brown woman funk in the heat of summer, old old old, and sunrise was a bloody sheet.

The time she took it in her mouth one morning while I was brushing my teeth, saying, *"This oughtta cool ya off."*

Times of mirth and merriment so raucous we should have died. Like the time we went to New York to her friend Jane's wedding. Jane was someone Dawn and Dee had known in college, one of the wild bunch, no holds barred. If any bitch on earth was not ready for marriage, it was Jane. Some industrial heir was the lucky guy, straight as an arrow; she played high stakes. Everybody was cool; only a few caught the look in our eyes, caught the smell of sex coming off us in the elevator, or on the veranda overlooking the Manhattan skyline. I distinctly recall seeing and hearing Dawn being interrogated by the bride on the balcony while Dee and I giggled in the corner, pressed close, so close I could smell her.

"Your sister's fucking that guy, isn't she, Dawn? I know it. I can smell it, for fucking Christ's sake! Come on, old girl, level with Jane. Is your sister fucking your whitey-white stepson, not less than a handful of weeks after you put his old man in the earth? If anybody could do it, Dawn, it's a sister of yours. Fess up."

And Dee just grinning the dirtiest, dopiest grin in the world, shaking her head back and forth, making a fist and putting it in front of her mouth. The old Lenny Bruce Rule of Survival Number Sixteen: *Deny, deny, deny.*

How can I describe the sheer joy of falling in with absolutely the wrong person? How can I recall the naked fun of breaking all the rules, not just singing about it? It was fun to scream our guts out when the spirit wanted out, fun to know we weren't fooling anybody, though we sure tried. Most of all, it was boundless fun to be madly in love with the last person on earth you should be in love with, and it was absolutely hysterical that we'd actually go after that love with all the passion we could muster, and that proved to be plenty.

"Sure you're not thirty?" she'd always say after a good workout.

"No. I'm not sure."

One day the inevitable happens. Time for Dawn and me to talk while Dee is downtown doing winter shopping with the kids. A bitter-cold day that makes us feel utterly alone, as if we're the only humans alive on earth. There's no yesterday, no tomorrow, only this afternoon unfolding beneath icy clouds and a merciless star.

We find ourselves facing each other over the same kitchen table where I used to find him in the morning sipping a cup of coffee, reading the mail, writing a poem, making a firecracker. Maybe he's wearing a red and white flannel shirt, the same one I wore to bed last night to stay warm with Delilah. Maybe he's wearing the same old black pants and black boots. Maybe the steam will rise from his cup of coffee and he'll say that's just how it is, what our lives are, a wisp of steam, a halo of breath. Maybe he'll be silent and I'll be solemn, respectful of his thoughts, eager to share a moment or two out back on the shooting range but not courageous enough to ask. Maybe I'll get my cup of coffee and sit across from him, holding the cup in both hands and watching the birds grab crumbs from the snow.

There is no need for small talk, explanations, qualifications.

We could probably walk away from this table knowing each other's thoughts without speaking, but there is a certain pleasure in meeting here. We've traveled so far and we have so much farther to go. Here is our chance to stop, look, listen. This moment is a poem, his and ours, written in stone and on the face of the wind. It will last forever and disappear the second we speak it. Our gentleness is so tender, I wonder if it will vanish when the words come, but I am not afraid. Dawn is holy, I am holy, Delilah is holy, the kids are holy, the snakes and the fucking alligator are holy beyond belief. God is alive and well this very minute in Hill House—I know because I can touch Him, I can feel His arms around us.

"Are you happy with Delilah?"

"Yes."

"I'm glad."

I've never heard such an awesome silence, not even in the desert, not on top of the Rocky Mountains, not in any woods, not in any meadow. I could give her a lifetime of love with one touch, one kiss, but of course I fight the urge to pull her close.

"He would have been proud," she says.

But some days I was filled with inexplicable terror, especially when I had to be alone in the house for too long. I'd close myself off in my room on the second floor, take a book off the shelf, or maybe even work on a poem. I'd sit at my desk and all of a sudden I'd realize my mind wasn't on that book or poem, it was racing around the house trying to find out if anyone had snuck in, if the dog was still sleeping at the bottom of the stairs, or had his throat been cut? I'd sit in that small room with the late winter sun pouring in, pull his Walther from its hiding place, gently slip in a full clip, and wait. For God knows what. After a while I might lie down on my ratty double mattress that took up most of the floor in what was still the laundry room. Even now I can see her going down on me, or me going down on her, in that bed, on so many afternoons before the kids came home from school and Dawn came home from work, as if I had a camera eye poised above our field of feathers.

I'd curl up in the late-afternoon sun, trying not to think of my dead father or the space he left behind, which I was—although I couldn't—wouldn't—have admitted then—trying so desperately to fill. Trying not to think of the emptiness I felt without him or the fullness I felt with him, because I knew he was still with us and always would be whenever we needed him, and sometimes when we didn't. Words are so weak when it comes to describing the distance between things and the soul.

Thinking only of the loaded gun on my pillow.

One afternoon I got a call while Dawn was at work (as a housing inspector for the township, no less, and she didn't know dick about inspecting houses). Dee was busy running errands. Betty Jean Number One wanted to meet me. She said she wanted to have something to remember him by—maybe his pillbox? Said he used to keep her pills in with his. I said sure. Why not? How intimate, how touching—matching pills.

She drove up to Hill House an hour later in her little red Triumph. She stood about five five, slim, modest build, brown hair and eyes. Okay so far. Her face was swollen from an auto accident, but she still had it.

I met her at the door. For no more than ten seconds I felt the power of my sex around me like a halo. Not a dominant power, an *attracting* power. Emanated at the right time in the right place under the right circumstances, a man could not fail to catch something, my dear departed dad once told me. Hopefully not a disease.

She kissed me. She held on. She looked up at me, and I felt the halo dissolve into thin air. But that was all right—it stayed long enough. Suddenly I felt very shy and weak in the knees. I didn't want to have to share this with Dee. That was one bridge I seemed incapable of crossing. One woman, one man. In some ways I'm remarkably old-fashioned.

I knew, of course, what she wanted.

"Would it help?" I said.

"Yes . . . you're so young and strong . . . I'm not much older than you, but I sure feel it. . . ."

I couldn't believe this! All through my teens it had been a very dry season, and now they were coming from miles around, in sexy little deathtrap sports cars. I tried to subdue my awe, act like this was nothing I couldn't handle, hadn't been through a hundred times before.

We drove to the other house, which was technically still his because he had actually managed to pay his rent a couple of months in advance. Probably the only time in his life and he couldn't be there to enjoy it. Typical.

The house had been stripped: bare walls, bare cabinets, bare floors. Our footsteps exploded in the cold afternoon air, the cold silence. We walked into the bedroom—what had once been his other bedroom, his bed away from home—had been filled with furious love sounds, maybe—and faced each other, almost warm in the haloes of our breath.

She took off her jeans, and I let mine fall. She pulled her blouse over her head, and I unbuttoned my shirt. She laid her coat on the bare pine floor, and I laid mine next to hers. Made pillows out of shirt and blouse, blankets out of pants and scarves. The trees had their aches and pains, and made sure we knew. The air tried to take the late-afternoon light, but failed, just another dead winter day.

Even now I swear I can't think of a feeling to match what I felt on mornings, ordinary mornings, when I'd wake with thick yellow sun pouring in the windows, remembering last night and how I'd crawled out of her bed, our bed, *theirs* when Dawn took the kids away for a weekend, and the den when she didn't. . . .

Stumbling out the back door and seeing Delilah watering the plants in the greenhouse with the broken windows, which I'd boarded up. Pure sex, pure love—it hardly mattered which—the way she watered and fed and cared for them. So much green in there it would bounce off the light, bounce off her thin white cotton blouse, caressing her as gently as she caressed those long thick ferns. I'd sit there sometimes for an hour before making a sound, just to have that simple pleasure all to myself. Wondering what it meant to have such fullness and such emptiness, not so much by turns but all at the same time.

. . .

We take a walk in the middle of the heaviest snowstorm these parts have seen in years, we step out the back door into the impenetrable American midnight, and we penetrate it. We head for the woods like Sioux trudging through the Dakotas, only unlike the Sioux we have no idea where we are or where we've just been or where we're going. But that's nothing new to us, so we just keep walking, silent, religious, suddenly aware that we are not alone, we're not in control, we're guests after all and who are we trying to fool, anyway? Nothing could fool these clouds, nothing could fool this awesome wind, nothing could fool these frozen trees, nothing could fool this mystical American midnight.

We can only allow this mystery to enter us for seconds at a time . . . the wild wind pushing us down down down into our silent selves. Soon we know we're defeated and turn back, back to the illusion of the hearth. She wraps her arms around my waist and hugs me from behind like we're riding some invisible motorcycle, our footsteps measuring not in feet but inches. I remember a sculpture I once saw of an Eskimo man, woman, and child hooked in the same embrace, caught in the same dance against death, lockstepping through the storm. Would you believe I knew just then the eternal power of being a man, the eternal power of being a woman, the eternal power of being a child, so happy to be alive on the face of this unhappy earth.

It took so long for me to break through his disguise, and even now it's difficult. How did he do it? Magic? Coercion? Fear? Some amazing acting ability? Some amazing ability to protect our illusions, feed our fantasies about ourselves, to keep the glamorous veneer in spite of aggression, rejection, cruelty, self-destruction? *Destroyer of All Worlds* doing what he did best, taking most of it with him, taking everything he could, every chance he had, and we made sure he had plenty of those. And we loved him for it! Loved every minute of it! It was never a question of giving him another chance; our supply was limitless, and he knew it.

Getting off on the idea that maybe he did kill those nine men with his metric Mauser on a fetid nightmare road in Venezuela, getting off on the idea that maybe he did blow away two bladed Chicanos. Getting off on glib megadeath, getting off on his wounded brain. A father who was not a father, who was once my older brother and now my younger brother, who was strange and not a stranger. A father of invention. A father I once loved, and now hated, and would eventually love again; and lost, or in a sense never had.

Sick with grief and love, sometimes I had the distinct, very frightening feeling I was glad he died when he did, that now I could find out who he really was, something I never could have done while he was alive. Almost as if by playing with one of his women I was playing out some grim, exhilarating charade of revenge, by tearing into her I was getting mine. Taking very good care of David, the only problem was that I was losing battles left and right and the cavalry was nowhere, nowhere in sight.

Dancing with Delilah was richer, deeper, than anything I'd ever known; it gave me a center I knew was false, I knew was a lie, but it was my lie, and it kept me alive. Would you hate me if I said I understand the men who feed smoke to women and children in far-off places in the name of God and country, who come back wondering why their wives have left them, their children can't look them in the eye? *Nothing in my life has ever arrived in small increments, it's always been stop or violent.* Like father, like son; full of life, full of death, full of lies lies lies.

Feeling she was mine, all mine, knowing all the time whose she'd always be, but what the hell. Giving something of myself that was so young and fresh, so sweet and tender, I knew I'd never see it again, a one-shot deal, the time of my life. It all became very clear the day she said:

"I used to think there were two kinds of people. The givers and the takers."

Once I asked her if any of her kinky friends ever went too far, and she said, "What's too far?"

Times when I let it all hang out and went with all the far-out things I'd like to do to her. Knowing full well that there probably wasn't anything I could think of that she hadn't already done a hundred times, that I had been until now a sexually sheltered nineteen-year-old, there were certain things of which I would always be innocent no matter how hard I'd try to shake that innocence; that she was my first real woman, the rest were just girls; that I was deeply afraid of and of course drawn to the deep end of the pool where she lived, and would eventually go under.

One day spring came rolling in, and that night, just for kicks, we rented a room in a sleazy motel somewhere out in the sticks. It didn't take long for us to get down to business.

"It doesn't matter why," Dee said with a little help from Jack Daniel's. "It's just something I want you to do. It's a gift for you that I never wanted to give to any other man, not even your father."

That beautiful silence peculiar to rented rooms gobbled up her words, along with every other night sound. I couldn't speak. Somehow she realized I would need a little encouragement as she turned on her side, her back to me.

"I'm not leaving this dump till this ass is *fucked!*"

Afterward she said, "You were baaaddd. You just took it. Didn't mess around."

Spring was no more intense than winter, and nothing was so close to us as coolness and the birds. We'd rock and roll deep into the night, we weren't even sad when we woke past noon to the sounds the snow made when melting, when our eyes opened in a choir of light. The light said it all. While winter had been dark and cold and made me very aware of all God's dangers, spring brought with it at least the promise of release.

And in a way, that spring was generous to us in the way farmers might speak of spring's generosity: It was very green, and warm, and wet, and somehow made room for more tenderness.

Once spring arrived, Otto would come by for the same reason I was there: He wanted to get into their pants. Like me, he always had an excuse. Talk about old times, share a drink, even offer Dawn a job. Once he offered to go into business with her running guns—said she could make $500 a week easy—but she refused.

It's afternoon in April and we get to talking, Attila leaning against my leg like a kid craving affection. We talk about

Derringers, my favorite gun. He lets me shoot his, which he keeps jammed against the front seat on the driver's side. Says he keeps it there because he picks up a lot of hitchhikers. One tried to rob him once.

"Shoot someone in the head with this," he says, "and the slug'll stay inside the skull, unlike a .38 or another kind of .22." As if I really care where the lead comes to rest, as long as it hits home. His Derringer shoots hollow-point Magnum .22s, which "travel at a higher velocity" than a .38 and therefore have greater "stopping power" than anything up to and including a .38. He says this a couple times, as if he really digs the idea. I get the creeps, start moving away. But he walks over to me, real close, and says what's really on his mind.

"I don't know if you know it, Dave, but I'm interested in Dawn *sexually*. I've been after her for years, even when your father was alive. But, no. Never gave me anything. Now, I don't want to pursue her if it's gonna bother you. I mean, because of your father's death and all."

As if I don't *know* it, in the biblical sense? Anything half-sexual that walks on two or four feet wants to fuck her.

"That doesn't have anything to do with me," I shrug, getting hot under the collar, fit to kill for my women and my castle and my fucking dog. "That's her decision—and yours. No, I'm not uptight about that at all."

Of course I wanna stick a ten-inch blade in his gut right here and now with Attila standing on the sidelines ready to applaud, but I try to finesse the situation by inviting him inside, be my guest, if she's not in bed already, I'll put her there for ya, *no problem*. But of course I'm really incapable of being cool when he or anybody else tries to make his or her move. I shake and sweat, get crazy inside.

What could Delilah possibly have seen in *me?*

"You're so much like him," she once said in a whisper after love, "and you're so different. It's like I can see him walking around inside you, and then I can see you walking around inside him. Someday those two men are going to become the same man."

I could feel a punch line forming in that lovely brown woman-brain, so I tried to beat her to it.

"And you want to be in bed with me when that happens, huh?"

"I can be serious, too, David Barry."

"You'd still want to take me for a test drive."

"Men think women don't know how to be serious, but it's really the other way around."

"Would you turn me away from your bedroom door?"

"I'm so glad you're not arrogant or conceited or egotistical," she said in a fading whisper, and fell asleep in my arms.

I could jerk her off on the train on the way to her friend's wedding, then a minute later talk world politics. I fit right in as if I'd been married to her twenty years.

I could lie and cheat without batting an eye.

I could tear her apart for lying and cheating.

I had long legs, strong arms, a good tongue, and a good cock that knew how to rock around the clock.

I was mean.

Funny.

Sad.

Young.

Old.

Good with a rifle. Ace with a pistol. Made bombs in the basement and sold them downtown to the boys who worked the pumps. Used the profits to keep food on the table.

I'd light a fuse and toss a few out the back door when I had something to say to God. Wouldn't wait around for answers.

I had balls.

I'd go up on the roof with the intention of fixing things up so someone would look at Hill House and be stupid enough to want to buy it. I'd paint under the eaves that hadn't been painted since the house was born, hanging down off the roof, no safety rope. I'd check out the gutters, and, finding them in despicable shape, do the only thing that made any sense—pry out the nails with a crowbar, kick out their rusted guts. After a few hours, I'd realize I might have solved the gutter problem but had trashed our lawn in the process. No matter. Haul the wreckage up to the woods,

maybe fifty feet from the house, and leave it for Mother Nature
to chew on for the next few hundred years. Eyeing the screen
door, I'd see that it, too, had a terminal case. Rip and toss, slash
and burn.

At the end of day, come to dinner, sweaty and tanned, saying
to Dawn and Dee, who'd grin from ear to ear:

"If your gutter offend thee, cut it off. If your screen door
offend thee, pluck it out."

I knew I was being awarded her personal Medal of Honor
when she'd say:

"You're getting personal, now stop that, you're getting too
familiar, now stop that!"

If I said I'd spank her if she wasn't a good girl and I'd spank
her if she was a good girl, she'd make an *mmmmmm* sound, do
a little hug and twist, shine with that grin, and say:

"You promise?"

Some promises I never could deliver, never had the chops to
go all the way, to serve all the dishes she requested—though,
Lord, there were plenty of times when I wanted to.

That was the highest one of all, discovering how receptive a
woman could be. There was the feeling that she could take anything I could dish out and come back for more ten minutes later.
Get inside, start the engine, gun it harderfastermeanerlonger
than anything that's ever swaggered on two paws and called itself
a man. Somebody once said the only way two people can be good
in bed is if they're both takers, taking all they can get. I don't
know. All I know is they were my Good Old Days and I don't
ever want to see them again.

Delilah would go out with a guy as long as she could stand him,
get as much out of him as she could, use his truck to go to Millville
for the day, sometimes even a bundle of cash up front, with
promises of more—all from some poor white sucker who would
do anything to have a taste of that brown sugar. I should know.
I was one of them.

He'd be too good for her, and in the end she couldn't stand to
see such one-sided abuse. I'd laugh along, too innocent and dumb
and screwed up to realize that I came from the same pot, the

same stock, as all those jokers and fools. I'd pay any price for an exotic fuck in these deadly boring badlands. Maybe she really loved me, maybe she didn't. I'd be an absolute idiot to make claims either way at this late date. I'm not even sure, after all this time and distance, that I felt anything more for her than lust, or some sort of compassion that got bent out of shape pretty quick, a schoolboy's possessiveness and downright hunger for anything that moved well and called itself female and would give itself to me.

There were fleeting moments when we shared something that can only be described as peace, when we seemed to flow into and through each other and all the sharp edges would dissolve at the slightest touch. We might go through hell to get there, but we got there.

I remember lying with her on my dirty mattress, Dawn and the kids out somewhere and the wolves somehow thrown off our trails. I remember lying on that mattress and making love for hours with the warm sun falling across the bed, falling across us, blessing us, holding us, golden and safe. If we talked at all, it was in a language that only the two of us could understand, the message now lost but the feelings not forgotten.

I remember long, slow nights when Dawn was out and we'd call the Chinese restaurant down by the highway. I would drive out late in the Buick to pick up something delicious to eat in bed. Fried shrimp was a favorite, pork fried rice was another. We would lie there in all that rubble, watching TV and eating till three in the morning, when the station would crash and we'd come to the tune of the "Star Spangled Banner." I can only remember one or two nights under that roof when we didn't make love. We were always hungry—for food or each other or both.

One warm afternoon I was sitting at my desk in front of a window, working on a new poem. She knocked quietly on the door, walked over to me, bent over behind me, and slid her long brown arms down my chest to my waist. I reached behind and held her thighs, and we stayed like that, silent, for what seemed like hours. For the first time in months I felt soft and beautiful and radiant. She said, "You look so sexy in that white shirt."

No woman had ever said anything like that to me.

. . .

And of course summer was the full flowering of our desire, a flower that brought with it all the stuff of summer: the endless buzz of endless bugs, heavy pockets of hot air that could take us under all by themselves, muffled crackling of old angers and new laughter falling on the beaten ground. By now, the edge of our love was so finely honed it no longer could be called a dumb blunt instrument. Now it looked and felt more like some exquisite razor, some rare blade from out of this world that would not announce its wounds with pain but instead gave you lots of little flowers, pretty red things that would, if you weren't careful, bleed you dry in the noonday sun. The edge of our love was by now so well defined, so finely honed, that we hardly ever had to use it, and when we did, it was more for sport than any real need.

And so it was perfectly fitting that for the Bicentennial Fourth, the biggest, most glorious Fourth of this century, we would celebrate, but not in the usual way. There would be no ground pieces, no aerial shells, no frills or fancy fluff. No, there would only be room for the essential, we would strip our celebration down to the leanest meat we could find: four last bombs to come out of the Black Dawn Bomb & Fountain Factory. Four 16mm film tins packed with homemade powders, each one equal to or greater than your average land mine, each one not really a symbol but the actual embodiment of our love for each other, ourselves, and what we had. Four—one for each of us.

I planted them halfway down the hill on the side facing the eastern horizon because I figured that side was closer to God, planted them with such love and care you'd have thought I was engaged in some ancient, arcane ritual that had been handed down to me in secret, for which the only payment would be the knowledge that I was the last keeper of the flame, the last of the ones who howled, the only one who saw that black cloud up ahead. And you would have been perfectly right, that was exactly how I felt; and when the first one went, it shook the house as well as the hill; and when the second one went, my only thought was that I hoped it was enough to shake him in his stony sleep, I hoped it was enough to say I'm picking up the pieces, I'm scattering them far and wide, farther and wider than you will ever know, ever could have known. That I am what I am, my father's son, and I am what you were and what you were not, what you never could have been, and on this day under heaven and all my days to come I thank you for this gift called Life, I thank you for the gift of your death.

I can see us now walking down to the reservoir for a midnight swim. She's had a little drink because it's the only way she can really cut loose, and she keeps falling against me like a dumb drunken bitch of a whore and I wanna slap her around, make her toe the line, let her know who's boss, and she just wants that total sex, that total smashing of body against body, soul into soul, she just wants to pull me down into the mud and I just want to throw her down into it and climb in for the ride. Bugs buzzing against our heads driving our brains insane, she's wearing hardly nothing and if someone shined his headlights now her gorgeous silhouette would shine through brighter than the midsummer moon. If you don't walk quieter and stop smashing into me I'm gonna get loud too and smash into you, and I mean it the sweat is burning my eyes, my temper is rising, it's the sexiest moment of our lives, lost out here in the blindfolded nightmare American dark with no protection but the heat and power of our sex, and that's powerful enough to scare anything away, better keep your distance, buddy, you might burn up while entering our atmosphere.

It's the sexiest moment of our lives and we milk it for all it's worth, even now I can taste it in the grinding between my nineteen-year-old white-boy teeth, don't call me boy 'cause I'm a man, my woman here'll tell ya, wontcha, honey? Tell the man how good you have it since you hooked up with me, go on, I'm waiting, I can stand here and listen and wait all night, I ain't taking one step till I hear the words come outta your sweet mouth.

But she can't stand still long enough to act this one out, she's gotta get wet, gotta get baptized in that green American midnight slime, gotta squish around in that muck get it between her toes in her hair between her teeth pull me down there with her and watch the bubbles climb out of our mouths, slow-motion, sink real slow, going down for the last time, hours later I'll taste that swamp, days later I'll taste that swamp, fucking years later I'll taste that fucking swamp when I'm with another woman, I'll never ever get it out of my nose, and still I gotta go for it, get it all tonight, this is summer and nothing is more important than summer.

So she goes in headfirst and I stand on the bank ashamed of my fear, ashamed of holding back—I haven't held anything back yet, so why start a bad habit now after it's taken so long to kick all the old ones, all the old restrictions on my teen-age soul? No, I don't wanna start no bad habits, least of all listen to fear, so I dive in, I *dive* into that fucking swamp of a reservoir and I'm not even drunk. And I can't believe it but my neck doesn't break on something hidden just below the surface, my feet don't slash on something sharp down there in the bottomless muck. No. I glide out under this American moon, I've got my feet and legs and cock and balls shoved down deep into the muck of America, and here's my hand reaching out across the water, and I'm not sinking, I'm floating, I'm free, I'm touching my golden brown lady under twilight's last gleaming, the moon smiling down, the stars winking and saying *go for it,* the air is perfectly still, this sweet silence is so perfectly unbearable I must scream her unbearably beautiful name.

Feeling the first cool breeze of autumn, knowing it's quite possible that for the rest of my life the only memory I'll have for the death of summer and birth of winter is what I feel now in Hill House, breathing air so cool and clean and crisp it hurts the brain, so sweet it'll never let me forget how much of a privilege it is just to breathe. Feeling the first cool breeze of autumn as I walk up to the target range where I hardly ever shoot now but listen for the small blue explosions of the past.

What is left looks around at what is left and decides it's time to quit, time to get going, time to go our separate ways or be cut down for the harvest. We have a conversation late one night. She asks how many times I've been in love. I say I've been in love with every girl I've made love with, and that's about three or four. She's ten years older and she's amazed. There are only three men she's ever really loved, two of them are gone and here I am, the third love, and she can feel how I'm already gone, gone for good, and there it is, she will love no more. She will go with other men, she might even marry, but it will be for something less than love, much less than love. We both know what that something is, even though we have no words for it and even if we did we wouldn't want to speak them.

And so we come full circle. What began as just another unbelievable love story has become something even more unbelievable: an axis, a reference point from which I will depart and to which I will never return, but that will always be with me, written on my face and stored behind my eyes and singing in my heart with all my other wounded and dead. And what will it be for her, what will it become? Will it be her axis, or will it be the place from which she will depart and to which she will never return, leaving nothing but herself behind?

23

Dad

I hope he's happier next time around. I hope he finds a nice girl and settles down for good and has a million kids and makes a lot of money, is a great success in the business world, a pillar of his community, a fine, upstanding citizen.

I always had the feeling, whenever I was around him, that some weight was getting heavier and heavier. I never knew what to call it because I was too young. He told me how this business project didn't work for that reason or this marriage failed for that reason or this new girlfriend drifted away for some other reason and this new invention didn't fly because of something totally out of his control. I never thought about the toll. I was nineteen. I knew a lot at that age, but I knew nothing about defeat.

My father must have been surprised—he must have been shocked—by how barren his life had become. He had planted no seeds. Or, he had planted many seeds. Some he let grow wild, some he trampled down, some he poisoned, some he tore out by the roots, and some he abandoned. That's one hell of a garden.

I think my father was shocked that it could really happen to him. He had played with death all his life, and now death was playing with him.

Some nights, some days, I feel you close. My heart beats a little faster, my chest tightens, I grow weak and strong at the same time. Are you here to tell me—tell me what? What could you possibly tell me that would have any meaning? I don't care anymore about your life, your death, your lies, your truth. I don't want your women anymore (long ago they gave up on me). I don't want your guns, books, films, knives, snakes, houses, debts, debris. I don't want your secrets or even your destiny. I couldn't give a shit about your myth, about the size of your cock. I couldn't care less about the age of your youngest child. I don't want to know your last words, don't want to remember how you looked in death, don't want to recall the minute details of your descent into the earth. I don't want to go to your cemetery and have to ask the groundskeeper where we put you a few centuries ago. I don't want to listen to his confusion over whether you are buried next to Moses Boozer or Our Baby. I don't want to be told that no one from your families has bought a marker for your grave—just under a grand; you'd think somebody would spring for you one last time. I don't want to have to tell the groundskeeper I'll be back in a year or so with the cash and a few choice words to cast in bronze.

If we meet tonight as strangers on a fetid nightmare road in Venezuela, or Vietnam, or Ghana, or Jamaica, or Cuba . . . I will not hesitate to string you up for all to see, I will laugh as you struggle for breath, as your face turns blue, as your bowels evacuate, as your cock blooms one last time. And what if the rope doesn't break? As some poet once wrote: Your neck will feel the weight of your ass. Your feet will dance in midair, your little black ankle boots with the pointed toes will curl and curl and curl in spasm after spasm of terrorist pain, your backward knees will be useless for helping you climb out of this tree and shifting gears in a foreign, sperm-shaped getaway car. Even if you could escape our guerrilla grip, your charisma would only help us find you in the Venezuelan or Vietnamese or Ghanaian or Jamaican or Cuban nightmare dark, your aura would only be a spotlight to lead us—to lead me and my band of merry Freedom Fighters—to your fantastically illuminated North American psychoactive flare of a CIA assassin soul. We would empty your pockets of scorpions and bird eggs and worms and other exotic creatures, and maybe, for foreign exchange, we would stuff them full of Gravel mines or loaded butane cigarette lighters or tiny metal bombs that explode on impact and scatter poison shrapnel, scatter enough poison shrapnel to take out a roomful of us gooks armed to the teeth with scimitars.

But we will trick you after all. We would not dare extract you so quickly. We will want you for our collection, we will keep you in a cage. So any death toys Made in U.S.A. that we stuffed into your pockets, that we taped to your balls, will be disarmed, sterilized. Your new home will be sanitized for your protection. The rope will break before your neck. Your carcass will crumple to the ground and you might break a gnome ankle or two, or twist one of your prehistoric knees, but it will all be a joke. Gothic gallows humor. Joke, joke. The wages of sin are more of the same.

We will build a cage and lock you up and call you Uncle. We'll know you're a horny sonofabitch because you wrote your own history, so you will not be without female companionship. A harem of baby Gaboon vipers, and maybe a few spitting cobras, will do quite nicely. We won't settle for the cocaine of porn to help you pass the time. We'll give you the real thing. We'll call her Betty Jean III.

You'll have your movies, your play, your fun and games.

And we'll have ours.